Research Methods in Sports Coaching

Research Methods in Sports Coaching is a key resource for any student, researcher, or practitioner wishing to undertake research into sports coaching. It takes the reader through each phase of the research process, from identifying valuable research questions, to data collection and analyses, to the presentation and dissemination of research findings. It is the only book to focus on the particular challenges and techniques of sports coaching research, with each chapter including examples, cases, and scenarios from the real world of sports coaching.

The book introduces and explores important philosophical, theoretical, and practical considerations in conducting coaching research, including contextual discussions about why it's important to do sports coaching research, how to judge the quality of coaching research, and how sports coaching research might meet the needs of coaching practitioners. Written by a team of leading international scholars and researchers from the UK, US, Canada, and Australia, and bridging the gap between theory and practice, this book is an essential course text for any research methods course taken as part of a degree programme in sports coaching or coach education.

Lee Nelson is a Lecturer in the Department of Sport, Health, and Exercise Science at the University of Hull, UK. His research and teaching interests include micro-politics, emotions, and pedagogy in coaching and coach education contexts.

Ryan Groom is Senior Lecturer in Sports Coaching at Manchester Metropolitan University, UK. His main teaching and research interests focus on qualitative research methodologies and social theory to explore power, identity, and interaction.

Paul Potrac is Professor of Sports Coaching at Edge Hill University, UK. His research and teaching interests focus on exploring the social complexity of sports coaching and coach education, with a particular emphasis on the political and emotional nature of practice.

D0232081

Research Methods in Sports Coaching

Edited by
Lee Nelson, Ryan Groom, and Paul Potrac

Routledge
Taylor & Francis Group

LONDON AND NEW YORK

First published 2014
by Routledge
2 Park Square, Milton Park, Abingdon, Oxon OX14 4RN

and by Routledge
711 Third Avenue, New York, NY 10017

Routledge is an imprint of the Taylor & Francis Group, an informa business

© 2014 for selection and editorial matter, Lee Nelson, Ryan Groom, and
Paul Potrac; for individual contributions, the contributors

British Library Cataloguing in Publication Data
A catalogue record for this book is available from the British Library

Library of Congress Cataloging in Publication Data
Research methods in sports coaching / edited by Lee Nelson, Paul Potrac,
Ryan Groom.
pages cm
Includes bibliographical references and index.
1. Coaching (Athletics)--Research--Methodology. I. Nelson, Lee. II. Potrac,
Paul, 1974-
GV711.R47 2014
796.07'7--dc23
2013033788

ISBN: 978-0-415-62680-4 (hbk)
ISBN: 978-0-415-62682-8 (pbk)
ISBN: 978-0-203-79754-9 (ebk)

Typeset in Garamond
by Taylor & Francis Books

Contents

List of figures and tables

Figures

Tables

Notes on editors and contributors

Editors

Lee Nelson is a Lecturer in the Department of Sport, Health, and Exercise Science at the University of Hull, UK. His research and teaching interests include micro-politics, emotions, and pedagogy in coaching and coach education contexts.

Ryan Groom is a Senior Lecturer in Sports Coaching at Manchester Metropolitan University, UK. His main teaching and research interests focus on qualitative research methodologies and social theory to explore power, identity, and interaction.

Paul Potrac is a Professor of Sports Coaching at Edge Hill University, UK. His research and teaching interests focus on exploring the social complexity of sports coaching and coach education, with a particular emphasis on the political and emotional nature of practice.

Contributors

Andy Abraham is a Principal Lecturer in the Carnegie School of Sports at Leeds Metropolitan University, UK. His research and teaching interests include professional education, practice, and decision-making.

Zoë Avner is a PhD candidate at the University of Alberta, Canada. Her research takes a poststructuralist approach to develop more ethical and effective coaching practices within performance sporting contexts.

Nick Caddick is a PhD student in the Peter Harrison Centre for Disability Sport at Loughborough University, UK. His main research and teaching interests are in qualitative inquiry and the health and well-being of combat veterans, physical activity, and the natural environment.

Martin Camiré is an Assistant Professor at the University of Ottawa's School of Human Kinetics in Ottawa, Canada. Dr Camiré is a researcher in the area of sport psychology and sport pedagogy and he is interested in examining how positive youth development can be facilitated in the context of school sport.

Bryna Chrismas is a Lecturer in Exercise Physiology in the Department of Sport and Exercise Sciences at the University of Bedfordshire, UK. Her research and teaching interests include exercise physiology with a particular focus on muscle damage and recovery, and the application of research methods and statistics in sport and exercise science.

Diane Culver is an Associate Professor in the School of Human Kinetics at the University of Ottawa, Canada. Her research relates to coach development in different contexts including disability sport and qualitative research. She teaches sport pedagogy and psychology.

Christopher Cushion is a Reader in Sports Coaching at Loughborough University School of Sport, Exercise, and Health Sciences, UK. His teaching and research interests focus on a sociocultural understanding of the coaching process and coach education and development.

Louise Davis is a Lecturer in Sports Coaching within the Department of Sport, Exercise, and Rehabilitation, Northumbria University, UK. Her research and teaching interests focus on the social psychology of coaching with particular interest in exploring interpersonal relationships, emotions in coaching, as well as individual differences.

Jim Denison is an Associate Professor at the University of Alberta, Canada. His research examines coach effectiveness in track and field through a Foucauldian lens. He is also Director of the Canadian Athletics Coaching Centre.

Brian T. Gearity is an Assistant Professor of Sport Coaching Education in the School of Human Performance and Recreation at the University of Southern Mississippi, USA. His research interests include coach learning, education, and effectiveness, qualitative methodologies, and understanding coaching through the work of Michel Foucault.

Wade Gilbert is a Professor and Sport Psychology Coordinator in the Department of Kinesiology at California State University, Fresno, USA. He is an active researcher and consultant in the areas of coach education, coaching effectiveness, and athlete talent development.

Luke Jones is a Lecturer in the Department of Sport, Health, and Exercise at the University of Hull, UK. His research takes a poststructuralist approach to examine the disciplinary nature of elite sport and how this effects athletes' retirement experiences.

Robyn L. Jones is a Professor at the Cardiff School of Sport, Cardiff Metropolitan University, UK. His research examines the complexity of coaching and how coaches manage the power-ridden dilemmas that arise. He has published several books and articles on coaching and pedagogy, and is the Editor-in-Chief of *Sports Coaching Review*.

Sophia Jowett is a Reader in the School of Sport, Health, and Exercise Sciences at Loughborough University, UK. Her research and teaching interests include psychosocial factors in competitive sport, applications of sport psychology in enhancing relationships, communication, and behaviors, as well as coaching-related issues.

John Lyle is a Professor of Sport Coaching at Leeds Metropolitan University, UK. His research interests are centered on conceptual development and modelling in sports coaching, and decision-making by coaches.

Graham McFee is a Professor in the Philosophy Department at California State University, Fullerton, USA and Emeritus Professor of Philosophy at the University of Brighton, UK. His major interests include the philosophy of Wittgenstein, philosophical aesthetics, and the philosophy of sport. He has published numerous articles across these fields, and nine single-authored books.

Clifford J. Mallett is Associate Professor of Sport Psychology and Coaching in the School of Human Movement Studies at The University of Queensland, Australia. His scholarship is focused on adaptive coach behavior mostly from a self-determination theory perspective and within the broad framework of positive psychology.

Phil Marshall is a Lecturer in Strength Conditioning and Undergraduate Director of Studies for the BSc Sports Coaching and Performance pro-gramme at the University of Hull, UK. He is currently undertaking PhD study exploring autoethnographical accounts of his own coaching experiences.

Adrian Midgley is a Professor of Sport and Exercise Physiology in the Department of Sport and Physical Activity at Edge Hill University, UK. His research interests include the psychobiological factors that help explain exercise tolerance during maximal exercise and the methodological aspects of cardio-pulmonary exercise testing. He teaches applied statistics to undergraduate and postgraduate students, and is a Fellow of the Royal Statistical Society.

Joseph Mills is a PhD candidate in the Faculty of Physical Education and Recreation at the University of Alberta, Canada. He is an accredited sport and exercise psychologist and his doctoral thesis is a Foucauldian analysis of high-performance endurance coaching.

Aidan Moran is Professor of Cognitive Psychology and Director of the Psychology Research Laboratory in University College, Dublin, Ireland. He has published widely in areas related to concentration, mental imagery, and expertise in sport performers.

Gareth Morgan is a Senior Lecturer in the Carnegie School of Sports at Leeds Metropolitan University, UK. His research and teaching interests include the areas of talent development, annual planning, and the development of players' psychobehavioral skills through coaching.

Bob Muir is a Senior Lecturer in the Carnegie School of Sports at Leeds Metropolitan University, UK. His research and teaching interests focus on the coaching process, coaching pedagogy and practice, coach education, learning, and professional development.

Laura Purdy is a Senior Lecturer in Coach Education at Edge Hill University, UK. Her research and teaching principally address the sociological and pedagogical aspects of coaching practice. Specifically, her publications have focused on the lived experiences of coaches and athletes in relation to the concepts of power and interaction.

Daniel Rhind is a Lecturer in Youth Sport within the Brunel Centre for Sport, Health, and Well-being at Brunel University, UK. His teaching and research interests focus on understanding the development of effective and healthy relationships in sport with a focus on the safeguarding of children.

Brett Smith is a Reader of Qualitative Health Research in the Peter Harrison Centre for Disability Sport at Loughborough University, UK. His research and teaching interests concern disability, qualitative methods, and narrative inquiry. He is Editor-in-Chief of the international journal *Qualitative Research in Sport, Exercise, and Health*.

Ronald E. Smith is a Professor of Psychology and Director of the Clinical Psychology Training Programme at the University of Washington, USA. His interests include research methods in clinical psychology, personality assessment and research, stress and coping, and sport psychology.

Frank L. Smoll is a Professor in the Department of Psychology at the University of Washington, USA. His research focuses on coaching behaviors in youth sports and on the psychological effects of competition on children and adolescents.

Andrew C. Sparkes is a Professor in the Research Institute for Sport, Physical Activity, and Leisure at Leeds Metropolitan University, UK. His research and teaching interests are grounded in methodological diversity and inspired by a continuing fascination with the ways that people experience different forms of embodiment over time in a variety of contexts.

William Taylor is a Senior Lecturer in Sports Coaching at Manchester Metropolitan University, UK, where he is responsible for postgraduate taught provision. His main teaching and research interests focus on the professionalization of sports coaching, and the use of poststructuralist theory in assessing the practice of coaching in the risk society.

Richard Tinning is Professor of Pedagogy in the School of Human Movement Studies, University of Queensland and Professor of Physical Education in the Faculty of Education, University of Auckland. His scholarly interests circulate around health and physical education, knowledge, teacher education, and pedagogy.

John Toner is a Lecturer in the Department of Sport, Health, and Exercise Science at the University of Hull, UK. His research and teaching interests include skill acquisition, expertise in sport performers, and pedagogy in sports coaching.

Pierre Trudel is a Professor in the School of Human Kinetics at the University of Ottawa, Canada. His main research area is coaches' development. In addition to coach development, his teaching interests include research methods and how to succeed in graduate studies.

1 Introduction

Lee Nelson, Ryan Groom, and Paul Potrac

Background and aims

Since 2000 there has been a significant increase in the publication of coaching-specific research. While sports coaching is not as developed as some of the more established sports science disciplines (i.e. sports psychology, sports sociology, sports physiology, and sports biomechanics) it is now recognized as a bona fide area of academic inquiry (Gilbert 2002; Gilbert and Trudel 2004; Potrac *et al.* 2013). This rise in scholarly activity has been accompanied by a growing number of academic institutions offering undergraduate and post-graduate sports coaching modules and courses. For example, according to Bush (2008) there are 217 sports coaching undergraduate degrees and 11 postgraduate programs in British universities. This trend can arguably be attributed to an increasing recognition of the role coaches play in shaping and facilitating the experiences of adults, adolescents, and children in a wide variety of sporting contexts (Cushion and Lyle 2011; Potrac *et al.* 2013).

It is in light of such developments that students are being offered the opportunity to complete coaching-specific investigations as part of their program of degree-level study. In spite of this, however, there has been a paucity of texts designed to develop coaching students' and neophyte researchers' understandings of research methods in relation to their chosen discipline area. Rather, individuals pursuing coaching research have, until now, had to refer to mainstream texts and books from other areas of the sports sciences. While numerous research methods resources exist, it has been our experience that coaching students have found it difficult to apply the topics, concepts, and discussions included within such texts to the investigation of coaching. It was because of such experiences that we decided to accept an invitation to compile this edited book.

In recognition of the above, this book is offered as a teaching tool for research methods courses on undergraduate and postgraduate coaching programs, as well as being a resource for more developed coaching researchers. The objectives of this book include: (a) helping coaching students to appreciate the importance of developing an understanding of this area; (b) introducing key topics, issues, and concepts in a discipline-specific way; (c) encouraging coaching researchers to give greater consideration towards research methods; and, finally, (d) stimulating interest in the academic investigation of sports coaching. To achieve these aims this book covers all facets of the research process. This includes how to design, conduct, and disseminate coaching research, and also how methodological decisions are inextricably underpinned by our respective philosophical beliefs as coaching researchers. Here, the book seeks to introduce readers to a range of philosophical stances, quantitative and qualitative methods of data collection and analysis, as well as forms of representation and dissemination.

Recognizing that the academic study of sports coaching (and coach education) comprises contrasting philosophical positions and preferred methodological designs, our intention was to help students and neophyte researchers to navigate the often contradictory and messy nature of coaching research. We hoped that doing so would enable readers to better understand the methodological options that are available when making research decisions. However, our choice to present a broad overview of methodological issues, alongside space restrictions, meant that omissions had to be made and limits were placed on the degree to which the topics included could be covered. Indeed, in an ideal world, we would like to have included a greater range of the modes of inquiry available to coaching researchers (e.g. action research, historical analysis, mixed method designs, narrative analysis, and visual sociology). However, we hope that the contents of this book will serve as a useful introductory text, offering a start (rather than an end) point in readers' exploration of research methods in sports coaching. Throughout the text, we would like the reader to consider the term sports coaching as an umbrella term for inquiry into sports coaching and, indeed, sports coach education.

While we wanted this text to convey not only the theory but also the practice of sports coaching research, it was not our intention to compile a simple 'how to' research methods book. Although guiding principles delivered in a contextually relevant way were considered to be important, our brief to the contributing authors was to write their respective chapters in a way that would help to evidence contrasting positions, initiate critical debates, and, perhaps most importantly, convey the often messy realities of research; features that we believe are underrepresented and underplayed in what are often sanitized accounts of such endeavors. Our goal was to develop a text that could help its readers to begin to grapple with contemporary methodological discussions, and understand the complex realities of conducting coaching research. To achieve these aims, we invited a number of scholars who have either contributed to the burgeoning field of coaching research, or research methods debates in the sports sciences more generally, to write the chapters in this book. We are extremely grateful for their respective contributions, and believe they have helped to produce what we hope will be an enriching and practically useful text for students and academics wishing to undertake research in coaching and, indeed, coach education.

The structure of the book

In terms of its structure, the book consists of twenty-three chapters that are presented in six distinct parts. Each of these chapters endeavors to link theory and practice through the utilization of standardized thematic formats. To this end, the following subheadings are principally utilized throughout the book (with the exception of three chapters located in Part I): (1) *Introduction and overview* (i.e. introduction to the concepts, definitions, and debates in the topic area being discussed), (2) *Applied issues and considerations* (i.e. those features that researchers should consider when addressing this aspect of the research process), and (3) *Reflections from the field* (i.e. rich and honest personal sharings about the messy realities of coaching research).

Part I: Philosophical considerations

The chapters in Part I (Chapters 2–5) provide the reader with a detailed exploration of what is frequently referred to as the paradigm debate. The part opens with an overview of discussions in this area (Chapter 2) before considering the three dominant paradigms, namely logical positivism (Chapter 3), intepretivism (Chapter 4), and poststructuralism (Chapter 5), in greater detail. Chapters discussing the three dominant research paradigms each employ the following structural format to ensure consistency of presentation and understanding: (1) *Research paradigm* (i.e. the philosophical and methodological foundations of the research paradigm), (2) *Implications for coaching research* (i.e. how the underpinning philosophical beliefs of the research paradigm impact on views about coaching and its investigation), and (3) *Case studies in sports coaching* (i.e. the discussion of coaching specific investigations that exemplify the research paradigm).

Part II: Preparing and initiating the research process

Part II (Chapters 6–10) addresses a number of issues that we believe that coaching researchers may wish to contemplate during the initial phase of a research project. More specifically, Chapter 6 discusses factors for supervisors and supervisee to consider when navigating the supervisory process. Chapter 7 provides a critical discussion of the strengths and limitations associated with different types of literature reviews, and the place of such reviews in the broader research process. Discussions then turn to the multiple interpretations and applications of theory (Chapter 8), as well as forms of representation (Chapter 9) in coaching research. The part ends with an exploration of research ethics and the notion of overt and covert studies (Chapter 10).

Part III: Quantitative approaches to coaching research

Part III (Chapters 11–14) focuses on the quantitative investigation of coaching. Chapter 11 specifically discusses the use of questionnaires. This is followed by

Chapter 12, which considers the application of systematic observation instruments. Chapter 13 then provides guidelines for the statistical analysis of quantitative data. The part closes with an exploration of those factors that should be considered when evaluating the quality of quantitative coaching research (Chapter 14).

Part IV: Qualitative approaches to coaching research

Part IV (Chapters 15–18) concentrates on the qualitative investigation of coaching. The part opens by exploring the use of interviews (Chapter 15). This is followed by a discussion of ethnographic research (Chapter 16). Chapter 17 provides guidelines for the analysis of qualitative data. The part closes with an examination of criteria that can assist with judging the quality of qualitative coaching research (Chapter 18).

Part V: Contemporary approaches to coaching research

In Part V (Chapters 19–21) the chapters introduce a range of contemporary approaches to coaching research. It should be noted that while the options presented in this part are arguably contemporary from a coaching research perspective, these approaches have a longer history of application within the broader field of social science. More specifically, this part provides a discussion of the writing of autoethnography (Chapter 19), discourse analysis (Chapter 20), and conversation analysis (Chapter 21). Collectively the chapters in this part provide relatively novel approaches to the investigation of coaching.

Part VI: Disseminating coaching research

The two chapters (Chapters 22–23) comprising Part VI attempt to prepare neophytes for disseminating their findings. Here, the oral presentation of research is the focus of Chapter 22, while Chapter 23 addresses the explicit and tacit rules of publishing coaching research in peer-reviewed journal articles and how cultural dynamics can influence research experiences.

Using the book

At its inception our goal was to design a text that could take the reader through the entire research process. We also acknowledged that readers would be at different stages of their respective research careers, and that depending on the readers current activities, interests, and purposes, some chapters would likely be considered more pertinent than others. It is in light of this that we set ourselves the challenge of trying to deliver a book that would provide a collection of stand-alone chapters which also collectively form a coherent whole. We hoped that such a design would cater for different uses of the book. For example, undergraduate students who are studying research methods for the first time might wish to work their way through each chapter of the book. More experienced coaching researchers might want to read those chapters that they identify as being of particular importance and interest, as and when they are deemed to be relevant. Additionally, we envisage that project supervisors might wish to recommend to their supervisees those chapters that they believe could aid the progression and development of their student(s).

While we have endeavored to produce a coherent book with a logical structure, it should be acknowledged that any edited text comprises a range of writing styles and approaches. We expect that many readers, especially those new to this area, may discover that the book's chapters contain various topics and terms that are unfamiliar to them. It has been our experience that developing an appreciation of research methods is much like trying to learn a new language. Learning the language of research methods, like trying to learn the language of any new research area, can often prove to be a challenging and daunting endeavor; we speak from experience. Nevertheless, it is our belief that this is a worthwhile pursuit, as developing an appreciation of research methods not only helps students to become more informed and critical consumers of scholarly texts, but also provides researchers with an underpinning knowledge base that can allow them to conduct their own research endeavors in an informed way. We hope that engaging with this book will help you, the reader, to become more familiar with the vocabulary of this language, and how and why an understanding of this area is so important.

References

Bush, A. (2008) 'Doing coaching justice: Promoting critical consciousness in sports coaching research', unpublished PhD thesis, University of Bath.

Cushion, C. and Lyle, J. (2011) 'Conceptual development in sports coaching', in L. Lyle and C J. Cushion (eds) *Sports Coaching: Professionalisation and Practice*, London: Elsevier, 1–14.

Gilbert, W. D. (2002) 'An annotated bibliography and analysis of coaching science: 1970–2001', *Washington, DC: American Alliance for Health, Physical Education, Recreation*, online, available at: www.aahperd.org/rc/programs/upload/grantees_coaching_science.pdf.

Gilbert, W. D. and Trudel, P. (2004) 'Analysis of coaching science research published from 1970–2001', *Research Quarterly for Exercise and Sport*, 75: 388–99.

Potrac, P., Gilbert, W. and Denison, J. (eds) (2013) *The Routledge Handbook of Sports Coaching*, London: Routledge.

Part I
Philosophical considerations

2 Philosophy of knowledge

Clifford J. Mallett and Richard Tinning

Introduction and overview

Understanding and evaluating coaching effectiveness is important for several reasons, including the development of coaching practice, the professionalization of coaching, and accountability. Moreover, the evaluation of coaching practice usually informs the recruitment and retention of coaches. Making evaluative judgments about a coach's contribution to the performance of an athlete/team is a complicated task. A key question is: How do we come to know about the quality of coaching practice? Furthermore, what kind of knowledge is considered generative in this process of coming to know? There are many ways in which we might examine this complex issue. One rather typical (and simplistic) approach is to consider a coach's win–loss record. Alternatively, we might consider how a coach has contributed to the athlete's competence and confidence. How should we decide what lens to examine this issue of judging coaching effectiveness? Where do I start? What evidence counts in making judgments about the quality of coaching? What forms of knowledge might be privileged in making those judgments? And, by whom?

There is a paucity of published research that reports systematic ways in which coaches are evaluated (Gilbert and Trudel 2004). So, how might we consider a program of research in understanding coaching effectiveness? In this chapter, we will discuss some of the ways of knowing about coaching practice; how we might examine what is known; what knowledge might assist in thinking about how coaching researchers engage in the research process; and finally, how different underpinning philosophical beliefs impact on views about coaching and the investigation of coaching practice.

Coaching and coaching research from a knowledge perspective

When we make judgments about coaching we are essentially valuing some things over other things. But what is the basis for making such value judgments? Part of the answer to this can be found in the pages of philosophy. When we think about knowledge we enter the world of epistemology. This word refers to the branch of philosophy that is concerned with the nature of knowledge (what it is), and how it is acquired (how do we get it). If you come from a background of science or psychology you might find some frustration with philosophy because many of the terms used do not have an operational definition by which you can 'nail' the concept. It is a different language and it might take a while to become familiar with it, understand what it means, and why it is considered important to understand.

There are different kinds of knowledge. Consider an athlete who knows how to pole-vault. This is an extremely complex movement task requiring considerable knowledge of the body in space, knowledge of force and when to apply it, among other aspects. The athlete needs such knowledge in order to execute the task. There is also the knowledge that someone might have about how to do a pole-vault without actually personally being able to perform the skill. Some relevant questions for coaching are: Does the athlete need to be able to perform as well as describe what they are doing when they perform? And, what of the coach? Does the coach need to be able to actually do the pole-vault? Or is it sufficient for the coach to understand the pole-vault and explain it to his athlete charge?

Being able to explain or describe something can be thought of as theoretically oriented knowledge. It is known as propositional (or knowing that) knowledge. *Propositional knowledge* is concerned with substantiating as true such statements as 'I know that the Norman conquest of England occurred in 1066' or 'I know that the run-up and pole-plant is a vital aspect of successful pole-vaulting'. *Practical knowledge*, on the other hand, is concerned with what Arnold (1988) called 'performative competence' such as 'I can draw a picture of a duck' or 'I can do a do a forehand volley in tennis'. As Arnold tells us '[w]hat is important to understand about these two types of knowledge is that each has its own rationality' (Arnold 1988: 21). 'Knowing-that' is a function of human theorizing and is concerned with the discovery of truths that are adequately supported by reason and experience, whereas 'knowing-how' is concerned with the rational execution of certain physical skills to a reasonable degree of competence. They are different expressions of human rationality.

Arnold also distinguishes between weak and strong senses of practical knowledge. Practical knowledge in the *weak sense* is where an individual can perform an activity (i.e. he or she is physically able to do something) but cannot articulate how it is done. Practical knowledge in the *strong sense* is where an individual is able to physically perform an activity or skill, but can also articulate or describe how it is done. Being able to identify and articulate how a performance was done is essential to the strong sense of practical knowledge. A key issue for sports coaching is the nature of the practical knowledge (weak or strong) that is required for coaching. At face-value it seems appropriate that a coach possesses practical knowledge in the strong sense, but it is not that clear cut.

Although there is knowledge about movement that can only be acquired through participation in movement, it is not clear to us whether or not such knowledge is absolutely essential to teach movement. Consider the kinesthetic understandings that result from participation in a particular activity. Knowing what it feels like to do a pole-vault might be useful in communicating to athletes what it might feel like when they launch themselves into the air on the end of a pole, but often those feelings are idiosyncratic or at least difficult to articulate in a way that makes sense to others. The key question here is whether being able to perform a given activity *necessarily* enables the coach to present the athlete with a greater range of explanations, analogies, teaching points which will facilitate learning the activity, than could be expected of a coach without personal practical knowledge of that movement.

This returns us to the issue of Arnold's weak and strong senses of practical knowledge. Clearly, practical knowledge in the weak sense is of limited ped-agogical value for a coach. And obviously, practical knowledge in the strong sense would be of advantage to a coach. However, would it be possible to possess knowledge of how a movement is performed *without* being able to perform it oneself? The answer is yes and one only needs to look at sports like gymnastics and freestyle skiing to recognize that many coaches do in fact possess extensive knowledge about particular movement skills *without* being able to perform the movements themselves. So, the essential knowledge for the coach is knowledge *about* (i.e. propositional knowledge) how to perform a practical activity and the corresponding ways of organizing the graded, progressive practice necessary to acquire the skill. Also being able to perform the skill might be a bonus, but it is not a necessity.

Another dimension of knowing is what Polanyi (1966) termed *tacit* knowledge. Tacit knowledge is an embodied 'know-how' and also includes feelings or kinesthetic understandings. For example, knowing how to ride a bike is something that for many people is tacit knowledge. They still can do it even after decades of absence from the skill because they still possess the tacit knowledge of the skill. Such knowledge includes what it feels like to ride a bike and is largely idiosyncratic and difficult to express in a way that others can actually experience it the same way. From a coaching perspective, tacit knowledge, while obviously important for the learner, is very difficult to pass on (transfer) to others. It is different in *kind* from explicit propositional knowledge that can be expressed in language and objectively confirmed.

Behind epistemology is an even more fundamental philosophical concept, namely ontology. Ontology is that part of philosophy concerned with the nature of reality, the nature of existence. Does something actually exist? And how would you know? In regard to knowledge, some begin with the ontological assumption that all 'worthwhile' knowledge is knowable. It is already 'out there' waiting to be discovered, measured, and otherwise apprehended by science. We can think of the elements in the periodic table, Kreb's cycle, and the structure of the atom as this sort of knowledge; knowable 'things' that have been discovered, measured, or otherwise understood through science.

There are others who reject the idea that reality exists outside our human, subjective understanding of it. For example, they argue that knowledge is socially constructed, meaning that we, as members of a culture, simply agree to what knowledge is. Typically agreement is made through language e.g. 'we can agree that this is a fish'. However, such agreement breaks down across languages. A fish is a *poisson* in French and a *pescado* in Spanish. The material animal we recognize as a fish (or *poisson* or *pescado*) exists independently of our naming it, but our *knowledge of it* is socially constructed within and through our culture.

There are many practical examples of knowledge obviously being socially constructed. Social practices such as democracy, religion, and sports are not things *of nature*. Rather they are things of culture; they don't exist independently of humans, indeed they 'exist' only because we humans have invented them. So, we can understand that a fish, or an ocean, *exists* in a different way from something like democracy or sports – they have a different ontology.

Ontologically, one's BMI is different from one's IQ. While both can be 'measured', one is determined by measuring things that have a particular *kind of existence* (mass and height might be thought of as 'real' in that they have a physical presence) whereas IQ is a measure of how we respond to certain questions none of which have a reality like height, for example. This may seem to have strayed a long way from the matter of judging coaching effectiveness and quality, but there is a link. We can think of the different criteria that might be used in judging coaching quality *as representing different ways of knowing* and even as having different ontologies.

If we judge coaching *effectiveness* by 'objective' measures such as win–loss ratio, our knowledge is of the kind that is propositional and objective. We can count or measure it and those data are objective and easily verified. If, however, we talk about coaching *quality* things get more complicated. Judgments of quality in coaching will usually include judgments of such non-objective things as interpersonal communication (coach to athlete), enthusiasm, creating an autonomy-supportive environment, empathy, and initiative, among others. These are *different realities* from those considered in effectiveness. Questions of quality ask questions of different kinds of knowledge and how you might come to know such knowledge. While it is possible to 'measure' these attributes of a coach's 'performance', the measures are of a different kind from a measurement such as win–loss ratio. Even though we can even train two observers to judge a non-objective measure such as enthusiasm with a high degree of agreement, the thing we are 'measuring' has a different ontological existence.

Applied issues and considerations

Researchers who set out to investigate coaching effectiveness or coaching quality will sometimes use different research traditions in their work. As will be seen in other chapters in this section, these traditions represent different paradigms, different philosophical and theoretical frameworks for thinking about and doing research. Paradigms orient and represent particular ways of thinking. They are grounded in certain assumptions about nature and reality; that is, they have different ontological geneses. Think for a moment about our way of thinking about the earth and its relation to the sun. The earth was, for many thousands of years, thought to be the center of the universe. This was the dominant paradigm until the sixteenth century when Copernicus published his *De revolutionibus orbium coelestium* (*On the Revolutions of the Celestial Spheres*). In this book Copernicus showed (mathematically) that the earth (and all the other planets) revolved around the sun. This heliocentric paradigm was a huge challenge to the dominant paradigm of the time.

Paradigms also operate in thinking about what we might call the non-physical world. For example, within the broad fields of psychology and psychiatry there are different paradigms with regard to the treatment of mental disorders. Freudian psychoanalysis emphasizes that human drives are an expression of innate sexual and aggressive impulses and that many mental disorders, such as neurosis, can be cured by going back (what Freud called the 'talking cure') to the early childhood events in the family. Behavior therapy, on the other hand, represents a different *paradigm* for treatment of mental disorders. It works on changing behaviors, and through it mental attitudes (Eysenck 1990).

Research is often classified by the paradigm that underpins the research process. We read of positivist, interpretive, and critical research paradigms in the world of researching into coaching. These paradigms reflect certain values, beliefs, and dispositions toward the social world. Early career coaching researchers should consider in which of these frameworks they situate their research studies. Moreover, it is essential that researchers are cognizant of the ontological and epistemological assumptions that underpin each of the three research paradigms and the subsequent implications these have for methodological decisions. It is important to consider these differing theoretical perspectives because they influence the research process – what questions are considered important and how they should be answered.

The *positivist* research tradition (see Chapter 3) is a paradigm that is dominant in the natural sciences (such as biology, physics, medicine) and it begins with the ontological assumption that there is a real world 'out there' that can be objectively measured. In coaching research the key goal of this paradigm is the prediction and control of human behavior (e.g. athletes' performance outcomes). Positivistic research tends to use quantitative data (but this is not a necessary and sufficient attribute to deem a research project as positivist). Often data (numbers) are treated to various forms of statistical analysis to determine whether results have occurred by chance or by some targeted intervention. Positivistic research in the social sciences has its roots in behavioral psychology and has been a dominant discourse in coaching science. This is unsurprising because particular ways of coaching are thought to control and predict desirable athlete behaviors (i.e. cause–effect relationships). In an attempt to enhance athletes' performance outcomes positivistic traditions are reflected in research that has examined the independent and interactive behaviors of coaches and athletes during the coaching process. Researchers aligned to the positivistic traditions have observed and measured coach behaviors in an attempt to design and test coach behavior interventions aimed at enhancing athlete outcomes. For example, in understanding why some coaches are more successful than others we might examine potential differences in their personality traits. In this examination we might use empirically supported measures (questionnaires), such as the NEO-PI-3 (McRae and Costa 2010). In collecting data on coaches' motivation we might use questionnaires such as the Coach Motivation Questionnaire (McLean *et al.* 2012) to assist our understanding of the relationship with coaches' behaviors. Finally, it is important to acknowledge that positivist researchers are often in search of a testable proposition; for example, successful coaches (compared with less successful coaches) are characterized by a specific personality profile.

Another increasingly popular research tradition comes from the social sciences and begins with a different set of assumptions about knowledge and reality. The *interpretivist paradigm* (see Chapter 4) sees reality as constructed by the individual – people experience things differently and hence the research process should try to uncover the meaning that individuals ascribe to an event or happening. Individuals make sense of their experiences in unique ways; however, this meaning-making is also subjected to a larger social influence (Macdonald *et al.* 2002). In more fully understanding 'events' questions associated with interpretivist inquiry will consider not only how people make sense of that experience, but also what underpins that meaning-making. This research tradition also assumes multiple subjective realities and can give voice to a range of research participants' subjective experiences. An interpretive researcher attempts to make explicit one's understanding of human meaning in constructing our dynamic social world. Typically (but not always) this research relies on qualitative type data such as interviews. Rynne and colleagues (2010), for example, used semi-structured interviews to gain an understanding of how high-performance sports coaches learned their craft in the workplace. In that research, scholarship (early career) coaches reported how their learning was influenced by (i) the roles they were afforded and not afforded; and (ii) the distribution of power in their relationship with head coaches. Researchers working with the interpretive paradigm might describe their work by such terms as phenomenology, ethnography, narrative inquiry, action research, or life history. Consistent with these research methodologies is the notion of socially constructed multiple truths. Unlike those from the positivistic research tradition, interpretivist researchers do not attempt to predict or generalize behavior, but attempt to understand subjective experience in the context of time and place.

Another paradigm that frames some coaching research is the *critical paradigm* (see Chapter 5). For researchers who position their work in the critical paradigm their issues of concern are those related to social justice and equity. This work is avowedly political in the sense that it sets out to make a difference to people's lives by exposing and challenging inequities and power relations. Topics of focus might include gender, sexuality, power, ability, social class, and/or ethnicity. Critical-oriented research most often, but certainly not exclusively, uses qualitative data. There are many theoretical tools used in critical-oriented research including: critical theory, poststructural theory, feminist theory, postcolonial theory, critical race theory, and critical ethnography. The work of Natalie Barker-Ruchti (2012) is illustrative of the critical paradigm applied to coaching research. Barker-Ruchti completed a qualitative study of elite level women's artistic gymnasts. She was concerned that the extreme training practices might be oppressive of young women and she wanted her research to contribute to exposing and challenging inequities and power relations between coaches and their charges. Her work drew on poststructuralist and feminist theories to understand the experience of young women in artistic gymnasts. What she found was that, for the young women in her study, the experience of being an elite gymnast was both oppressive and emancipating *at the same time.* Critical researchers in coaching science ask questions about their own and others' assumptions and purposes to challenge reproductive coaching practices and promote opportunities for structural and behavior change.

It is important to acknowledge that individually these research paradigms are insufficient to enable the investigation of all possible research questions in coaching science. Researchers from the three paradigms have the potential to provide complementary and rich understandings of key questions in sport coaching and therefore research findings from all paradigms should be valued for their unique and overlapping contributions to answering those important questions. Understanding these research paradigms, and their underpinning ontological and epistemological assumptions, is underscored because they provide a framework for thinking about and conducting coaching science research in a rigorous and systematic way. But we should also acknowledge their limitations.

Reflections from the field

As a practical example of research that illustrates some of the many issues regarding epistemology and ontology outlined above, let us consider the work of Kelly and Hickey (2008) as represented in their book *The Struggle for the Body, Mind and Soul of AFL Footballers.* While not research into coaching per se, what Kelly and Hickey did was to investigate what an athlete needed to become a modern Australian Football League (AFL) player. In the process they were researching the development of a professional footballer *identity*. In their case a football identity comprised three dimensions: body, mind, and soul. They determined that football clubs set out to shape not only the *bodies* of their young players (as represented by measures of physical development and performance) but also their *minds* (developing their 'football brain', and their coach-ability or receptivity to being coached) and their *soul* (as represented by their character, work ethic, courage, moral judgment).

The data they collected for their research was in the form of words, thoughts, and ideas of coaches, recruiting staff, players, and executives from clubs and peak groups responsible for the industry. The data were collected in interviews, focus group conversations, and written in documents. The type of data they used is important. How, for example, do you 'get at' the notion of soul? While judgments about the *body* can be made by objective measures of BMI, running and kicking performance (their reality is 'out there' waiting to be measured), and judgments about *mind* might use objective measures of personality traits (although in this case they did not measure personality), there are no such measures of the *soul*. Rather, the soul is a social construction and relies on the agreement in a particular social context as to what its various characteristics might be. For example, what is meant by courage? If someone who dives to retrieve a ball in a very dangerous situation never perceives the situation to be dangerous, is he showing courage?

The AFL have produced a *Recruiting Operators Manual* that is used to quantify and compare talent in the recruiting process. It lists fourteen performance areas; ten for the body (including for example pace, endurance kicking ability, etc.), one for the mind (football smarts), and four for the soul (including football character, leadership, and self-discipline). Each player is given a rating 1–5 (poor to rare, a 4 being excellent) on each of these 'measures'. What might seem obvious to the reader already, given the discussion above, is that the things included in this list are not all of the same *kind*. Moreover, what it takes *to know* certain performance characteristics is also different in kind. For example, knowing a player is 'excellent' in terms of pace is determined simply by means of an objective measurement of speed over distance (sub 2.95 seconds for 20 meters). However, to be rated 'excellent' for football character requires a different type of knowledge. In this case a player is rated as 'excellent' if he 'Plays and trains at a high level of mental and physical intensity. Enjoys training and club environment'. There is no measurement because the nature of character is of a different kind from speed. The 'variable' of football character is socially constructed and the judgment purely subjective.

A similar scenario would evolve in considering all of the 'variables', aspects, or dimensions that might make up a quality coach. While some aspects might be measureable, others require an agreement across subjective judgments. Reconciling these different kinds of knowledge is a dilemma to be resolved for those who want to make a judgment of coach's work.

A question for the coaching field in general is: to what extent are certain types of knowledge privileged over other types and if so what are the implications? For example, is objective measurement (as knowledge) privileged over subjective judgment? Are researchers' emotional investments in particular ways of knowing helpful or a hindrance in judging quality coaching? One useful way of thinking about his issue is through the *Stats versus Stories* challenge. Think for a moment about some of the most important decisions you have made in your life. Now think about *how* you made the decisions. In all situations we are usually bombarded with 'evidence' that we can use to assist in making a decision. Some of the 'evidence' will be anecdotal, usually in the form of stories that are passed around. Still other forms of 'evidence' will be available in the form of statistics (e.g. population data). If they contradict each other, how do you make a judgment, how do you choose?

In thinking about a research project in coaching science, it is important first to ask a good question. In making that decision one should also consider the purpose of the research. The question should drive the research process. Once the key research question is decided scholars should choose the most appropriate framework for coming to know about that question. It is interesting to observe that over the past decade or so there has been a growing coaching research literature that is based on the interpretive paradigm. Typically such empirical research is reported as case studies, narratives, and autoethnographies. These studies are called *idiographic* (a term used to describe the effort to understand the meaning of contingent, unique, and often subjective phenomena) and they give detailed accounts about a small number (perhaps one) case (athlete, coach, or event). The findings from such research are not generalizable to the population of coaches or athletes or even all similar events. However, although they might be idiosyncratic, they provide a valuable window into the world of coaching that cannot be obtained by research using other research methods. The important thing is not which research paradigm is best, but an acknowledgment that they each provide different versions of 'truth' and all contribute to our knowledge of coaching.

References

Arnold, P. (1988) *Education, Movement and the Curriculum*, London: Falmer Press.

Barker-Ruchti, N. (2012) *Women's Artistic Gymnastics: An (Auto-)ethnographic Journey*, Basel: Gesowip.

Eysenck, H. (1990) *Rebel with a Cause: The Autobiography of Hans Eysenck*, London: W.H. Allen & Co.

Gilbert, W. D. and Trudel, P. (2004) 'Analysis of coaching science research published from 1970–2001', *Research Quarterly for Exercise and Sport*, 75: 388–99.

Kelly, P. and Hickey, C. (2008) *The Struggle for the Body, Mind and Soul of AFL Footballers*, Melbourne: Australian Scholarly Publishing.

Macdonald, D., Kirk, D., Metzler, M., Nilges, L. M., Schempp, P. and Wright, J. (2002) 'It's all very well, in theory: Theoretical perspectives and their applications in contemporary pedagogical research', *Quest*, 54(2): 133–56.

McLean, K. N., Mallett, C. J. and Newcombe, P. (2012) 'Assessing coach motivation: The development of the coach motivation questionnaire (CMQ)', *Journal of Sport & Exercise Psychology*, 34: 184–207.

Polanyi, M. (1966) *The Tacit Dimension*, Chicago: University of Chicago Press.

Rynne, S., Mallett, C. J. and Tinning, R. (2010) 'The learning of sport coaches in high performance workplaces', *Sport, Education and Society*, 15: 331–46.

3   Logical positivism

Ronald E. Smith and Frank L. Smoll

Research paradigm

In our Youth Enrichment in Sports (YES) project that has spanned more than three decades, we have focused on interactions between coaches and young athletes. We have been concerned with identifying coaching behaviors that underlie athletes' desirable psychosocial characteristics and with developing an evidence-based intervention program that trains coaches in creating an athletic environment that enhances coach–athlete and peer interactions, increases the pleasure of participating, enhances self-esteem, fosters adaptive achievement goals, reduces performance anxiety, and decreases the percentage of young athletes who drop out of sports.

In this chapter, we discuss the role of measurement in our basic and applied research, theory testing, and program evaluation. In this work, we have chosen to use observational methods as a major research tool to measure what coaches do during practices and games and to assess how these behaviors (as well as athlete-perceived coaching behaviors and coaches' behavioral self-perceptions) relate to athletes' reactions to their athletic experience. We first discuss the beliefs and assumptions that underlie this approach. To achieve our objectives, a number of important assumptions had to be spelled out. Some were philosophical and others were methodological.

Theory, research, and intervention are reciprocally related

A distinction is often made between basic and applied science. Basic science is usually defined as the development of theories and the discovery of knowledge for its own sake, whereas applied science involves the applications of knowledge derived from basic science for the solution of practical problems, like developing an evidence-based coaching intervention. These relations do not simply involve a one-way causal path from knowledge or theory to application. Instead, they involve two-way, or reciprocal, relations between theory, research, and interventions. This means that each of the three facets has a causal impact on the others and is, in turn, influenced by them. Thus, our theories deepen our understanding and guide our research, and our research, in turn, is the most important influence on theory development and testing (see Chapter 8). Our theories also affect the interventions we develop, but the success of these interventions reflect, in part, the adequacy of our theory. If the interventions do not work, this may mean that our theory needs revisions. Finally, the link connecting intervention and research is also a reciprocal one. Consequently, our research provides leads for intervention, and sound outcome research allows us to assess the efficacy of the interventions and, perhaps, to identify the aspects of the intervention that are responsible for its success. In turn, the nature of the intervention dictates the outcome variables that we focus on and the way the evaluation is conducted. Attending to these three reciprocal linkages helps to ensure that our theories, research, and applied activities will support one another and advance our field as a scientific and applied discipline.

Without good measures, we have nothing

Measurement is the *sine qua non* of scientific activity. A theory consists of a set of concepts (theoretical constructs such as coach behaviors, self-esteem, perceptions, or anxiety) and propositions stating how they are assumed to be related to one another. Without reliable and valid measures of our scientific concepts, we cannot operationally define them in a manner that allows us to test relations among them. For example, we cannot study self-esteem (a construct) without some external measure of it, such as a scale that produces a 'self-esteem' score. Even when research is atheoretical, we cannot study a topic like coaching behaviors without adequate measures of it. And, where interventions are concerned, the nature of the intervention dictates the outcome variables that we focus on and the way the evaluation is conducted. Thus, measurement is at the core of all scientific activity, be it in psychology or in other sciences.

Multimethod and quantitative measurement is optimal

Several different measurement approaches can be taken in coaching research. For example, if we want to know how coaches behave, we can ask the coaches what they do and how often, ask the athletes the same questions, or observe the coaches and record what they actually do. As explained below, the theoretical model that guided our research required that we develop ways of measuring the same behaviors at all three levels in a way that resulted in numerical, or quantitative, indices of the behaviors. Thus, we applied a multimethod approach that involved self-reports (from the coach), reports by others (from the athletes), and objective measures of observable behaviors. Many researchers recommend the multimethod approach (e.g. Campbell and Fiske 1959).

We are committed to this type of *quantitative* research. As data, we favor numerical scores that we can subject to statistical analysis. Other researchers, some of whom describe their work in this section (see Chapters 4 and 5), use *qualitative* measures in which they interview people and then either describe what the people said or develop a categorical system to organize (and sometimes, to quantify) the verbal responses. As you shall see, we used this method ourselves to find out 'what's happening out there' as a preliminary basis for developing our quantitative measures. But this was only a means to fulfilling our quantitative goal.

Our underlying philosophy, typical of most scientists, is known as *logical positivism*. Logical positivism combines *empiricism* – the idea that observational evidence is indispensable for knowledge – with a set of scientific methods for drawing conclusions from data. This approach differs from a reliance on intuition, reason, and logic that is embodied in many philosophical and theological approaches to knowledge. Logical positivism arose in the 1920s as a school of philosophy that was primarily concerned with the logical analysis of scientific information. A key principle was *verifiability*, the assertion that a scientific statement is meaningful if and only if it can be proved true or false on the basis of experience. In this view, we know the meaning of a statement if we understand on the basis of empirical evidence (not intuitive reasoning) the conditions under which it is true or false. Somewhat later, it was recognized that verifiability was too strict a criterion, for even empirical evidence cannot prove that a proposition is true, for some future observation may show it to be false. This led to the newer criterion of *falsifiability*, which stated that it must be possible to prove that a theoretical proposition or empirical generalization is *not* true. A single (or several) inconsistent observation(s) can thus cast doubt on a theoretical proposition and possibly require a revision of a theory. Such revisions help to establish the limiting conditions under which theoretical propositions (propositions involving constructs) or empirical generalizations (relations between empirical observations) hold.

To logical positivists, metaphysical statements by their very nature are not empirically verifiable and thus are outside of the realm of scientific discourse. They are the province of philosophy. However, some philosophical assumptions (for example, Freud's proposition that unconscious processes powerfully influence behavior) can serve as a basis for hypotheses that can be tested empirically if the constructs involved can be operationally defined, as is occurring in cognitive and social psychology using such operations as priming and implicit attitude measures to access unconscious processes (Bargh and Morsella 2008). Other propositions (such as non-belief or belief in the existence of God or beliefs in determinism or free will) are philosophical assumptions that cannot be subjected to empirical test. It should be noted, however, that scientific activity is frequently based on overriding assumptions, such as the assumption of determinism that provides the basis for empirically studying 'laws of nature.'

Finally, scientific theories, as mentioned above, are axiomatic systems with *rules of correspondence* that establish relations between theoretical terms (constructs) and observations that are used to bring the constructs into the empirical realm (i.e. operationally defined measures). A theory is by its very nature deductive in that general propositions are applied to particular instances. In addition to its ability to be tested (falsifiability), the value of a theory is in part defined by the range of different domains in which it can be applied.

'Experiential knowledge' is no substitute for evidence-based practice

There are several routes to knowledge and sound practice in sport psychology. One is personal experience. Indeed, informal observations are typically the first stage in the process of scientific inquiry. People notice something of interest and try to figure out why it occurred, or they draw conclusions from their personal observations. This is a good starting point, but *experiential knowledge* cannot be the end point for an ethically grounded science of sports psychology. The reason is that personal judgment and conclusions can be fraught with sources of error, including self-serving biases that selectively reinforce already existing beliefs and mental operations that cause us to make misjudgments about probabilities. Indeed, psychologist Daniel Kahneman won the 2002 Nobel Prize in Economics for his pioneering research on the fallibility of human judgment, even by so-called experts in their fields. And for more than sixty years, we have known that simple mathematical formulas for combining clinical data to arrive at decisions often trump expert judgment by even highly experienced clinicians. William Grove and Paul Meehl (1996) surveyed 136 empirical studies across a wide range of fields that compared expert judgments and predictions with actuarial methods in which a simple mathematical equation or an actuarial table based on past research was used to make a prediction. They found that in only eight instances did the experts do better than the actuary, and that in sixty-four of the studies, the actuary did significantly better than the experts. Their explanation is that while the human brain excels at reasoning and generating theoretical propositions, it has great limitations in other activities:

> The human brain is a relatively inefficient device for noticing, selecting, categorizing, recording, retaining, retrieving, and manipulating information for inferential purposes ... The human brain is functioning as merely a poor substitute for an explicit regression equation or actuarial table. Humans simply cannot assign optimal weights to variables, and they are not consistent in applying their own weights.
>
> (Grove and Meehl 1996: 315–16)

Given the demonstrated fallibility of human observation and decision-making, we cringe when some sports psychology practitioners reject the need for scientific study of an intervention based on the faulty notion that, 'I do not need to test it, because I know it works from my own experience.' The pages of history illustrate well the folly that can result from this way of 'knowing.' For example, in the Middle Ages the expert observations of inquisitors served as the basis for a treatise, *Malleus Maleficarum*, written by two Dominican monks, that gave explicit guidelines for identifying a witch. On the basis of these principles, more than 100,000 persons were put to death as witches (Kraemer and Sprenger 1487/1970). In the history of medicine, experiential knowledge has served as the basis for procedures that physicians 'knew' were effective from their clinical experience, including purging, blood-letting, blistering, and lobotomies. Unfortunately, for their patients, these treatments were later shown through empirical research not only to be ineffective, but also dangerous and sometimes fatal.

Today, all major medical and psychological organizations champion *evidence-based practice*. This means that all interventions (whether medical, pharmacological, or behavioral) should be based on firm empirical evidence and should have demonstrated efficacy based on outcome research. The gold standard for testing interventions in the psychological and health sciences is the *randomized clinical trial*, in which participants are assigned randomly to an intervention condition or to a control condition designed to rule out other possible reasons for improvement. We believe that this standard is essential in testing sports psychology intervention programs.

Implications for coaching research

Applying the principles discussed above in our own research resulted in a five-phase approach to studying and modifying coaching behaviors.

Phase 1: Developing a conceptual model

Our work began in the 1970s when we constructed a theoretical model based on what we knew from previous research (or suspected on the basis of scientific theories) about the factors that influence coaching behaviors and their effects on young athletes. Importing concepts and methods from other areas of psychology is known as *translational research* (Smith and Smoll 2011). We knew from the start that we were dealing with a very complex social environment and that it was going to be a challenge to capture all of the complex factors involved. The model that evolved over time is presented in Figure 3.1. It depicts a broad conceptual view of coaching behaviors and other situational and individual difference variables that are assumed to influence children's reactions to their athletic experience reactions (attitudes toward the sport, their experience, the coach, and teammates), as well as the hypothesized causal relations (shown by arrows) among these coach, child, and situational factors (Smoll *et al.* 1978; Smoll and Smith 1989). The model assumes that children's evaluative reactions to what the coach does are mediated by their perceptions and recall of the coach's actual behaviors (i.e. the *psychological situation* that they create in their own minds). Likewise, as indicated by the bidirectional arrows between the perception/memory component of the model and the evaluative component, we assume that children's evaluative reactions help color their perceptions and memories of coaching behaviors.

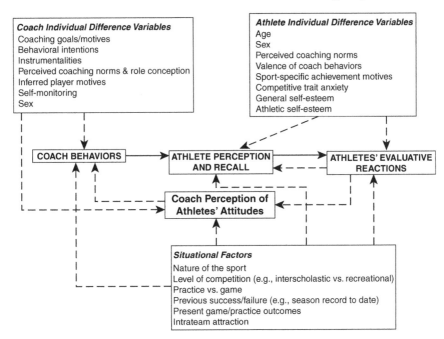

Figure 3.1 A model of adult leadership behaviors in sport and hypothesized relations among situational, cognitive, behavioral, and individual difference variables (adapted from Smoll and Smith 1989)

Phase 2: Developing measures

The next step was to adopt or develop measures of the constructs in the model. The central task was to develop coaching behavior measures. The model required that we develop measures of the actual behaviors engaged in by the coach, as well as measures of those same behaviors as perceived by the athletes and by the coaches themselves. Coaches engage in countless acts. Which ones should be the focus of measurement? At the behavioral level, we wished to develop a behavioral assessment system that trained observers could use to code coaches' behaviors during practices and games. We began by using the method of naturalistic observation. A group of researchers, situated at various vantage points, observed soccer, basketball, and baseball coaches during practices and games, verbally reporting what they saw (the situation and the coach's behavior) on tape recorders during designated time intervals. The thousands of descriptions were then typed onto individual index cards and categorized. We found that the observers agreed closely on their verbal reports of corresponding situations and behaviors, and that a relatively modest number of categories could capture the vast majority of behaviors. We called the resulting coding system the Coaching Behavior Assessment System (CBAS; Smith *et al.* 1977). The CBAS categories are presented in Table 3.1.

Table 3.1   Coding categories of the Coaching Behaviors Assessment System

Class I. Reactive Behaviors to Defined Situations

A. Responses to Desirable Performance
  1. POSITIVE REINFORCEMENT (R)
  2. NONREINFORCEMENT (NR)

B. Responses to Mistakes/Errors

  3. MISTAKE-CONTINGENT ENCOURAGEMENT (EM)
  4. MISTAKE-CONTINGENT TECHNICAL INSTRUCTION (TIM)
  5. PUNISHMENT (P)
  6. PUNITIVE TECHNICAL INSTRUCTION (TIM + P)
  7. IGNORING MISTAKES (IM)

C. Responses to Misbehaviors
  8. KEEPING CONTROL (KC)

Class II. Spontaneous Behaviors

A. Game-related

  9. GENERAL TECHNICAL INSTRUCTION (TIG)
  10. GENERAL ENCOURAGEMENT (EG)
  11. ORGANIZATION (O)
B. Game-irrelevant

  12. GENERAL COMMUNICATION (GC)

Reactive behaviors are those that occur in response to designated situations, whereas spontaneous ones are initiated by the coach.

In order for a coding system to be useful for research and provide valid measurement, observers must be trained to use it in a uniform fashion. We therefore developed a detailed training manual with examples of the coding categories, a programmed learning component, and graphic (cartoon) representations of the behaviors. We also developed an accompanying video that enabled us to test observers' codings of representative behavior sequences of coaching behaviors depicted by an actor. These training materials allowed us to train observers to a high level of interobserver agreement (see Chapter 12). When they had demonstrated competence in using the system, observers were sent to the sports environment to collect data. The observers situated themselves in the spectator areas and recorded each coaching behavior as it occurred, using the codes (e.g. *R* for Positive Reinforcement or *P* for Punishment). During contests, observers also recorded the score at designated intervals (in baseball, at the end of each half-inning) so that we could determine how coaches behaved during various types of competitive situations (for example, while winning or losing). We found that the average coach engaged in about 200 codable behaviors during a typical youth baseball or basketball game.

The conceptual model required that we also develop measures of coach and athlete perceptions of the coach's behaviors as well as an objective behavioral coding system. As an example, the behavior of Positive Reinforcement was measured in a multimethod manner at all three levels, as shown below:

CBAS Training Manual definition of Positive Reinforcement

POSITIVE REINFORCEMENT or REWARD (R). A positive reaction by the coach to a desirable performance or effort by one or more athletes. It should be noted that R may be verbal or non-verbal in nature.

Examples: (a) A coach says, 'Way to go,' or 'Good play, Jerry,' after a good play.

(b) The coach claps or pats a player on the back after a good play, such as getting a hit, or scoring a goal, or trying hard.

Athlete item for coach's use of Positive Reinforcement:

Coaches reward or praise athletes when they do something well or try really hard. Some coaches give a lot of *Reward* while others do not. How often did your coach *Reward* you for good plays or effort? Circle the number that indicates how often your coach *Rewarded* you. (Rated on a scale ranging from 1, *never* to 7, *almost always*)

Coach self-report item for Positive Reinforcement:

Coaches reward or praise athletes when they do something well or try really hard. Some coaches give a lot of *Reward* while others do not. How often did you *Reward* your athletes for good plays or effort? Circle the number that indicates how often you used *Reward*. (Rated on a scale ranging from 1, *never* to 7, *almost always*)

As our research program proceeded, we developed measures of the coach and player individual difference variables included in the conceptual model (Figure 3.1). This allowed us to assess individual difference variables that influenced how coaches behaved and how athletes responded to various classes of coaching behaviors. For example, we found that the athlete's level of self-esteem was an important influence. Athletes who were low in self-esteem were far more affected by the supportive behaviors of Positive Reinforcement and Mistake-contingent Encouragement because of their stronger need to feel good about themselves (Smith and Smoll 1990).

Behavioral measures, self-reports, and reports of others' behaviors all have their advantage and potential disadvantages. Behavioral measures (see Chapter 12) provide the most 'objective' method and are preferred for this reason by many researchers. However, the value of a behavioral assessment system depends on whether it captures the most important classes of behavior and whether observers are able to use it accurately. In the CBAS, the behavioral categories are quite broad, and there are issues with the breadth of categories. For example, reinforcement for good performance and for effort are lumped together in a single category, but they may have different impacts on athletes. Another issue, known as *reactivity*, refers to the fact that people may control and modify their behavior when they know that they are being observed. To counter reactivity, we do not use the data collected from the first game we observe. This provides a period of acclimation, and coaches have reported that they soon become oblivious to the presence of an observer. It is also note-worthy that, in most instances, we can record only a sample of the coach's behaviors over the course of the season. In our research, for example, despite the fact that we obtained a behavioral profile of coaches that exceeded 1,000 behaviors, we cannot be sure we did not miss important behaviors occurring during the many games we did not record. These and other factors could influence the validity of the behavioral data.

Self-report (see Chapter 11) is the only way that we can assess people's perceptions and other aspects of personal experience. Self-report measures also have their disadvantages, however. People are not always candid in their responses. Some measures are susceptible to individual differences in people's readiness to respond in a socially desirable fashion in their self-descriptions or ratings of others. There may also be distortions in recall of events that occurred some time ago, and asking athletes or coaches to give a summary response of their behaviors over an entire season can yield a very imprecise response unless the behaviors occurred in the very low or very high ranges of the rating scale. Thus, no measure is perfect, and in most areas of psychology, measurement precision is much more challenging than in the medical or physical sciences.

Case studies[1] in sports coaching

Having developed measures that met acceptable scientific standards, we were ready to proceed to the last three phases of our research, which involved: (a) assessing relations between coaching behaviors and young athletes' evaluative responses, (b) using this information to develop an intervention for coaches, and (c) evaluating the effects of the coach training program. As we describe these facets of our work, keep in mind that none would have been possible without valid measures of the constructs in our conceptual model.

Phase 3: Studying the effects of coaching behaviors

The CBAS provided us with the tool we needed to assess the actual behavior of coaches and to discover how they impacted young athletes. In large-scale observational studies, trained observers coded more than 80,000 behaviors of some 70 coaches during baseball and basketball games. At the end of the season, we interviewed and administered questionnaires to nearly 1,000 children who had played for the coaches to measure how their sport experience had affected them (Smith and Smoll 2011). We found clear relations between coaching behavior profiles and many aspects of the young athletes' experiences, including how much they liked playing for the coach, how much fun they had, and how their feelings about themselves were affected. As noted earlier, we also found that youngsters low in self-esteem were especially affected by their relationship with the coach (Smith and Smoll 1990).

In early studies, we examined relations between season-long totals of CBAS behaviors and children's reactions to their coaches. When behavioral profiles were created involving all behaviors over the entire season, relations were found, but they were more modest than we expected. However, coaches differ not only in how frequently they exhibit CBAS behaviors across all situations combined, but they also show individual differences in how they respond in particular situations, such as when things are going well or badly for their teams. In more recent research, we have studied how these situation–behavior patterns (which we call *behavioral signatures*) are related to other variables, such as athletes' attitudes toward their coach. For example, we focused on the psychologically disparate situations of winning and losing during games. We found that the frequency of supportive behaviors (reinforcement and encouragement) was significantly related to end-of-season liking for the coach only when these behaviors occurred while the team was winning ($r = .50$). Supportive behaviors that occurred while losing were unrelated to liking for the coach ($r = .09$). The opposite pattern occurred for punitive behaviors. Punitive behaviors during losing game situations were negatively related to liking for the coach ($r = -.37$), but unrelated when they occurred while winning. When we examined the behavioral profiles of the most-liked and least-liked coaches, a notable pattern emerged. When games were tied or very close, the two groups of coaches did not differ in their rates of supportive and punitive behaviors, but this changed noticeably when their teams were losing or winning. When losing, least-liked coaches engaged in high rates of punishment, whereas best-liked coaches had below-average rates of punitive behaviors. When their teams were winning, the least liked coaches had very low rates of supportive behaviors, whereas the best-liked coaches had extremely high rates (Smith *et al.* 2009).

This result adds a layer of complexity to the study of coaching behaviors. It suggests that the unit of analysis that should be studied is not behaviors across all situations, but rather behaviors-within-situations. As social cognitive theories have long asserted, both behavior and its effects are a function of interactions between the person and the situation.

One other finding deserves mention. We obtained three different measures of coaching behaviors: those that were observed using the CBAS, athletes' ratings of how frequently their coaches behaved, and coach ratings of their own behaviors. When we examined relations among these three measures, we found that the athletes' ratings corresponded much more closely to the actual observed behaviors than did the coaches' self-reports. Indeed, coaches seemed quite unaware of their behavior profiles. As we shall see, this finding has important implications for both coach training and for the evaluation of coach interventions.

Phase 4: Developing a scientifically based coaching intervention

The basic research performed in Phase 3 gave us a scientific basis for deriving behavioral guidelines for coaches that could be used in providing a better

sports experience for youngsters. In Phase 4, we developed a psychoeduca-
tional program called Coach Effectiveness Training that became the basis for
an evolved current version, known as the Mastery Approach to Coaching
(MAC; Smoll and Smith 2014). The newer program name reflects an
increased emphasis on what our Phase 3 findings showed: the best outcomes
for children occurred when coaches establish what is known as a mastery
motivational climate. A mastery climate defines success in terms of effort,
personal improvement, enjoyment of the activity, and mutual support of team
members. This is contrasted with an ego climate, where success is defined
as winning contests and outperforming others, and where unsatisfactory
performance is punished.

Behavioral guidelines in the MAC intervention strongly encourage mastery
climate behaviors and discourage the use of criticism and excessive control
that mark an ego motivational climate (Smoll and Smith 2014). Knowing
that coaches cannot change their behavior without being aware of what they
do (and that coaches are generally unaware of their own behavior patterns),
the MAC also instructs coaches in how to monitor their adherence to the
guidelines. Because the research-derived guidelines are relatively few, the
intervention can be administered as an educational workshop that lasts less
than two hours, plus a printed manual that lists the coaching 'do's and don'ts'
and contains a behavioral self-monitoring form. Recently, in order to increase
program dissemination, we have developed a video version of the workshop (see
<*www.y-e-sports.com*> for a preview).

Phase 5: Evaluating the effects of the intervention

No matter how compelling and logical a program might seem to be, we
cannot conclude that it is effective in producing its intended effects. Accordingly, in Phase 5, we and other investigators have compared trained (MAC)
and untrained (control group) coaches and their athletes in a series of experimental outcome studies. To assess the effects of the intervention, we
measured how the coaches behaved and the effects the training had on their
athletes. Consistently, we found that the MAC training program had positive
effects on both the coaches and the athletes who played for them on such
factors as liking for the coach and teammates, increases in self-esteem and
reductions in sport performance anxiety, and development of mastery-oriented
achievement motivation. The athletes reported that their coaches established a
mastery climate, and they themselves showed increases in mastery achievement
goals and decreases in ego goal orientation (Smith and Smoll 2011).

In addition to these positive findings on athlete self-report measures,
we also examined an important behavioral measure, namely, whether or not
athletes dropped out of sports the following season. Sport attrition studies have
linked negative coach–athlete relationships as an important factor in athletes'
decisions to discontinue sport participation. We found that, in accordance
with previous dropout research, 26 percent of the athletes who played for

untrained coaches were not playing sports the following season, compared with only five percent of the athletes who played for MAC trained coaches (Barnett *et al.* 1992).

As noted earlier, the randomized controlled experimental design is the gold standard for evaluations in medicine and science. Although qualitative testimonials from coaches and practitioners are of interest, they are no substitute for experimental demonstrations of program efficacy. We have already seen that coaches have limited awareness of how they behave, so their reports are not as compelling as observed behavioral evidence of change. Likewise, programs that are promoted as 'scientifically based' because they are based on scientific data obtained in other areas of psychology cannot be considered to be *evidence-based* until the program itself is evaluated in randomized trials. By this scientific criterion, it is unfortunate that the MAC intervention is the only coach training program among many that has been evaluated in this manner and shown to have positive effects on coaches and athletes. Though space does not permit a detailed description of the validation research, abstracts of these studies and embedded video examples of coach (and parent) training materials can be found on the YES project web site (www.y-e-sports.com).

Note

1 It is important to note that in the context of this chapter the term 'case study' refers to investigations that exemplify our logical positivist approach to research rather than a methodology for studying sports coaching.

References

Bargh, J. A. and Morsella, E. (2008) 'The unconscious mind', *Perspectives in Psychological Science*, 3(1): 73–9.

Barnett, N. P., Smoll, F. L. and Smith, R. E. (1992) 'Effects of enhancing coach–athlete relationships on youth sport attrition', *The Sport Psychologist*, 6: 111–27.

Campbell, D. T. and Fiske, D. W. (1959) 'Convergent and discriminant validity by the multitrait-multimethod matrix', *Psychological Bulletin*, 56: 81–105.

Grove, W. M. and Meehl, P. E. (1996) 'Comparative efficiency of informal (subjective, impressionistic) and formal (mechanical, algorithmic) prediction procedures: The clinical–statistical controversy', *Psychology: Public Policy and Law*, 2: 293–323.

Kraemer, H. and Sprenger, J. (1487/1970) *Malleus Maleficarum*. New York: Bloom.

Smith, R. E. and Smoll, F. L. (2014) *Sport Psychology for Youth Coaches: Developing Champions in Sports and Life*, Lanham, MD: Rowman & Littlefield, 227–48.

Smith, R. E., Shoda, Y., Cumming, S. P. and Smoll, F. L. (2009) 'Behavioral signatures at the ballpark: Intraindividual consistency of adults' situation–behavior patterns and their interpersonal consequences', *Journal of Research in Personality*, 43: 187–95.

Smith, R. E. and Smoll, F. L. (1990) 'Self-esteem and children's reactions to youth sport coaching behaviors: A field study of self-enhancement processes', *Developmental Psychology*, 26: 987–93.

——(2011) 'Cognitive-behavioral coach training: A translational approach to theory, research, and intervention', in J. K. Luiselli and D. D. Reed (eds) *Behavioral Sport Psychology: Evidence-based Approaches to Performance Enhancement*, New York: Springer.

Smith, R. E., Smoll, F. L. and Hunt, E. (1977) 'A system for the behavioral assessment of athletic coaches', *Research Quarterly*, 48: 401–7.

Smoll, F. L. and Smith, R. E. (1989) 'Leadership behaviors in sport: A conceptual model and research paradigm', *Journal of Applied Social Psychology*, 19: 1522–51.

——(2014) 'Conducting evidence based coach training programs: A social-cognitive approach', in J. M. Williams and V. Crane (eds) *Applied Sport Psychology: Personal Growth to Peak Performance* (7th ed.), Boston: McGraw-Hill.

Smoll, F. L., Smith, R. E. and Hunt, E. (1978) 'Toward a mediational model of coach-player relationships', *Research Quarterly*, 49: 528–41.

4   Interpretivism

Paul Potrac, Robyn L. Jones, and Lee Nelson

Research paradigm

Like the other paradigms discussed in this book (see Chapters 2, 3, and 5), interpretivism provides a particular belief system for thinking about and conducting research. In this respect, it serves as an umbrella term for a variety of theoretical and methodological positions. Since 2000, the interpretive perspective has been increasingly adopted to underpin inquiry in the evolving academic field of sports coaching. This growing subscription to interpretive approaches could arguably be attributed to the unavoidable realization of the limits associated with understanding and representing sports coaching from a largely reductionist, logico-positivist position (Jones *et al.* 2004; Jones *et al.* 2011; Potrac *et al.* 2013).

The premise of this chapter is to outline the basic tenets of interpretivism, before presenting it as a lens through which coaching can, and perhaps should, be considered. Towards this end, we initially provide a brief overview of interpretive inquiry as related to its ontological, epistemological, and methodological assumptions. Following this, we discuss some of the practical considerations that researchers may wish to consider when conducting research into coaching (and coach education) from an interpretive standpoint. In the final section of this chapter, we discuss our experiences of conducting interpretive coaching research. Here, the focus is placed on how we came to adopt the interpretive stance in our work, in addition to highlighting the often messy and emotional process(es) of working in this way.

The interpretive paradigm: Ontology, epistemology, and methodology

While the application of interpretive approaches to coaching research is relatively new, the interpretivist paradigm itself has a long history encapsulating a range of intellectual traditions. These include *verstehen* (Weber 1947), phenomenology (Husserl 1965; Schütz 1970; Heidegger 1962; Merleau-Ponty 2004), symbolic interactionism (Mead 1934; Goffman 1959; Blumer 1969; Stryker 2002), and ethnomethodology (Garfinkel 1967), among others. Philosophically, the interpretive paradigm provides a radical alternative to the positivistic orthodoxy that can still be witnessed in some corners of sports coaching research. Interpretivism fundamentally rejects the belief that the social world (e.g., people, cultures, social practices, and social institutions) can be examined and understood through the assumptions and methodologies natural scientists use to examine the physical world. In illustrating this point, Popkewitz (1984: 41) noted that, 'to an atom, the language of culture means nothing. However, to people immersed in Azanda or American life, the ideas, concepts and languages of interactions create ways of expressing and defining the possibilities and limitations of human existence.' The interpretive perspective then, is 'founded on the premise that the social world is complex' and 'that people [e.g., coaches, athletes, and coach educators], including researchers and their research participants, define their own meanings' within respective social, political, and cultural settings (Jones and Wallace 2005; Markula and Silk 2011: 31; Purdy and Jones 2011).

It is important to emphasize at this early juncture that *understanding* the (naturally subjective) experiences of individuals and groups lies at the heart of interpretive inquiry (Coe 2012). As such, a key point of philosophical separation between positivism and interpretivism relates to how each approaches the task of examining and explaining human behavior (Bryman 2012). Here, rather than generating nomothetic or lawlike accounts of action that can be used to make future predictions (as would be the case with positivistic research), interpretive inquiry is concerned with discerning how individuals make sense of their experiences and actions (Bryman 2012; Coe 2012). That is not to say that those working in the paradigm are only interested in explaining isolated personal agency, as such work is 'undertaken with reference to the interpretive understanding of social (i.e., collective) action' (Bryman 2012: 30). In terms of its ontological, epistemological, and methodological underpinnings, the interpretive paradigm generally adopts an internalist-idealist/relativist ontology (i.e., there is no reality independent of perception), a subjectivist epistemology (i.e., knowledge is subjective and socially constructed), and an idiographic methodology (i.e., the focus is on the individual case) (Sparkes 1992; Markula and Silk 2011; Coe 2012). From an ontological perspective then, interpretivism rejects the view that the social world consists of 'hard, tangible and relatively immutable facts that can be observed, measured and known for what they are' (Sparkes 1992: 20). Instead, interpretivist researchers subscribe to the view that the social world is something that is constructed within individuals' 'subjectivities, interests, emotions, and values' (Sparkes 1992: 25).

Simply put, interpretivists argue that what exists in the social world is what an individual thinks exists (Coe 2012; Markula and Silk 2011; Sparkes 1992). However, interpretivism does not suggest that 'the mind creates what people say and do' (Smith 1989: 74), or that the social world only exists in people's heads. Rather, interpretivists argue that it is the mind that influences 'how we interpret movements and utterances' inclusive of 'the meanings we assign to the intentions, motivations, and so on of ourselves and others'

(Smith 1989: 27). Indeed, it is here, in the realm of meaning-making, that interpretivism is often seen as staking its claim; a position which naturally makes the application of more scientific methods inappropriate as explanatory frameworks (Lazar 2004; Seale 2012). However, although the emphasis is on personal meaning-making, this does not reflect a call to take up an uncritical relativist cudgel, an 'anything goes' attitude (as some have suggested). Social life can never be so contingent. Rather, interpretivism argues for meaning to be founded in social consensus, which is inherently subject to processes of contestation and disorder. Such consensus has been termed or described as many things; for example, social understandings, 'structural universals' (Lévi-Strauss 1963), 'intersubjective agreements' (Schütz 1972), and 'ethno-methods' (Garfinkel 1967) among others. Although they can be acknowledged as commonly understood rules which guide social life, interpretivists view them not as imposed independent structures, but rather as 'created by individuals in the course of their everyday lives', which only (through means of power) come to be regarded as objective and external (Scott 2009).

Not surprisingly then, the interpretive paradigm recognizes that our perception of reality may be influenced by a number of political, cultural, and social factors that support the construction of such shared understandings (Stryker 2002; Howell 2013). Social reality, from this perspective, is the product of how people individually and collectively make sense of (or *interpret*) the social worlds in which they live (Smith 1989; Markula and Silk 2011). Subsequently, this process of sense-making is not considered to be a fixed and stable phenomenon, but is capable of changing based upon an individual's experiences and his or her sense-making capacities (Sparkes 1992). Additionally, the meaning that an individual attaches to episodes in the social world is open to revision, as he or she may revisit and re-interpret their own and others' behaviors in a variety of different, sometimes contradictory, ways (Biesta *et al.* 2011; Goodson *et al.* 2010) (this was a point recently articulated by Jones [2013] directly related to coaching).

Although many consider that generalizations cannot be drawn from interpretive research, Williams (2000) produces an interesting counter-argument. Here, he states that if one takes a broad meaning of 'generalization' as a 'general notion or proposition obtained by inference from particular cases' (Williams 2000: 212), then interpretive research is packed with generalizations. In fact, in many ways, the point of such work is to infer from specific instances something about a culture; what Berger (1963) termed seeing the general in the particular. Although he accepts Denzin's (1989) and Guba and Lincoln's (1982) claims about the idiosyncrasy of context providing too many indeterminates within interpretive research to allow any meaningful generalization to take place, Williams (2000) makes the case for *moderatum* (i.e., moderate) generalizations. The bases for such generalizations lie in the (relative) cultural consistency of the social world, a consistency which makes social life possible (Williams 2000). Indeed, and echoing a point made earlier, even Denzin in this respect talked of a 'situated structuredness', thus giving credence to a 'shared world of meaning' (Williams 2000: 220). The purpose of bringing this issue to the fore here is not to position our precise agreement with it, but to raise consideration of the wider value of interpretive research over and above the immediate context of engagement.

In terms of its underpinning epistemology, the interpretive paradigm is based upon the supposition that knowledge is socially constructed. In rejecting the positivistic view that an external reality can be objectively investigated through a set of value-neutral research procedures, the interpretive perspective suggests that there 'can be no brute data ... on which to found knowledge or verify our positions' (Sparkes 1992: 27; Markula and Silk 2011). Instead, the only way to explore the realities that exist in people's minds is through subjective interaction, especially as it relates to the impact of a person's biography, and the related values and theories (both implicit and explicit) that he or she subscribes to (Sparkes 1992; Kelchtermans 2009). Consequently, those adhering to an interpretive approach hold to the view that research is a subjective, interactive (or transactional), and co-constructed activity involving both the researcher and the researched (Guba and Lincoln 1994; Howell 2013). On this point, Manning (1997: 96) outlined how such research 'is interactive in the way the researcher's questions, observations, and comments shape the respondent's actions', as well as how the participants' responses influence the analysis and interpretations of the researcher. Consequently, the final research report, paper, or thesis is the product not only of the researcher's relationships and interactions with participants in the field, but also of the analytical capacities and choices of the research 'team', and their understandings of, and subscription to, particular guiding theories (Guba and Lincoln 1994; Denzin and Lincoln 2005; Markula and Silk 2011). As interpretive researchers then, while the research participants' experiences lie at the core of inquiry, we recognize that we cannot 'hope to see the world outside of our place in it' (Sparkes 1992: 27).

In terms of investigative design, interpretive researchers utilize hermeneutic (or dialectical) methodologies to interactively explore and subsequently interpret the experiences of others (Guba and Lincoln 1994). The focus is on the depth and detail of data collected from small populations, as opposed to prioritizing a breadth of data to formulate generalizations (Mukherji and Albon 2012; Howell 2013). The emphasis is thus placed on the production of 'thick description' (i.e., rich and highly detailed accounts about what is seen, heard, and felt) and 'thick interpretation' (i.e., the analysis of events within a research context) (Geertz 1973; Denzin 1989; Howell 2013). This often entails spending an extended period of time with an individual or group utilizing a wide range of qualitative methods that include ethnography, a variety of interview techniques (e.g., life history/biographical, structured, unstructured, focus groups), narrative inquiry, and the analysis of written (e.g., diaries and personal documents) as well as non-written sources (e.g., photographs and pictures) (Sparkes 1992; Markula and Silk 2011; Howell 2013) to understand the subjects' meanings of lives as lived. These methods can be used in isolation or in conjunction with each other. For example, a researcher exploring the experiences of newly appointed assistant coaches may wish to combine biographical interviews with the analysis of participant diaries (depending, of course, upon the stated aims of the investigation). However, it is important to recognize that, in interpretive research, 'the researcher cannot come to a study with a pre-established set of neutral procedures but can only choose to do some things as opposed to others based on what seems reasonable, given his or her interests and purposes, the context of the situation, and so on' (Smith 1989: 157). Perhaps the key point to highlight is that data collection in interpretive research is 'not a reporting process guided by a specific set of techniques' but is, instead, acknowledged as an 'inquiry process carried out by human beings' (Wolcott 1990: 191–202).

Unlike in positivist inquiry, where various standardized instruments are used, interpretive researchers 'are themselves the primary research tool with which they must find, identify and collect data' (Ball 1990: 157). As such, it is expected that interpretive researchers adopt a reflexive approach to their work, which can be understood as developing a greater understanding of oneself within a research project (Lincoln and Guba 2000; Markula and Silk 2011). This often entails the careful consideration and documentation of the researcher's relationships with participants in the field, how they believe these relationships might influence the nature of the data collected, the choices made in terms of identifying and collecting further data, and, finally, the researcher's analysis and subsequent interpretation of the data gathered (Ball 1990; Sparkes 1992; Mukherji and Albon 2012).

Implications for coaching research

Naturally, the ontological, epistemological, and methodological assumptions of the interpretive paradigm influence how researchers who subscribe to them carry out their work into coaching and coach education. For example, rather than trying to develop objective truths and predictive theories about what coaching is or ought to be, interpretive researchers seek to explore the experiences of coaches and other key contextual stakeholders (e.g., coach educators, athletes, performance analysts, and physiotherapists, among others). Indeed, hypothesis testing and functional modeling is very much the anti-thesis of interpretive research. Alternatively, the emphasis lies in providing insights into the social complexities of studied phenomena; into generating knowledge for understanding (Jones and Wallace 2005) as a *precursor* for practical action (a principle that many coach education policy makers still fail to grasp).

One of the strengths of the interpretive perspective is that it allows researchers to better consider, for example, how coaches and coach educators may come to variously understand, and choose to respond to, the ambiguities and pathos inherent within their respective settings (e.g., Jones, Armour and Potrac 2003; Jones and Wallace 2005; Potrac and Jones 2009; Purdy and Jones 2011; Potrac *et al.* 2013). Indeed, we believe that an interpretive approach to coaching allows valuable insights into how 'emotion, cognition, self and context, ethical judgment and purposeful action' are 'all intertwined' in the experiences of practitioners (Kelchtermans 2005: 996; Potrac *et al.* 2013). Such understandings can help us to move beyond largely inhuman representations of coaching that continue to litter the literature.

Recent studies have variously illustrated these issues within the context of coaching research (e.g., Potrac and Jones 2009; Toner *et al.* 2012; Nelson *et al.* 2013; Nelson *et al.* 2014). For example, Toner *et al.*'s (2012) work illustrated the co-constructed nature of narrative understanding and how our perceptions of events, people, and phases of time may change in relation to ongoing social interaction with others. Similarly, Nelson *et al.* (2013; 2014) and Potrac and Jones (2009) highlighted how researchers are ultimately responsible for the reconstruction and representation of the narratives of those they study. Finally in this context, Purdy and Jones' (2013) paper drew attention to the strategies and identities that researchers may construct in order to steer their fieldwork towards desired ends.

A further related issue here is the emotional nature of conducting interpretive research. This is because, according to Lee-Treweek (2000: 128), qualitative research 'is people work and is, therefore, also emotional work'. As such, it is arguably not possible for us to 'switch off' personal needs and emotional reactions because we are conducting a research study (Stoler 2002; Dickson-Swift *et al.* 2008). In this regard, human inquiry could be considered to be an intellectual and emotional activity that is 'felt deeply' (Gilbert 2001: 9). Indeed, researchers may not only feel a gamut of different emotions as they work (e.g., joy, confusion, anxiety, sadness, pride, and frustration), but they may also have to make decisions about which emotions to show, suppress, or make themselves feel (Hochschild 1983; Dickson-Swift *et al.* 2008; Purdy and Jones 2013). In a similar vein, researchers may also have to manage the emotions of their research participants; something that is seldom documented in completed theses and sports coaching papers. Hence, although researched accounts sometimes 'deal with how hurdles blocking entry were successfully overcome and emergent relationships cultivated', the 'emotional pains of this work are rarely mentioned' (Shaffir *et al.* 1980: 3–4). It is an area that certainly needs further attention.

A final consideration here is the need to recognize that the interpretive paradigm is an encompassing term for a diverse range of theoretical approaches to understand individual meaning-making (Markula and Silk 2011; Howell 2013). For example, we have been largely inspired by the writings of Erving Goffman (e.g., Jones 2006; Potrac and Jones 2009; Jones *et al.* 2011 among others). In drawing upon Weber's (1947) notion of *verstehen*, Goffman's (1959, 1961, 1963, 1967, 1969) dramaturgical sociology illustrates how individuals engage in strategic interaction and manipulate their presentation of self based upon the meanings they have constructed in, and of, various social encounters. However, there is a range of alternative approaches that could be utilized. These include the symbolic interactionist perspective developed by scholars from the Chicago School of Sociology (see Roberts 2006). Symbolic inter-actionism focuses on the use of language and how individuals are engaged in a process of actively interpreting and responding to a variety of symbols in their everyday lives (Roberts 2006; Markula and Silk 2011). Equally, phenomenology provides another means of exploring individual sense-making, especially as it relates to notions of space, time, and our understandings of the world in which we live (Howell 2013). The original work of Husserl (1965), which is known as philosophical or transcendental phenomenology, has been followed by alternative strands of related inquiry proposed by Heidegger (1962/2004), Schutz (1970), Merleau-Ponty (1999), as well as the ethnomethodological approach developed by Garfinkel (1967). Coaching researchers, then, need to consider where (theoretically as well as methodologically) they locate themselves within the interpretive paradigm, and to consider the implications this may have for the ways in which they conduct their respective research endeavors.

Case studies in sports coaching

The decision to engage in interpretive coaching research was initially driven by our experiences as coaches, and our related dissatisfaction with the rationalistic, technical, and largely unproblematic academic representation of what we actually did. This was further accentuated by our mixed reactions to material that we encountered on coach education and coach development workshops and programs. While useful in terms of providing us with some insightful technical and tactical knowledge and ideas, the wider overall message about the nature of coaching just didn't ring true to us. As coaches, we felt that we were exposed to, and had to contend with, multiple realities, problems, tensions, joys and interpretations held by various people. There never seemed to be a time when a homogenous reading of others and events was actually evident. Coaching messages were understood in different ways at different speeds by different groups and people. Hence, we saw coaching as characterized by ambiguity, non-linear learning, relationships, micro-politics, and emotion. Although this reality is contested by some who, despite any supporting empirical evidence, insist that coaching is pretty straightforward, not surprisingly our research agenda came to focus on the everyday contested experiences of coaches, coach educators, and athletes.

An example of resulting work was our paper addressing the micro-political nature of coaching (Potrac and Jones 2009). Here, we sought to reconstruct Gavin's (a pseudonym) experiences as a head coach of a semi-professional football team, especially in relation to the micro-political nature of his interactions with key contextual stakeholders. While Gavin's experiences are presented in the form of a realist tale (see Chapter 9), we acknowledge that, as researchers, we ultimately constructed the text (Richardson 1990; Sparkes 2002). Within this paper, we utilized social theory in the forms of micro-politics (Ball 1987), micro-political literacy (Kelchtermans 2005), and the presentation of the self in everyday life (Goffman 1959) as sense-making frames to develop a suggested reading of Gavin's coaching experiences. We believe this study provides a useful illustration of how an interpretive approach can be used to produce insights into, and interpretations of, the ways in which Gavin experienced, understood, and variously responded to the fluid and dynamic political terrain at Erewhon F.C.

More recently, work developing the metaphor of coaching as orchestration (e.g., Jones *et al.* 2013; Santos *et al.* 2013) has also provided an example of interpretive inquiry. Building on earlier studies (e.g., Jones and Wallace 2005, 2006), Santos *et al.* (2013) utilized interviews to explore if and how coaches 'orchestrate'. The work was both inductive and deductive in nature, in that its questions (and subsequent answers) were both related to the study's aims, yet allowed a degree of freedom to the coaches to express themselves as they saw fit. Similarly, although the analytical process was largely inductive (that is, building from the ground up), the researchers were directed towards 'what to look for' in the data by the given objectives. In addition, what the research was trying to ascertain was the meanings within the interviews, as opposed to the words spoken. Throughout the work then, strong elements of interpretation were evident. Although this may seem like a 'freedom road', where everyone's interpretation is of equal value, to follow it would be to misjudge the paradigm's intention. As stated earlier, interpretation takes place within tacitly understood boundaries, social rules that guide how we act in relation to each other. To better understand the meanings within the interviews then, the authors undertook a process (to varying degrees) of personal and collective reflexivity and critique, as they sought to interpret the interview data obtained.

While it may not be apparent within our papers, we can certainly subscribe to the view that interpretive inquiry (and research in general) is an emotional affair. Far from being an objective and dispassionate activity, we have 'felt' and very much continue to 'feel' our research. For example, we have engaged with participants whose tales have moved us to considerable sadness, while we have vicariously shared the joys of others. Indeed, we have found that fieldwork can be an intense, anxiety-ridden affair that entails considerable self-presentation (Shaffir *et al.* 1980; Purdy and Jones 2013). Similarly, the challenge of writing narratives, making sense of data, and subsequently publishing our work is accompanied by a spectrum of emotions, some of which are positive, some of which are not (see Chapter 23). Nevertheless, we believe that attempting to understand and interpret the experiences of individuals within various coaching and coach education settings is a rich and rewarding activity.

Finally, while we have written this chapter about the interpretive paradigm, and have subscribed to its basic tenets in our research work, this does not mean that we ignore other ways of thinking about social life. For example, while we have used Goffman's dramaturgical sociology considerably as a sense-making coaching lens, we have, in recent years, increasingly engaged with a variety of theoretical positions (e.g., see Jones *et al.* 2011; Jones 2009; Jones *et al.* 2013;

Potrac and Marshall, 2011; Potrac *et al.* 2013; Purdy *et al.* 2013; Nelson *et al.* 2013, 2014). Indeed, while some have seen this 'movement' as decorative theorizing, we view it as honoring a state of academic inquiry; of continuously thinking and challenging ourselves and others to produce higher-quality coaching research. Hence, we make no apology in stating an intention to continue engaging in interpretive research, with the ultimate objective of furthering sports coaching knowledge.

References

Ball, S. J. (1987) *The Micro-politics of the School: Towards a Theory of School Organization*, London: Methuen.

——(1990) 'Self-doubt and soft data: Social and technical trajectories in ethnographic fieldwork', *International Journal of Qualitative Studies in Education*, 3(2): 157–71.

Berger, P. (1963) *Invitation to Sociology*, New York: Anchor Books.

Biesta, G., Field, J., Hodgkinson, P., Macleod, F. and Goodson, I. (2011) *Improving Learning through the Lifecourse*, London: Routledge.

Blumer, H. (1969) *Symbolic Interactionism*, Englewood Cliffs: Prentice-Hall.

Bryman, A. (2012) *Social Research Methods* (4th ed.), Oxford: Oxford University Press.

Coe, R. (2012) 'The nature of educational research: Exploring the different understandings of educational research', in J. Arthur, M. Waring, R. Coe and L. Hedges (eds) *Research Methods and Methodologies in Education*, London: Sage Publications, 5–14.

Denzin, N. (1989) *Interpretive Interactionism*, London: Sage Publications.

Denzin, N. and Lincoln, Y. (2005) *The Handbook of Qualitative Research* (3rd ed.), Thousand Oaks, CA: Sage Publications.

Dickson-Swift, V., James, E. L. and Liamputtong, P. (2008) *Undertaking Sensitive Research in the Health and Social Sciences: Managing Boundaries, Emotions and Risks*, Cambridge: Cambridge University Press.

Garfinkel, H. (1967) *Studies in Ethnomethodology*, Englewood Cliffs: Prentice-Hall.

Geertz, C. (1973) 'Thick description: Toward an interpretive theory of culture', in C. Geertz (ed.) *The Interpretation of Cultures*, New York: Basic Books, 3–30.

Gilbert, K. (2001) 'Introduction: Why are we interested in emotions?', in K. Gilbert (ed.) *The Emotional Nature of Qualitative Research*, London: CRC, 3–15.

Goffman, E. (1959) *The Presentation of Self in Everyday Life*, New York: Doubleday.

——(1961) *Asylums*, Garden City, NY: Doubleday.

——(1963) *Stigma: Notes on the Management of Spoiled Identity*, Englewood Cliffs: Prentice-Hall.

——(1967) *Interaction Ritual: Essays on Face-to-face Behaviour*, Garden City, NY: Doubleday.

——(1969) *Strategic Interaction*, Philadelphia: University of Pennsylvania Press.

Goodson, I., Biesta, G., Tedder, M. and Adair, N. (2010) *Narrative Learning*, London: Routledge.

Guba, E. and Lincoln, Y. (1982) 'Epistemological and methodological bases of naturalistic enquiry'. *Educational Communication and Technology Journal*, 30: 233–52.

——(1994) 'Competing paradigms in qualitative research', in N. Denzin and Y. Lincoln (eds) *The Handbook of Qualitative Research*, London: Sage Publications, 163–94.

Heidegger, M. (1962/2004) *Being and Time* (trans. J. MacQuarrie and E. Robinson), Oxford: Blackwell.

Hochschild, A. R. (1983) *The Managed Heart: Commercialisation of Human Feeling*, Berkeley: University of California Press.

Howell, K. (2013) *An Introduction to the Philosophy of Methodology*, London: Sage Publications.

Husserl, E. (1965) *Phenomenology and the Crisis in Philosophy*, New York: Harper & Row.

Jones, R. (2009) 'Coaching as caring ('The smiling gallery'): Accessing hidden knowledge', *Physical Education and Sport Pedagogy*, 14(4): 377–90.

——(2013) *Towards a Theory of Coaching: The Learning Order*. Invited presentation given at the European College of Sport Science (ECSS), Barcelona, Spain, June 26–29.

——(2006) 'Dilemmas, maintaining 'face' and paranoia: An average coaching life', *Qualitative Inquiry*, 12(5): 1012–21.

Jones, R., Armour, K. and Potrac, P. (2003) 'Constructing expert knowledge: A case study of a top-level professional soccer coach', *Sport, Education, and Society*, 8(2): 213–29.

——(2004) *Sports Coaching Cultures: From Practice to Theory*, London: Routledge.

Jones, R., Bailey, J. and Thompson, A. (2013) 'Ambiguity, noticing, and orchestration: Further thoughts on managing the complex coaching context', in P. Potrac, W. Gilbert and J. Denison (eds) *The Routledge Handbook of Sports Coaching*, London: Routledge, 271–83.

Jones, R., Potrac, P., Cushion, C. and Ronglan, L. T. (2011) *The Sociology of Sports Coaching*, London: Routledge.

Jones, R. and Wallace, M. (2005) 'Another bad day at the training ground: Coping with ambiguity in the coaching context', *Sport, Education and Society*, 10(1): 119–34.

Kelchtermans, G. (2005) 'Teachers' emotions in educational reforms: Self-understanding, vulnerable commitment and micro-political literacy', *Teaching and Teacher Education*, 21: 995–1006.

——(2009) 'Career stories as gateway to understanding teacher Development', in M. Bayer, U. Brinkkjaer, H. Plauborg and S. Rolls (eds) *Teachers' Career Trajectories and Work Lives*, London: Springer, 29–47.

Lazar, D. (2004) 'Selected issues in the philosophy of social science', in C. Seale (ed.) *Researching Society and Culture* (2nd ed.), London: Sage Publications, 7–20.

Lee-Treweek, G. (2000) 'The insight of emotional danger: Research experiences in an home for elderly people', in G. Lee-Treweek and S. Linkogle (eds) *Danger in the Field: Risk and Ethics in Social Research*, London: Routledge, 114–32.

Lévi-Strauss, C. (1963) *Structural Anthropology*, New York: Basic Books.

Lincoln, Y. and Guba, E. (2000) 'Paradigmatic controversies, contradictions, and emerging confluences', in N. Denzin and Y. Lincoln (eds) *The Sage Handbook of Qualitative Research* (2nd ed.), London: Sage Publications, 97–128.

Manning, K. (1997) 'Authenticity in constructivist inquiry: Methodological considerations without prescription', *Qualitative Inquiry*, 3(1): 93–115.

Markula, P. and Silk, M. (2011) *Qualitative Research for Physical Culture*, London: Palgrave.

Mead, G. H. (1934) *Mind, Self and Society: From a Standpoint of a Social Behaviourist*, Chicago: University of Chicago Press.

Merleau-Ponty, M. (1999) *Phenomenology of Perception*, London: Routledge.

——(2004) *The World of Perception*, London: Routledge.

Mukherji, P. and Albon, D. (2012) *Research Methods in Early Childhood: An Introductory Guide*, London: Sage Publications.

Nelson, L., Potrac, P., Gilbourne, D., Allanson, A., Gale, L. and Marshall, P. (2013) 'Thinking, feeling, acting: The case of a semi-professional soccer coach', *Sociology of Sport Journal*, 30: 467–86.

Nelson, L., Potrac, P. and Groom, R. (2014) 'Receiving video-based feedback in elite ice-hockey: A player's perspective', *Sport, Education, and Society*, 19(1): 19–40.

Popkewitz, T. (1984) *Paradigm and Ideology in Educational Research: The Social Functions of the Intellectual*, Lewes: Falmer Press.

Potrac, P. and Jones, R. (2009) 'Micro-political workings in semi-professional football coaching', *Sociology of Sport Journal*, 26: 557–77.

Potrac, P., Jones, R., Gilbourne, D. and Nelson, L. (2013) 'Handshakes, BBQs, and bullets: A tale of self-interest and regret in football coaching', *Sports Coaching Review*, 1(2): 79–92.

Potrac, P., Jones, R., Purdy, L., Nelson, J. and Marshall, P. (2013) 'Coaches, coaching and emotion: A suggested research agenda', in P. Potrac, W. Gilbert and J. Denison (eds) *The Routledge Handbook of Sports Coaching*, London: Routledge, 235–46.

Potrac, P. and Marshall, P. (2011) 'Arlie Russell Hochschild: The managed heart, feeling rules, and emotional labour: Coaching as an emotional endeavour', in R. Jones, P. Potrac, C. Cushion and L. T. Ronglan (eds) *The Sociology of Sports Coaching*, London: Routledge, 54–66.

Purdy, L. and Jones, R. L. (2011) 'Choppy waters: Elite rowers' perceptions of coaching', *Sociology of Sport Journal*, 28(3): 329–346.

Purdy, L. and Jones, R. L. (2013) 'Changing personas and evolving identities: The contestation and re-negotiation of researcher roles in field work', *Sport, Education and Society*, 18(3): 292–310.

Purdy, L., Potrac, P. and Nelson, L. (2013) 'Trust, distrust and coaching practice', in P. Potrac, W. Gilbert and J. Denison (eds) *The Routledge Handbook of Sports Coaching*, London: Routledge, 309–20.

Richardson, L. (1990) 'Narrative and sociology', *Journal of Contemporary Ethnography*, 19(1): 116–35.

Roberts, B. (2006) *Micro-social Theory*, London: Palgrave.

Santos, S., Jones, R. and Mesquita, I. (2013) 'Do coaches orchestrate? The working practices of elite Portuguese coaches', *Research Quarterly for Exercise and Sport*, 84: 263–72.

Schütz, A. (1970) *On Phenomenology and Social Relations: Selected Writings* (ed. H. Wagner), Chicago: University of Chicago Press.

——(1972) *Common Sense and Scientific Interpretation of Human Action*, Netherlands: Springer.

Scott, S. (2009) *Making Sense of Everyday Life*, London: Polity Press.

Seale, C. (2012) *Researching Society and Culture* (3rd ed.), London: Sage Publications.

Shaffir, W., Stubbins, R. and Turowetz, A. (1980) *Fieldwork Experience: Qualitative Approaches to Social Research*, London: Sage Publications.

Smith, J. (1989) *The Nature of Social and Educational Inquiry: Empricism versus Interpretation*, Norwood, NJ: Albex Publishing Corporation.

Sparkes, A. C. (1992) 'The Paradigms Debate', in A.C. Sparkes (ed.) *Research in Physical Education and Sport: Exploring Alternative Visions*, London: Falmer Press, 9–60.

——(1995) 'Writing people: Reflections on dual crises of representation and legitimation in qualitative inquiry', *Quest*, 47: 158–95.

——(2002) *Telling Tales in Sport and Physical Activity: A Qualitative Journey*, Champaign, IL: Human Kinetics.

Stoler, L. R. (2002) 'Researching childhood sexual abuse: Anticipating effects on the researcher', *Feminism and Psychology*, 12(2): 269–74.

Stryker, S. (2002) *Symbolic Interactionism: A Social Structural Version*, Caldwell, NJ: The Blackburn Press.

Toner, J., Nelson, L., Potrac, P., Gilbourne, D. and Marshall, P. (2012) 'From "blame" to "shame" in a coach–athlete relationship in golf: A tale of shared critical reflection and the re-storying of narrative experience', *Sports Coaching Review*, 1(1): 67–78.

Weber, M. (1947) *The Theory of Social and Economic Organisation*, New York: Free Press.

Williams, M. (2000) 'Interpretivism and generalisation', *Sociology*, 34(2): 209–24.

Wolcott, H. (1990) 'Ethnographic research in education', in R. Jaeger (ed.) *Complementary Research Methods for Research in Education*, Washington, DC: American Educational Research Association, 327–53.

5 Poststructuralism

Zoë Avner, Luke Jones, and Jim Denison

Research paradigm

Recent years have seen a growing interest and turn to poststructuralism and postmodernism in the field of coaching research. Coaching research scholars (e.g. Shogan 1999, 2007; Denison 2007, 2010, 2011; Lang 2010; Denison and Avner 2011; Denison *et al.* 2013; Gearity and Mills 2013) have increasingly moved coaching research in this direction by primarily drawing on the work of French poststructuralist Michel Foucault to critically examine sport coaching and high-performance sport in order to develop pragmatic interventions to help coaches become more effective. The purpose and scope of this chapter is to provide an introductory guide to poststructuralist theory for researchers interested in conducting sport coaching research from this perspective. To do so, we have organized this chapter into three distinct parts.

Here, we discuss the main tenets and key concepts of poststructuralism, its historical roots and major scholars. We also discuss the ontological and epistemological assumptions adopted by poststructuralist thinkers, their preferred methodological approaches, as well as their definition and use of theory. Following this, we consider the implications and key practical considerations for coaching researchers choosing to adopt a poststructuralist perspective to conduct coaching research and disseminate coaching knowledge. We specifically focus on how a poststructuralist framework shapes understandings of the purposes of coaching, coach education, and coaching research as well as research practices. Finally, the first and second authors discuss their experiences of conducting coaching research from a poststructuralist perspective. Luke Jones will share his experience conducting interviews with semi-professional soccer players to understand and critically examine their experiences of sporting retirement, and Zoë Avner will share her experience conducting a Foucauldian discourse analysis of coaching websites to inform a study related to university coaches' understanding and use of 'fun' within their coaching practices.

The poststructuralist movement originated in contemporary French philosophy and gained influence through the work of French theorists like Michel Foucault, Jacques Derrida, and Gilles Deleuze. Poststructuralism marked a strong paradigmatic shift away from the main tenets, and epistemological and ontological assumptions of positivism, but also of humanism/interpretivism and critical theory and their respective articulations of power, knowledge, truth, and reality. Despite its numerous theoretical strands, poststructuralist/ postmodernist theorists overlap in their rejection of universal metanarratives (e.g. positivism), dualistic understandings of power (e.g. critical theory) and the humanist self (e.g. humanism/interpretivism) (Markula and Silk 2011: 46).

A poststructuralist theoretical framework rests on specific epistemological and ontological assumptions about the nature of reality and truth. In contrast to positivist researchers who consider knowledge, reality, and truth as objective and singular, and consequently, consider their role as researchers to uncover and reveal reality/truth through the linear application of the scientific method, poststructuralist researchers understand knowledge to be contextual and 'reality' and 'truth' to be multiple and subjective.

When poststructuralist researchers talk about reality and truth as multiple and subjective, they are not denying the existence of a material reality (e.g. gravity). What they do deny, however, is the positivist claim that it is possible for researchers to be 'objective' and that there is a singular reality/truth out there 'waiting to be discovered' and revealed through the scientific method of inquiry. For poststructuralist researchers, research is inevitably influenced by the social, and thus always contextual and subjective whether scientific or sociological.

What further differentiates poststructuralist researchers from post-positivist or interpretivist/humanist researchers, for example, who also believe that truth/reality is subjective, is their belief in multiple realities and that knowledge, reality, and truth are produced through 'discourses' rather than found. Discourse is a key poststructuralist concept, which corresponds to dominant ways of understanding a particular social field (e.g. sports coaching), as well as understanding the dominant practices within a particular social field (e.g. sports coaching practices) (Markula and Silk 2011; see Chapter 20).

Furthermore, poststructuralist theorists believe that discourses are produced through dynamic and fluid (albeit non-egalitarian) power relations, which frame our understanding of the social world. Thus for poststructuralist researchers all knowledge, truth, and reality is inevitably political (in the sense that it is tied to power relations) and all human beings are involved in their production since all human beings are a part of power relations. In this way, poststructuralists do not endorse a divide between structure and agency.

While poststructuralist theorists, including Foucault, have developed many theoretical concepts to better understand and critically engage with our social worlds in order to promote social change, we chose two specific post-structuralist concepts to elaborate on: power relations and discursive formations. We believe these concepts provide the most useful starting points for coaching researchers wishing to engage in sport coaching research from a poststructuralist perspective.

Power relations and discourses

One of Foucault's most significant contributions to social theory was to provide a substantial alternative theorization of power to the commonly accepted dualistic understanding of power developed by Marx and advocated by critical theorists. In contrast to Marx's view of power as hierarchical, and as a substance that a dominant/ruling class holds and imposes on a dominated powerless class, Foucault (1978, 1979) saw power as relational, fluid, and inseparable from the production of knowledge/truth/reality. Thus, according to Foucault, a coach does not 'have power' over a 'powerless' athlete. Rather, a coach and an athlete are both active (albeit often unequal) participants in a power relation.

While a power relation might be fluid and mobile, it is not 'free' in the sense that it is both regulated and produced through discourses or 'ways of knowing, which are perpetuated through our everyday practices' (Markula and Silk 2011: 48). These everyday practices thus provide the limits and possibilities for understanding and practicing sport coaching. These coaching and sporting discourses can be 'subjected' or 'marginalized' or they can become 'dominant' and problematically reified as 'universal' coaching/sporting truths (Denison and Avner 2011).

However, to map discourses within a discursive field (e.g. sport coaching) does not imply dividing dominant discourses from subjected ones as if discourses were fixed, permanent, and monolithic entities. Rather discursive 'mapping' (Foucault 1981) entails retracing how various discursive elements are systematically joined and distributed to produce certain objects as intelligible within a specific socio-historical context (e.g. our current modern understanding of sport coaching and its related practices).

What Foucault's (1973, 1978, 2003) various discursive mappings allowed him to show is that modern society and individuals are produced through a combination of scientific and individualizing discourses. Similarly, our present understandings and practices of sport coaching are produced within the confines of dominant scientific discourses shaped and supported by the sport sciences and dominant individualizing discourses shaped and supported by individualizing knowledges like sport psychology and pedagogy. While, according to Foucault (Dreyfus and Rabinow 1983), no discourse is in and of itself 'good' or 'bad', they become problematic when naturalized and accepted as universal truths and when they are no longer critiqued or questioned.

For instance, a physiological/biomechanical understanding of the body and performance is not 'wrong' or 'bad'. However, these knowledges, which have been formed under particular conditions, only provide a partial understanding of the body and performance that is largely based on a modernist body/mind split where the body is viewed as a machine. This dominant metaphor and modernist understanding of the body in turn influences coaches to teach individual technical skills in linear, standardized, and incremental ways, which may not always be the most effective. For example, these pedagogical practices are likely to frame athletes' understandings of their own bodies as objects to be controlled, managed, and 'transcended' through disciplinary practices.

Some of the many problematic effects which can result from this bio-mechanical and reductionist understanding of the body and skill acquisition at the level of individual athletes include a normalization of pain and injuries, the production of overly compliant docile bodies, an increasing feeling of alienation from one's body and one's sporting practice, and even the onset of depression and early sporting retirement (Shogan 1999, 2007; Denison 2007, 2010). While these dominant scientific and modernist discourses have potentially very problematic effects on athletes, they also have problematic implications for coaches and the coaching profession at large as they tend to produce compliant and docile coaches and work against the development of critical thinking and innovation in coaching (Denison and Avner 2011).

While it is important to understand how coaches, athletes, and sport coaching researchers are constrained and subjected through various coaching/sporting discourses, it is equally important to understand that they also play an active role in the production and re-production of these power relations and coaching and sporting discourses. Thus, coaches, athletes, and researchers can effect change within the current power relations of performance sport, providing they become critically aware of the problematic effects of these dominant discourses within coaching and sporting contexts and of their own role in the perpetuation of unbalanced power relations within these specific contexts (Denison and Avner 2011).

In what follows, we examine some of the key implications of post-structuralist theory and of Foucault's concepts of power relations and discourse for sport coaching researchers choosing to adopt this perspective and theoretical framework.

Implications for coaching research

The ontological and epistemological assumptions that underpin post-structuralism influence how poststructuralist coaching researchers understand the practice of coaching and coach education, the purpose of research into coaching and coach education, and how they go about investigating coaching and coach education. For example, since poststructuralist researchers reject the main tenets of positivism (of reality and truth as objective and singular; see Chapter 3), the focus of poststructuralist sport coaching researchers cannot be to uncover and reveal the 'truths/reality' of sport coaching (e.g. what sport coaching fundamentally is). Nor is it, based on this, to prescribe a set of 'best coaching practices' for coaches to follow and apply. Rather, poststructuralist sport coaching researchers aim to reveal the power relations involved in the production and dissemination of coaching knowledge, the ways these impact how we understand and practice sport coaching, and finally some of the problematic effects of these dominant ways of understanding and practicing sport coaching.

Furthermore, as Markula and Silk (2011) emphasized, the poststructuralist researcher actively participates in the production of knowledge/truth/reality: 'each individual is a part of power relations and thus, part of the negotiation, circulation and alteration of discourses' (Markula and Silk 2011: 51). This relational and productive understanding of power necessarily carries within it important and complex ethical implications for poststructuralist coaching researchers, and it should inform each and every step of one's research from the formulation of the research question all the way to the dissemination of the findings.

Since for poststructuralist researchers no aspect of the research process, or the production of research knowledge, is ever 'neutral', it is important that they continuously consider the ethical implications of their research actions (their potential benefits but also their potential dangers, limitations, and problematic consequences). Thus, to take ethics seriously within post-structuralist research requires an ongoing critical questioning of one's use of power as a sport coaching researcher, which goes beyond the traditional ethical requirements of research boards and more obvious ethical considerations related to research participants in interviews/participant observations. It also requires an ethical commitment to minimize unbalanced power relations both through one's research into coaching and coaching education, but also *within* the research process itself.

Importantly, while poststructuralist coaching researchers often use post-structuralist theoretical concepts to map/better understand, and critique the field of sport coaching, they can also use their theoretical frameworks to promote theory-driven social change within the field of sport coaching. As Markula and Silk (2011) emphasized, the purpose of poststructuralist research can be threefold:

1) To understand/map the discourses which shape our understandings of the social world and our individual and social practices;
2) To critique the problematic effects resulting from dominant discourses.
3) To develop theoretically driven pragmatic interventions to foster more ethical practices.

Whether coaching researchers choose to map, critique, or enact social change depends partially on the scope of their research project, but also on the previous literature and knowledge of a particular discursive field. A coaching researcher would thus first need to 'map' the discourses of sport coaching before he/she is able to critique these or develop theoretically driven pragmatic interventions to enact positive, theory-driven change within a specific coaching/sporting context and the larger discursive field of sport coaching (Markula and Silk 2011).

While most qualitative research paradigms overlap in the methods available to researchers, there are some methods which are less suited to the epistemological and ontological underpinnings of poststructuralist research. For example, since poststructuralist researchers do not believe in an objective/singular real-ity/truth, they will be unlikely to use surveys, which are more common within positivist and post-positivist research paradigms. In addition, while most qualitative research paradigms typically use research methods such as interviews, observations, or textual analyses, there are differences in the way poststructuralists use these research methods to gain research knowledge, as we will show in the final part of this chapter.

Along with differences between how they use various research methods to gain/produce research knowledge, there are also significant differences between the criteria research paradigms use to evaluate what constitutes 'good' research. In general, poststructuralist criteria for evaluating research tend to be 'more fluid', open-ended, and plural than for example post-positivist research criteria (e.g. validity and generalizability) and the methods employed to guarantee these criteria are met (e.g. triangulation). Poststructuralist research criteria mostly encompass concerns with 'the theoretical contribution of the research, as well as the process and impact on the community' (Markula and Silk 2011: 220).

In the final part of this chapter we draw on two pragmatic examples of doctoral research projects conducted from a poststructuralist/Foucauldian perspective to contextualize the above discussion and illustrate some of these key principles and the implications of poststructuralist research.

Case studies in sports coaching

Luke Jones' case study

Benefits of poststructurally influenced coaching research

As I investigated how to design my doctoral study, which examined enforced retirement from British working football, I was surprised that the negative experiences of retiring athletes had seemingly stayed unchanged despite over sixty years of sport retirement research from an array of social science perspectives. How could this be the case? It was clear that many sport psychologists had spent a great deal of energy attempting to help this population, but, realistically, there were limited signs that any real changes had taken place. My exposure to poststructuralist thinking, and specifically the theoretical tools of Foucault, allowed me not only to consider why there has been limited progress in the field of sport retirement, but importantly for this chapter, it enabled me to design an interview guide capable of investigating the working realm of professional football as a 'modern discipline' and how this might influence players' retirement experiences.

Interview guide

In my poststructuralist study into retirement from working British football, it was not my intention to identify a universal truth about retirement, or how to prescribe the best 'retirement pathway' for retiring athletes. Rather, I was motivated to uncover how the disciplinary techniques present in British working football dictate a player's experiences both during and after his career. In order to achieve this objective, it was necessary to develop an interview guide capable of generating a discussion that, rather than focusing on identifying an individual's characteristics as a retiree, would instead strive to uncover the disciplinary nature of football's coaching practices and inherent relationships in order to analyze how these might impact a player in retirement.

Foucault (1979) noted that power operates 'by fabricating individual bodies into social order' (Markula and Pringle 2006: 73). As a result of being exposed to disciplinary power, individual bodies become normalized into useful bodies capable of performing a necessary task. In the case of football, this means being able to perform a specific 'function' with regularity on the pitch. In his text *Discipline and Punish: The Birth of the Prison*, Foucault (1979) outlined how disciplined bodies are created 'through the use of space, through selection of suitable activities, through the organization of time and through the composition of forces' (Foucault 1979: 74). This text provided a great resource for me to create informed questions capable of interrogating the elements of a football career that each retiree had experienced, in order to discover the long-term consequences of these experiences in retirement.

Rather than simply developing an interview guide to 'measure' the retiree's adjustment to life after sport, my questions focused on how these men were exposed to certain disciplinary spaces as they worked, the particular types of activities they were prescribed, what their daily routines included, and how coaching expectations changed throughout their development as players. My participants' responses allowed me to isolate multiple moments in the lives of professional football players and consider how, in these moments, power was enacted upon their bodies. These discussions also allowed me to establish and analyze the effects of disciplinary power and what this might mean in retirement. By designing an interview guide this way, I was able to analyze the disciplinary mechanisms responsible for the distribution of disciplinary power in working football and their consequences for retired players.

Zoë Avner's case study

My doctoral project addresses the following research question: how do Canadian university coaches understand and promote fun within their coaching practices? To address the first part of this question (coaches' understanding of fun) I decided to conduct a Foucauldian discourse analysis of key coaching websites and educational programs. Mapping how fun is discursively deployed within university coaching discourses as a first step to address my research question was necessary, since no studies had done this to date.

In keeping with my poststructuralist/Foucauldian theoretical framework and its specific ontological and epistemological assumptions, my goal was not to discover the 'truth' of fun for university coaches (as positivist researchers might seek to do) or how university coaches might experience fun in various ways (as humanist/interpretivist researchers might seek to do), but rather to contextualize fun within the specific power relations of university sport. More specifically, by engaging in a Foucauldian discourse analysis of key coaching websites and educational programs, I sought to develop a better understanding of 'the range of possibilities' for understanding and practicing fun within the specific power relations of university sport, as well as what the various effects of fun are within this specific sporting context.

One of the great attractions to me of a poststructuralist/Foucauldian framework is that it enables researchers to 'problematize' what is usually taken for granted and/or seen as unproblematic (in this case how 'fun' is apolitical, innocuous, and desirable, and something that all coaches should seek to promote within their specific coaching contexts). The poststructuralist step of 'problematizing' is part of the research process which seeks to (re)politicize specific aspects of sport coaching and taken-for-granted coaching 'truths' to the end of developing more effective and ethical coaching practices (Denison and Avner 2011).

The 'doing' of my Foucauldian discourse analysis followed Markula and Silk's (2011) guidelines for conducting a Foucault-inspired discourse analysis of texts compatible with poststructuralist ontological and epistemological assumptions and with a Foucauldian articulation of power as fluid, relational, and productive and operating through the 'tactical uses of discourses' (Liao and Markula 2009: 40). This discourse analysis method can be broken down into five distinct yet interrelated stages of analysis. They involve identifying various discursive elements (objects, enunciations, concepts, and theories), and a final stage that involves connecting the identified theories to power relations within specific social and sporting contexts.

Objects are 'the specific topics to which texts refer' (Liao and Markula 2009: 42), while enunciations are essentially where these topics are talked about. In my project, the object of my textual analysis was fun in university coaching. The enunciations for my analysis could have potentially included popular coaching magazines, websites, and manuals designed for the 'performance coach'. However, following Patton's (2002) criterion-based sampling, I chose to focus specifically on two coaching programs/models supported and discussed in two major Canadian coaching websites: the National Coaching Certification Program (NCCP) on the Coaching Association of Canada (CAC) website, and the Long Term Athlete Development (LTAD) model on the Canadian Sport for Life (CS4L) website.

Concepts are, according to Foucault (1972), the various discursive elements that may be linked together in order to produce intelligible theories about a specific object. In my research project, concepts refer to the various elements that can be grouped together in order to produce intelligible theories about fun and coaching in a university context. Theories are how individualized groups of statements 'link with general domains of statements' (Markula and Silk 2011: 131). In my case, theories are individualized groups of statements related to fun and coaching in a performance sport context.

The final stage of my Foucauldian discourse analysis of selected coaching texts involved connecting these various theories of coaching to a set of dominant knowledges/'sciences' (e.g. sport physiology, bio-mechanics, and sport psychology) and its related practices (e.g. periodization). And then lastly, I connected these dominant sciences and practices to the power relations of university sport in order to ascertain the discursive possibilities for understanding and practicing fun in university sport.

Connecting these dominant knowledges and practices to power relations not only allowed me to understand the range of current possibilities for understanding and practicing fun in university sport, but also to problematize the effects of the current discursive articulation of fun in university sport. In other words, it enabled me to understand how fun intersects with dominant understandings of the body and movement, and people and relationships in university sport (i.e. how 'fun' is strategically produced to support dominant scientific and disciplinary practices in performance sporting contexts), and also the potential problematic effects that derive from this articulation of fun in university sport (e.g. athlete and coach docility, and the reification of unbalanced power relations).

References

Denison, J. (2007) 'Social theory for coaches: A Foucauldian reading of one athlete's poor performance', *International Journal of Sports Science & Coaching*, 2: 369–83.

——(2010) 'Planning, practice and performance: The discursive formation of coaches' knowledge', *Sport, Education & Society*, 15: 461–78.

——(2011) 'Michel Foucault: Power and discourse: The 'loaded' language of coaching', in R. L. Jones, P. Potrac, C. J. Cushion and L. T. Ronglan (eds) *The Sociology of Sports Coaching*, New York: Routledge, 27–39.

Denison, J. and Avner, Z. (2011) 'Positive coaching: Ethical practices for athlete development', *Quest*, 63: 209–27.

Denison, J., Mills, J. and Jones, L. (2013) 'Effective coaching as a modernist formation: A Foucauldian critique', in P. Potrac, W. Gilbert and J. Denison (eds) *Routledge Handbook of Sports Coaching*, London: Routledge, 388–99.

Dreyfus, H. L. and Rabinow, P. (1983) *Michel Foucault: Beyond Structuralism and Hermeneutics*, Chicago: University of Chicago Press.

Foucault, M. (1972) *The Archaeology of Knowledge and Discourse on Language*, New York: Pantheon Books.

——(1973) *The Birth of the Clinic: An Archaeology of Medical Perception*, New York: Vintage Books.

——(1978) *The History of Sexuality, vol. 1: An Introduction*, New York: Vintage Books.

——(1979) *Discipline and Punish: The Birth of the Prison*, New York: Vintage Books.

——(1981) 'The order of discourse', in R. Young (ed.) *Untying the Text: A Post-structuralist Reader*, London: Routledge, 145–58.

——(2003) *Abnormal: Lectures at the Collège de France (1974–1975)*, New York: Picador.

Gearity, B. and Mills, J. (2013) 'Discipline and punish in the weight room', *Sports Coaching Review*, 1: 1–10.

Lang, M. (2010) 'Surveillance and conformity in competitive youth swimming', *Sport, Education, and Society*, 15: 19–37.

Liao, J. and Markula, P. (2009) 'Reading media texts in Women's sport: Critical discourse analysis and Foucauldian discourse analysis', in P. Markula (ed.) *Olympic Women and the Media*, Basingstoke: Palgrave Macmillan, 30–49.

Markula, P. and Pringle, R. (2006) *Foucault, Sport, and Exercise: Power, Knowledge and Transforming the Self*, New York: Routledge.

Markula, P. and Silk, M. (2011) *Qualitative Research for Physical Culture*, Basingstoke: Palgrave MacMillan.

Patton, M. Q. (2002) *Qualitative Research*, London: John Wiley & Sons.

Shogan, D. (1999) *The Making of High Performance Athletes: Discipline, Diversity and Ethics*, Toronto: University of Toronto Press.

——(2007) *Sport Ethics in Context*, Toronto: Canadian Scholars' Press.

Part II

Preparing and initiating the research process

6 Navigating the research process

Wade Gilbert, Martin Camiré, and Diane Culver

Introduction and overview

The purpose of this chapter is to discuss key issues that university supervisors and students must consider when conducting sports coaching research. Although many resources are available to guide students through the research process (Gratton and Jones 2004; Locke *et al.* 2007; Thomas *et al.* 2011), in this chapter we discuss research guidelines in the context of conducting undergraduate or graduate sports coaching research.

It is useful to initiate the dialogue by clarifying the expectations and requirements of student research at the bachelor's, master's, and doctoral level. The research project requirement of a Bachelor's degree is typically written during the final year of the program. The aim of the research project at this level is to get students to demonstrate a deeper approach to learning by using research methods to delve into a topic of interest. The undergraduate research project is valuable in helping students develop analytical and evaluative skills in addition to serving as preparation for graduate research. Research projects at the Master's level are substantial pieces of individual research meant to demonstrate that students can work in a scholarly manner and are acquainted with the literature in their area of interest. A Master's research project should be an original contribution to the field, through which students demonstrate advanced knowledge in a specialized area, higher order analytical skills, and rigorous and independent thinking. Research at the Doctoral level constitutes significant contributions to knowledge and embodies the results of original investigations that are of such quality as to merit publication in peer-reviewed scientific journals.

As is the case in most other fields, navigating the coaching research process is characterized by emotional ups and downs, uncertainty and misunderstandings, but ultimately triumph for those who see the process through. In order to minimize the negatives and maximize the positives, students and supervisors must, from the onset, ask themselves fundamental questions if their desire is to create and nurture a collaborative partnership. As it relates to students, a first question should be: What characteristics do I want in a supervisor? A competent supervisor is, among other things, someone who: (a) has technical expertise, (b) is personally active as a researcher, (c) is encouraging, (d) responds promptly to problems, and (e) is available (Sambrook *et al.* 2008). Students should strive to find supervisors who can offer the technical and emotional support necessary to successfully navigate the research process. Students should also consider supervisors' (a) academic reputation, (b) research funds, (c) willingness to support students' career development, and (d) tendency to sometimes use students as sources of labor to advance their own research agenda (Zhao *et al.* 2007).

Once a decision has been made to work with a specific supervisor, students should ask themselves: How much input do I have in selecting my research topic? In the field of coaching science students are sometimes given the opportunity to select their topics, but, as Hasrati and Street (2009) discussed, the culture is different in other fields such as engineering and science where topics are often assigned by supervisors who want their students to work on their funded projects. Therefore, students' degree of topic selection is an essential matter that should be discussed openly at the beginning of the partnership.

Supervisors also have important questions to reflect on in order to make educated supervision choices. A fundamental question all supervisors should ask themselves is: What is the appropriate degree of involvement in a student's work? Baratz Goodman (2006) explored this question in-depth and on the one hand states that overbearing supervisors who simply tell students what to do compromise autonomy and initiative. On the other hand, giving students too much autonomy goes against most students' desire for guidance. Ideally, a balanced approach integrating aspects of autonomy and guidance is desirable. Supervisors should aim to facilitate the journey by providing resources to make students' plans achievable while reminding them that, ultimately, they must work diligently to achieve their desired end goal (Todd *et al.* 2006).

Another important aspect supervisors must consider is: How do I provide honest feedback without sounding overly critical? Excessive criticism from supervisors has been associated with feelings of inadequacy, loss of confidence, and non-completion of dissertations (Li and Seale 2007). To avoid undue hardship, supervisors should clearly communicate expectations and provide students with constructive feedback that does not solely address deficiencies but deliberately offers concrete ways to improve.

Applied issues and considerations

Reflecting both on suggestions from the literature reviewed in the previous section and our collective experiences, we have arranged the supervised coaching student research process into ten steps. We present these ten steps in chronological order to illustrate a typical, and recommended, sequence of events for students and supervisors.

Step 1: Reflecting on sports coaching topics of interest

Prior to approaching potential supervisors, we encourage students to reflect on sports coaching topics that are of personal interest. Although students, particularly at the undergraduate level, may be required to select from a predefined list of sports coaching topics when deciding on a focus for their research, they should still critically examine their topic choice prior to taking any further action. At this initial step, we often require students to write a 1–2-page personal reflection paper on their topic and explain how the topic directly relates to their career goals. Given the typical heavy workload university students carry it is common for students to select a topic of convenience. In order to maintain the discipline and persistence required to complete a research project it is critical that students avoid a hasty topic selection. The reflection paper also allows the supervisor to make an initial assessment of the student's motivation and ability to write.

Step 2: Searching for shared spaces of interest

Once students have clearly identified coaching topics of interest, we recommend they then start to move outward in their search for potential 'shared spaces of interest' with university faculty members. The eventual success of coaching student research depends not only on the student's personal interest in the topic, but also on the availability of a qualified and willing research supervisor. By 'qualified' we mean a supervisor familiar with the current literature on the topic. By 'willing' we mean a supervisor demonstrating an interest in the topic, the student, and who has the time to collaborate. We have found that an effective method for students to determine a potential supervisor's qualifications and willingness is by scheduling a brief interview with the person in question. A faculty member is more likely to be willing to collaborate with students who conduct this interview in a professional manner. Students should use this opportunity to (a) say why the topic is relevant to their career goals – this shows the faculty member that the student has given serious thought to the topic and is likely to persist, (b) ask questions of the faculty member that demonstrate some background reading or research on the faculty member's qualifications – ask about specific papers or projects the faculty member has completed or other supervised student research in which he or she has participated, and (c) present a draft of a timeline for completing the project – this demonstrates that the student is organized and appreciates the time commitment required for completing a research project. In essence, the student should treat this faculty interview as an audition, realizing that the faculty member will be using the session to subtly evaluate the student's ability to complete supervised research.

Step 3: Revising the research topic and writing the purpose statement

After meeting with the selected – or assigned in many undergraduate cases – supervisor, the student should have a clearer understanding of what is known about the topic and recommended areas of future inquiry. This will allow the student to narrow his/her focus and write a very specific purpose statement.

For example, in step 1, the student may have identified 'coaching effectiveness' as a research topic. In step 3, insights gleaned from the supervisor interview may now allow the student to write a purpose statement such as 'to examine the role that coach interpersonal skills play in athlete satisfaction'.

Step 4: Systematically searching the literature

With a supervisor on board and a clear purpose statement, the student is now ready to embark on a systematic review of the literature (see Chapter 7). Regardless of the student's research experience, we recommend that students schedule an appointment with a research librarian. Literature search technologies and tools are constantly evolving and although the supervisor most surely can provide initial guidance, it is important that students become familiar with the most current and efficient literature search methods. We regularly find that after meeting with a research librarian, our students end up teaching us a few new search tricks! This step provides an important opportunity for building trust and collaboration between the student and the research supervisor as the student starts to contribute more to the partnership. During the literature review process, students will need to develop or use tools for managing and organizing the literature. Thesis proposal and research methods texts provide examples of literature summary tables (Locke *et al.* 2007; Thomas *et al.* 2011). Graduate students in particular may benefit from learning how to use reference management software. Dozens of options are available to students, including some that are free of charge (Wikimedia Foundation 2012).

Step 5: Writing Chapter 1 and research questions

Armed with a stack of journal articles, book chapters and other theses or dissertations, students are now ready to start writing Chapter 1 (Introduction) of their research project. We have found that students often struggle with initiating the writing process. Research writing – like any learned skill – requires practice and coaching. Supervisors should strive to provide specific and frequent guidance during this step and pay particular attention to student frustration that typically surfaces. Up to this point in the research process, the student likely has not written much other than a self-reflection paper on their topic. Now, we are requiring them to move closer into the 'researcher' role and actually start writing a research paper. This can be an extremely intimidating shift, particularly for students who struggle with writing confidence or skills. We have found that the most effective way to help students embrace the writing process is to require them to write evolving frequent drafts of Chapter 1. During this step, we often meet weekly with students to provide feedback and encouragement. We use this step to teach students to let go of 'getting it right' and simply focus on 'the next best step'. Supervisors need to keep in mind that this may be the first time the student has 'performed' for a faculty member in this way. It can be very intimidating for a student to share her writing with someone she holds in high regard such as a faculty member – who may be a globally recognized expert on the research topic. During this step, students are also required to write formal research questions.

Step 6: Writing Chapter 2 and creating a conceptual framework

Chapter 2 of a research project is often referred to as the 'Review of Literature' chapter, but we prefer 'Conceptual Framework'. Each university will have its own guidelines for formatting a research project and in our experience 'Review of Literature' seems to be the standard for Chapter 2. However, the review-of-literature chapter needs to move beyond a mere summary of the literature to include a conceptual organization of the literature and a critical discussion about the limitations of previous research. Commonly, students writing Chapter 2 produce a surface analysis of the literature; that is, students will read a series of journal articles and then summarize them (e.g. study A found this, study B found this, study C found this, etc.). We encourage students to look across their summary and reorganize it according to common themes. For example, for a review of interpersonal relationships and coaching effectiveness, common themes might be coach–athlete relationships, team cohesion, emotional intelligence, and autonomy-supportive motivational climates. We have also found it helpful to require students to create a one-page graphical display of their conceptual framework presenting common themes and the connections between them. Students can include these displays in their written research proposals and oral presentations.

Step 7: Selecting a research design and writing Chapter 3

At this point in the research process, the focus shifts to articulating how the research questions will be answered. It is critical that students and their supervisors keep the research questions close at hand during this step, because these questions should drive all research design decisions. Other considerations determining the selection of research design and methods are: researcher training, limitations of existing research on the topic, and the context. Here the student and supervisor must critically examine feasibility given the particular contextual restrictions (e.g. Can the student actually collect the data needed to answer the research questions within the required timeframe?). Given that all student research projects will be restricted by graduation timelines, a research project timeline must be written and agreed upon at this step. Scaling-back or changing research methodologies may be necessary, possibly meaning that the results of the research will have less of an impact on the field, and may not be publishable, but we believe the primary focus of undergraduate research should be to help students gain exposure to the research process and develop research skills.

Step 8: Defending the research proposal

Although typically a requirement for graduate student research, under-graduate students may also be required to present their research proposals (see Chapter 22). While graduate students frequently present their research proposals in formal, department, or university-wide forums, undergraduate students could find themselves having to present their proposal to peers in a class setting. We encourage our students to attend other students' proposal presentations as this provides them with relevant examples of students completing this important step. As with writing, we have found that many students become quite anxious at the prospect of having to orally present – or in their minds, defend – their research proposal. Requiring students to practice their presentations in our research groups and classes has proven to help students alleviate some of this anxiety. Regardless, we have found that even our most capable and well-prepared students still experience pre-presentation anxiety. As many of our coaching students have taken a wide range of classes in kinesiology and sport science, we remind them to use the skills they learned in their classes, such as developing pre-competition (presentation) routines, breathing exercises, visualization, and engaging in regular physical activity.

Step 9: Conducting the research

At this step in the research process, students typically experience a sense of elation and renewed energy for their research. Preparing the research proposal may take months – or even years in the case of some doctoral students – so it is natural for students to relax a little bit. While it is important to encourage students to celebrate reaching this step, it is also important for supervisors and students alike to watch for 'researcher drift'. We have found that without continued formal and regular supervision – and a written timeline for research completion – it is common for students to slowly drift away from their research. This should not be surprising as students will have had to sacrifice some other areas of their life in order to reach step 9 – maybe holding off on travel or cutting back on leisuretime activities. It is natural for students to want to catch up on these missed experiences. Thus, giving students a small break to 'reload' for the next phase of their research has been helpful. However, supervisors will have to be diligent to bring students back to focusing on their research in order to finish in a timely manner. It is critical at this point for the supervisor and the student to revisit the research project timeline created in step 7. We correspondingly recommend that students scale-back, if possible, other life commitments during this step in the research process. Data collection rarely proceeds as planned and students will need maximum flexibility in their schedules in order to adapt and respond to unanticipated research events. Coaching research involves interacting with people (coaches, athletes, administrators) who typically lead extremely busy lives that require frequent adaptations based on a myriad of potential coaching issues (athlete injuries or life issues, scheduling revisions, facility issues, tournament and playoff contingencies, travel changes, etc.). Of course, conducting the research also involves the process of analyzing the data and writing the research report. We have found it helpful to require students to focus on completing regular, short, drafts of their research reports. Although challenging for the supervisor because frequent feedback is required, this ensures the student stays on task and allows for small errors, or issues, to be detected and addressed often.

Step 10: Disseminating research results

Regardless of the student's level of study every student will be required to disseminate the results of their research in some fashion. For the undergraduate student, it may mean a written summary and/or a poster presentation in a class. For the master's student, it likely will mean at a minimum an oral presentation to the research committee and a conference presentation. Doctoral students can add to the master's student requirements multiple manuscripts and book chapters. Each of these dissemination options will require continued coaching from the supervisor that may extend well beyond the student's time at the university where they conducted the research. This step is where we have frequently noticed breakdowns in the student–supervisor collaboration resulting in limited or no dissemination of the research. It is difficult both for the student, who has moved on either to additional studies or a full-time job, and for the supervisor, who has likely started the entire research process again with other students. For graduate students and supervisors in particular, it is important to set out a written timeline for disseminating research results and clearly identify the role that each person will play. Students and their supervisors should identify specific conferences and journals that both fit – and are appealing to – the research team's career objectives and interests.

Publishing is an important endeavor in the career progression of academics, and authorship is often a contentious issue the effects of which can be curtailed if students and supervisors come to an agreement on shared roles and responsibilities (see Chapter 23). Many authorship guidelines have been produced (e.g. International Committee of Medical Journal Editors), offering criteria for authors submitting manuscripts. Generally, these guidelines state that authorship should be given to those who substantially contribute to one or more phases of the research process (i.e. conception, design, data acquisition, analysis, interpretation, drafting, revising). Burks and Chumchal (2009) have developed a decision tree to assist in determining whether undergraduate students have earned authorship depending on their level of involvement.

Reflections from the field

In this final section, we share the story of a graduate (master's level) student who completed a coaching thesis in 2012. The main actors in the story are

Wade Gilbert (the first author of this chapter) and a female graduate student we will call Madelyn. Madelyn's story provides a good representation of the ten steps outlined in the previous section, as well as the emotional highs and lows that are common to conducting student coaching research.

The story begins with the student approaching me early in her first semester of graduate school. I used the first meeting to gauge Madelyn's commitment to her career objectives and interest in conducting coaching research. While questioning her about her background, interests, and career goals, I learned she was a former university student-athlete with aspirations of becoming a collegiate coach. I also learned that her primary motivation for meeting with me was driven by a compulsory assignment for her Research Methods course: to identify a topic of interest and write a research proposal. Like so many other students we meet at this point in the research process, her focus could be best described as 'all over the place'. She was confused. She was not convinced she wanted to conduct a thesis, although the idea seemed appealing (in our Master's program, students choose between a thesis, a project, or a written exam for their culminating experience). The 30-minute meeting left us with a 'shared space of interest' (step 2), and moved her toward writing a one-page topic statement paper for her Research Methods class (step 1). We decided to focus on 'elite team sport coaching effectiveness'; still deliberately broad but at least delimited to 'elite' and 'team sport' contexts.

Off she went armed with new confidence – she had found a topic and a willing supervisor. No formal decision was made yet by Madelyn about actually conducting a thesis or me agreeing to supervise her if she did pursue a thesis. We did, however, agree to meet again in two weeks, by which time Madelyn had emailed me her topic statement paper. At this meeting, I provided her with feedback on the paper and pushed her to clarify her focus area. It was evident she was not able to identify or articulate one specific area. At this point, I shared details about some of my current projects, including a multi-year study with our collegiate women's basketball coach. This intrigued Madelyn because although basketball was not the sport she excelled in or intended to coach, it was a team sport she had played and the young coach of the basketball team was gaining national recognition. I invited her to attend one of our basketball research meetings (with two other graduate students and one other faculty member). I also started to provide her with some literature to read. Madelyn's homework after that meeting was to read the papers, revise her topic statement, write a purpose statement, and start searching the literature on her own (steps 3 and 4). I could tell at this point that Madelyn was excited about the prospect of working together, joining the basketball research group, and clarifying her topic area. It was at this point that I too became enthused about the possibility of collaborating with this graduate student. We had started to develop a good working relationship and rapport. I felt a connection between us and sensed that it would be fun and rewarding to work with this graduate student.

Madelyn connected with the basketball research group and, ultimately, we decided her research would focus on analyzing coaching behaviors during games. Another student had started working on analyzing practice behaviors for his coaching thesis. This illustrates an example of a student and I negotiating the selection of a research topic that fulfilled both of our needs and interests. Around this time I formally accepted Madelyn's request for me to serve as her research supervisor. We continued to meet weekly, alternating between an individual meeting and a basketball research group meeting. Madelyn completed a draft of her research proposal as part of her Research Methods course (steps 5, 6, and 7). At this point in the process everyone was happy and optimistic. The challenge now was to help Madelyn sustain the focus required to revise and finalize the written research proposal and successfully defend it in front of her thesis committee. It was during this phase – which spanned approximately six months – that Madelyn's focus, and enthusiasm, for the research varied widely. One week writing was going well and she felt she made an important breakthrough. The next week nothing was accomplished, writing was put off, other commitments took priority, or she simply was feeling burned out from all the reading and writing. The story continued like this – up one week, down the next – for several months. I believe Madelyn was reassured – and ultimately succeeded – in large part because I balanced her emotional rollercoaster with my emotional stability. I was in my eleventh year of supervising graduate students at that point in my career, and had experienced this situation many times previously. If not for this prior experience, I'm certain I too would have become extremely frustrated and overly emotional about the wild swings in Madelyn's focus and accomplishments. No doubt early in my career supervising graduate students I would have 'forced' things with Madelyn, perhaps pushing her too hard when she missed deadlines or perhaps even dropping her from my research team. Having supervised dozens of graduate student research projects now, I've come to accept Madelyn's scenario as the norm, not the outlier, when supervising student research projects. As supervisors, we need to continually remind ourselves what it felt like when we were ourselves students. Only through this type of regular reflection can we adequately empathize with our students and help put their struggles in perspective. Why wouldn't we expect them to experience wild swings in focus and emotions while undertaking the complex and messy process of designing a research project? Even now as a seasoned researcher myself, I regularly experience the 'highs' and 'lows' of the research process, so why would it be any different for a novice researcher?

Every time Madelyn and I met we reviewed her thesis timeline – what needed to be done by when in order to propose her research on the specific date we identified early in the research process. The date was based on several factors, including her intended date of graduation and the collegiate basketball schedule. I strongly advise all supervisors to write out formal research timelines with suggested dates for completing pieces of the project (selecting a thesis committee, scheduling a proposal presentation date, identifying when data will need to be collected, reviewing department and university calendars to determine when a thesis will need to be defended and deposited in order to graduate on time, etc.). I do this with all of my students now and it is perhaps the most effective tool I've found to help students and supervisors alike navigate the student research journey.

Madelyn successfully defended her research proposal (step 8) half-way through her two-year program. This was a joyous moment and confirmation that all the hard work was paying off. She fully invested herself into conducting the research (step 9) because it was intrinsically motivating. Her methodology involved videotaping collegiate basketball games and interviewing the head coach and the athletes. This was her strength; it was familiar ground for her compared to the world of academic research. The data collection emotional high was then followed by a data analysis and writing emotional low. Again, this is a pattern I have noticed repeatedly with students completing supervised coaching research. Madelyn's energy and focus was once again waning as she tried to balance the time intensive nature of her method (coding video tapes of 2–3-hour basketball games) with the very real need to secure a post-graduation job. Although earlier in the research process Madelyn entertained the possibility of pursuing a Doctoral degree, through the research journey she realized that her real passion – and strength – was coaching itself, not studying coaching. This of course drained some enthusiasm from completing the research project as it was difficult for her to make a clear connection between spending hours upon hours coding basketball tapes and landing a job as a collegiate coach in another sport. Again, in our weekly meetings I constantly brought her back to our research timeline to instill a sense of urgency. I also actively searched for local opportunities for Madelyn to present emerging results of her research. This included an on-campus graduate research symposium and a regional physical education and sport conference (step 10). I firmly believe these small wins helped push her over the research finish line. I am pleased to report that Madelyn successfully defended her coaching thesis and is now employed as a head collegiate team sport coach. It should be clear from this vignette that supervised coaching research is cognitively and emotionally taxing for supervisor and student alike. This is why we believe it is so important to find a 'shared space of interest' early in the process of navigating supervised student coaching research. The 'shared space of interest' represents a 'safe zone' for supervisor and student – an island, if you will, in the turbulent and choppy sea of research. It should also be clear that supervised student coaching research requires a commitment to relationship building. Supervisor and student are agreeing to embark on a journey that will test both of them equally. A successful outcome is much more likely if the supervisor and student enjoy spending time together because both parties will have to invest considerable time and energy in the relationship.

Drawing on current literature and personal experience from collaborating with our undergraduate and graduate students, we used this chapter to share suggestions for navigating ten steps in the coaching student research process.

Madelyn's story illustrates the typical emotional highs and lows that can be expected in the research journey. We believe the steps, and practical tips, provide coaching students and their supervisors with a guide for initiating and successfully completing sports coaching research.

References

Baratz Goodman, S. (2006) 'Autonomy and guidance in doctoral advisement relationships: a dialectical study', *The Humanistic Psychologist*, 34: 201–22.

Burks, R. L. and Chumchal, M. M. (2009) 'To co-author or not co-author: How to write, publish, and negotiate issues of authorship with undergraduate research students', *Science Signaling*, 2: 1–7.

Gratton, C. and Jones, I. (2004) *Research Methods for Sport Studies*, London: Routledge.

Hasrati, M. and Street, B. (2009) 'PhD topic arrangement in 'Discourse communities of engineers and social sciences/humanities', *Journal of English for Academic Purposes*, 8: 14–25.

Li, S. and Seale, C. (2007) 'Managing criticism in Ph.D. supervision: A qualitative case study', *Studies in Higher Education*, 32: 511–26.

Locke, L. F., Spirduso, W. W. and Silverman, S. J. (2007) *Proposals that Work: A Guide for Planning Dissertations and Grant Proposals* (5th ed.), Thousand Oaks: Sage.

Sambrook, S., Stewart, J. and Roberts, C. (2008) 'Doctoral supervision … a view from above, below and the middle!', *Journal of Further and Higher Education*, 32: 71–84.

Thomas, J. R., Nelson, J. K. and Silverman, S. J. (2011) *Research Methods in Physical Activity* (6th ed.), Champaign, IL: Human Kinetics.

Todd, M. J., Smith, K. and Bannister, P. (2006) 'Supervising a social science undergraduate dissertation: Staff experiences and perceptions', *Teaching in Higher Education*, 11: 161–73.

Wikimedia Foundation (2012) *Comparison of Reference Management Software*, Online. Available <http://en.wikipedia.org/wiki/Comparison_of_reference_management_software > (accessed 12 December 2012).

Zhao, C. M., Golde, C. M. and McCormick, A. C. (2007) 'More than a signature: How advisor choice and advisor behaviour affect doctoral student satisfaction', *Journal of Further and Higher Education*, 31: 263–81.

7 Reviewing the literature

John Lyle

Introduction and overview

The purpose of this chapter is to explore the characteristics, strengths, and weaknesses of reviews of academic literature, and how they may be used to generate research ideas in sports coaching. Critical analysis and interpretation of the literature can be a valuable and rewarding journey, providing both an overview of the current state of knowledge and a series of signposts to further study. On the other hand, it may point up the systemic limitations of academic inquiry to date in that field and generate a sense of 'so much more to be done'.

This is not a guidebook on writing a literature review, whether from an undergraduate, postgraduate, or experienced academic perspective. The underlying question is how the literature can be used to generate ideas for research. There is ample insight into what constitutes a sound review of literature and what a good research question might comprise. The issue is whether the latter is construed from the former. Does the review provide a precedent for the study? Our starting point, therefore, is that research should be 'premised' on something; there should be an academic context for a research study – why do this, why in this way, and why now? For this, we need to appreciate how reviews of literature are designed and written, and the extent to which they can be relied on for a comprehensive, unbiased account of the available literature.

The content of the chapter should be useful to undergraduate and post-graduate students, although in practice the undergraduate dissertation process often makes limited use of systematic reviews of literature. Nevertheless, it is necessary to have an appreciation of compiling and interpreting reviews, and using them to stimulate research ideas. There are a number of existing texts designed to help the undergraduate student with the preparation of dissertations and written in a sports context (for example, Andrews *et al.* 2005; Tenenbaum and Driscoll 2005; Gratton and Jones 2010; O'Donoghue 2010; Thomas *et al.* 2010). In this chapter we adopt a critical approach to the strengths and limitations of a number of types of literature review, and how they may be used to generate research ideas.

Purpose of reviews

Keary *et al.* (2012) provide a useful definition, characterizing the literature review as providing 'a basis for consolidating research findings within a specific area into a cohesive document that gives a clear indication of current progress, limitations and future directions of the research stream' (Keary *et al.* 2012: 239). More concisely, Tranfield *et al.* (2003) identify the purpose of a review of literature as 'to map and access the relevant intellectual territory' (Tranfield *et al.* 2003: 207). However, there is no definitive list of purposes. These include scoping the research field, narrowing a research problem, creating a conceptual map, identifying potential variables for study, identifying gaps in the existing field, cataloging common research methodologies, identifying key researchers and studies that have influenced the field, and generating new perspectives. As a result, researchers should be able to avoid repetition, conceive of potential new studies that would contribute to the field, and reinforce their familiarity with appropriate methods (Randolph 2009).

The reader needs to understand why a review might be written. For example, commercial clients are generally output-oriented (they want 'answers') and require client-focused, targeted, usually narrow questions. On the other hand, many researchers focus on what is termed 'exploratory' research, others on professional practice deficits, templates from other fields, or simply academic introspection. There is also government/funding body research in which the relevance of the study and accompanying methodological approaches are likely to be scrutinized very closely.

At this early stage, we need to distinguish between a stand-alone literature review in which the objective is to provide a comprehensive account of the research field, or part of that field, and the more selective supporting review of literature that normally accompanies an academic paper. Reviews of literature accompanying a published study may be selective and designed to demonstrate awareness of the area, key texts and trends, support for the rationale and methodology, and to show that the intended research will contribute something new to the field (Levy and Ellis 2006). It might be argued that the latter is a justificatory exercise designed to show the reader that the author is aware of recent and influential sources, in addition to introducing and supporting a key theory or method. Such a review might be considered more of a 'rationale for' the study in question. We might expect that these more selective and partial accounts would have had a catalytic impact on the generation of research ideas, but they are often written 'after the fact' and some caution needs to be exercised. In the main we are concerned with the type of comprehensive but focused review that is intended to provide an overview of the 'state of knowledge' in a particular field of study.

Types of literature review

It is helpful to distinguish between a stand-alone review of literature and one that accompanies published papers or a dissertation. This is important because the latter may be accessed by students as potential sources of research ideas. In addition, one of the challenges is to attempt to synthesize literature that may contain prescription, opinion, empirical studies, policy statements, and both primary and secondary sources, thus illustrating the advantages and dis-advantages of the narrower systematic review. It brings reliability to the review, but is likely to represent only a small fraction of the academic writing available. The term 'critical' is often appended to the word review. This implies that some evaluative and appraising commentary can be expected, particularly about individual studies, but also about the strengths and limitations of the general coverage of the subject matter. It is partly this critical interpretation, in addition to the collation and integration of sources, that distinguishes the review from a simple catalog of sources, usually termed an annotated bibliography.

Reviewing the literature may be a systematic or less systematic process. The former implies adhering to 'systematic review' practice (see Higgins and Green 2008) or comprehensive surveys of literature based on sound review practice. However, reviewing the literature may also be a partial process: for example, (a) finding a precedent for a 'spark of an idea', (b) confirming that there is sufficient existing literature to provide a 'scaffold' for an idea, (c) identifying methodological pitfalls or limitations in previous work, (d) comparing initial expectations with previous findings, (e) identifying contradictions, or (f) mapping the key authors.

A key distinction is that between narrative analysis of literature and systematic review. The systematic review is considered the most appropriate for policymakers in the health sciences, as it evaluates the weight of evidence in health-related interventions. The narrative review relies on the author's evaluation, judgment, and linguistic skills in synthesizing the literature and providing a summary of the evidence. In their overview of literature reviews, Tranfield *et al.* (2003) point to the limitations of traditional narrative reviews: not being exhaustive, lacking a satisfactory mechanism for aggregating and collating the 'messages' from what are increasingly diverse and contradictory studies, lacking rigor, and biased by the researcher/reviewer's purposes. The emphases, combination, and integration of research outcomes, research methods, theories, or applications provide the 'stamp' of a particular review. Thus, a critical review of methodologies to justify a researcher's approach is clearly different from an integrative and comprehensive review of outcomes intended to influence policymakers, or a critical review of theory developed in a historical context. You should be wary of the difference between 'a persuasive argument' and an unbiased account of the literature.

Systematic review is designed to produce transparent, reproducible (bias-free) reviews, most often associated with randomized controlled trials or interventions. This, of course, privileges the positivist paradigm (see Chapter 3), and is commonly associated with meta-analysis, which is a statistical procedure for synthesizing findings in order to enhance the 'power' of single studies. One of the key elements in a systematic review is that the searching of the literature is comprehensive and the selection of studies is based on reproducible keywords and search terms, thus ensuring that the final choice of studies is not biased by the reviewer's attempts to 'make a case'. Organizations such as the Cochrane Collaboration establish rules and guidelines for systematic reviews (Higgins and Green 2008). The 'rules' of the systematic review have evolved systematic review tools that are acknowledged as the most convincing evidence in health-related research, and demand certain conditions: for example, common research questions, acceptable research methods generally interpreted as randomized controlled trials, and strict rules of inclusion that favor relevant interventions, populations, and rigorous methodologies. These rules often significantly limit the number of relevant studies. The systematic review (or any other stand-alone review) is a complex and sizable research project, not an adjunct to another paper.

There have been attempts to apply systematic review principles in fields beyond the health sciences: for example, management (Tranfield *et al.* 2003) and higher education (Bearman *et al.* 2012). The Campbell Collaboration promotes systematic review in education, crime, and social welfare studies (www.campbellcollaboration.org). The Evidence for Policy and Practice Information and Coordinating Centre (EPPI) has developed and applied these principles and approaches (statistical, narrative, and conceptual synthesis) to public policy research (www.eppi.ioe.ac.uk). The systematic review has been applied to a wider range of research questions, paradigms, methods, and evidence (Gough *et al.* 2012). Thus the EPPI guidelines enable the researcher to rely on a systematic approach, without an overly restrictive set of inclusion criteria:

- An explicit search strategy (Databases, plus specialist websites, internet search engines, personal contacts; note in particular 'research' carried out for public bodies that may not be published or less easy to access)
- An explicit strategy for inclusion and exclusion
- Mapping and refining (describing the field)
- Appraising and synthesizing quality (judgment on quality and relevance leading to an assessment of the weight of evidence)
- Synthesizing study findings (This may involve statistical meta-analysis, narrative, or conceptual synthesis)
- A narrative (Structured narratives or summary tables; different types of research can be combined).

The non-systematic review relies on a different form of aggregating and interpreting evidence (that is, not simply the statistical evidence). This has been described as an 'integrative review' (Whittemore and Knafl 2005) and involves searching for patterns and interrelationships. It may be helpful to create a visual form of display of the evidence, before embarking on analysis and interpretation. Whittemore and Knafl suggest that analysis should comprise noting patterns and themes, clustering, comparing and contrasting, and identifying unusual patterns. It is important that the conclusion should address contradictory evidence, and seek for generalizing statements that encompass lesser groups of evidence. A salutary lesson is that students generally have access to the short report or published article, which is an even more condensed form of review, and differs considerably from a full 'technical' report (100 pages is the EPPI recommendation).

Applied issues and considerations

Issues in conducting a review

Most research methods textbooks address the mechanics of conducting a review, and provide specific advice on, for example, searching databases (Keary *et al.* 2012). No matter the type of review, there are some common steps or principles (Webster and Watson 2002; Levy and Ellis 2006):

(a) Identify the focus or purpose of the review. Is it a stand-alone review or supporting a specific piece of research? Can you focus the review in order to help identify keywords and sifting of sources?

(b) Create an auditable process (stop bias or acknowledge it). Identify the keywords (and combination of words) to be used in the search, the databases to be used, keep a record of the number of 'hits', and the use of individual sources to generate further sources should also be described.

(c) Create search parameters. What constitutes an acceptable paper? You may specify by date, scale and composition of research population, methods used, forms of analysis, or theoretical underpinning.

(d) Search for literature (note the difference between comprehensive, selective, representative, empirical, and eclectic reviews). Carry out the search remembering to record each step of the process. Likely databases are *Sport Discus*, *PsychInfo*, *Sociological Abstracts*, and *ZETOC*.

(e) Sort and classify sources. This is an inductive process that will help you to interpret the literature. This may reflect older–newer, empirical–conceptual, strong–weak findings, or methodological procedures. Remember that papers are likely to fall into more than one category.

(f) Identify a means of comparing or aggregating findings. This will be helped by the previous step. This is particularly relevant if accumulation of statistical evidence is to be used; narrative analyses rely on comparing findings in the context of similar or dissimilar classifications.

(g) Analyze the evidence (for example, statistical or narrative). Create themes, linkages, argument strings, and overviews, and decide how to display your findings (this may include tables or illustrative diagrams).

(h) Provide an evaluative summary. It is important to relate any summative evaluation or overview to the purpose of the review. Incorporate an element of critical appraisal, and attend to the weight of evidence, the strength of the literature, and new insights.

A further issue is the quality of the sources being reviewed. Likely factors will be (bearing in mind the nature of the study) the quality of the journal, the peer-standing of the authors, how often it is cited by others (but consider carefully the distinction between a 'supporting reference' and an exploration and incorporation of ideas – in addition to the frequency of self-citation), and, in particular, the 'strength' of the findings. It is important to distinguish between conceptual papers, in which the authors argue for the primacy of a particular interpretation or possible contribution of a theory or model, and empirical studies. There will also be factors associated with the methods employed. For example, does the sample population most appropriately illustrate the concepts involved; how well does the treatment/intervention mirror practice; is the measure of effectiveness convincing; is there a commonality of practice in the sample population of coaches; does the qualitative analysis delve beyond the accumulated statements of the subjects? In coaching studies a key question is the extent to which evidence is drawn from coaches' realistic *in situ* practice.

The interpretation of the findings is an opportunity for critical appraisal. When reading the review, (a) do you agree with the conclusions? (which texts have been particularly influential in focusing the conclusions), (b) has the author acknowledged any interpretive bias, (c) how strong are the sources on which the authors rely, (d) have the authors reinterpreted the original sources, relied on secondary sources, or merely referred to the findings, (e) are the authors helpful in identifying unanswered questions, and (f) is it clear that the authors have adhered to good review practice in conducting the review?

The method of synthesizing the research findings depends on the nature of the evidence. The systematic review attempts to aggregate comparable studies, whereas the narrative review may attempt to integrate findings from a more diverse range of studies. Another example is a realist synthesis (Pawson and Tilley 1997), in which the researcher investigates the underlying factors or facilitating circumstances rather than the program or intervention outcomes.

Research questions

Given the time and resources available to undergraduates, the most common approach is to replicate existing research in interesting, available, or problematic contexts. In general there is a two-phase approach to the use of literature in an undergraduate dissertation, but in my experience this is rarely a genuine trawling for ideas. Having identified a subject in which they have some interest, students are often directed by a supervisor to an initial set of readings in order to clarify relevant concepts, widen their horizons, and begin to tease out a research question. They may then be asked to review a more extensive but more focused selection of readings to provide ideas for appropriate methods and procedures, and to begin to shape their expectations (all of this being dependent on the nature of the study). The final version of the review of literature in the dissertation is evaluated for the extent to which it demonstrates familiarity with the field of study (language, concepts, methods, theories, developmental status), provides adequate underpinning for theories and concepts on which the study relies, has an element of interpretation (identifies common themes, trends, gaps), and provides a basis for comparing the new study's findings to existing findings.

It would not be unreasonable to argue that a research question satisfactorily executed should have a positive impact on policy or practice. However, this need not always be the case; clearly conceptual and theoretical research is also necessary. The following are some self-check questions about appropriate research questions. Can the question be satisfactorily addressed (feasibility, resources, available methodology, and the competence to execute it)? Is the question couched in appropriate language? The focus in qualitative research might be about meaning, significance, emergent theory or a description of social phenomena, whereas the focus in quantitative research is likely to involve the manipulation of independent and dependent variables and the relationship between them. Can the question be subdivided into five or six sub-questions that will help to scope the methodology? Have you established that the question needs to be asked? Is there an element of originality? Will it lead to replicable, accountable research practice? Are you satisfied that the findings will add to theory, help to solve problems, or has practical relevance (although concerns about relevance, applicability, or generalizability may not be a researcher's priority)?

Although some research ideas may genuinely emerge from reading the literature, others owe their genesis to supervisors, first-hand practical problems, commercial interests, continuation of previous research, empire-building, or opportunism. We might reasonably argue that questions are less likely to reflect a genuine gap in the literature and more likely to reflect a personal agenda. Researchers are constrained by familiar paradigms, and may also be conscious of the weight of existing research, and schools of existing research, or the influence of well-cited researchers (see Rangeon *et al.* 2012).

While it is rare for the research questions themselves to emerge directly from a literature review, the review can provide a working framework that will act as a catalyst for generating new ideas. The research questions are a final stage in a process that may begin with a literature review in which untested correlations between variables, new research populations, or conceptual limitations are identified. We may most often depend on the reviews of other researchers, but engaging in the review process ourselves increases familiarity with the literature, identifies the weaknesses (not highlighted by more selective reviews), permits a more detailed examination of methodologies, and allows us a more personal weighing of the evidence.

Reflections from the field

The literature associated with sports coaching is too diverse to support systematic review based on empirical findings. Although it has improved considerably in the past 15–20 years, many authors have noted its limitations – for example, inadequate conceptualization, epistemologically driven sub-groups, and difficulty in associating coaching behavior with athlete performance (Gilbert and Trudel 2004; Cushion and Lyle 2010; North 2013). Sport coaching is an enormously broad field of study (professional development, delivery practice, interpersonal relationships, social context, and coaching expertise – in addition to sports specific and performance-related issues). A realization that coaching practice can only be understood at the level of the particular, its distinctive and disconnected domains, role-specific behavior, and its human and emotional elements have contributed to a lack of unity and coherence in the literature. Indeed, it might be argued that small groups of researchers have created self-justificatory literature sets. Without wishing to be critical, researchers in fields such as coaching efficacy, coach–athlete relationships, leadership, or systematic observation studies could usefully 'take stock' of the contribution of their literature to coaching practice or the continuous advancement of 'coaching theory'.

There have been relatively few attempts at systematic review of coaching-related subject matter. These few studies have served to reinforce the not-uncommon conclusion that few papers satisfy the inclusion criteria. For example, in a review of the effectiveness of interpersonal coach education interventions Langan *et al.* (2013) could identify only four studies. Reviews have also been conducted into coach learning (Cushion *et al.* 2010), coach education (Trudel and Gilbert 2006; Lyle 2007a), mentoring (Jones *et al.* 2009), and professional development (Taylor and Garratt 2008; Griffiths and Armour 2012). The result is that literature reviews associated with sport coaching, although conducted within a set of systematic procedures, tend to be eclectic, narrative accounts. Indeed, the term 'academic review' (for example, Bailey *et al.* 2010) reflects the absence of a sufficiently coherent and methodologically sound, as well as dissociative, literature. Students should also note that the published sources may be distillations of reviews conducted elsewhere (for example, Martindale *et al.* 2005) and extensive use of literature sources is often used to scaffold a 'case' (for example, Duffy *et al.* 2011).

My involvement in a number of reviews (for example, Lyle 2007b, 2009; Cushion *et al.* 2010) has reinforced the lessons identified above. In fields of study such as coaching, there is limited consensus on research methodology, and the absence of a consensual research agenda provokes a divergent rather than convergent analysis/review (Tranfield *et al.* 2003). In addition, at this stage of academic writing in coaching, there is a significant amount of 'prescription', rather than weighing of empirical evidence. This leads to narrative reviews in which the net is cast widely to capture relevant sources from coaching and other fields, but the interpretations and conclusions require meta-synthesis rather than meta-analysis. In one review of decision-making research (Lyle and Vergeer 2013), a keyword search leading to over 400 sources resulted in fewer than thirty empirical studies in a twenty-year period, and these varied hugely in quality and focus. Griffiths and Armour (2012) provide an insightful summary, '[the] research lacks robustness, rigor, and a theoretical grounding from which to design future studies' (Griffiths and Armour 2012: 2), and 'the quality of the evidence base was poor in terms of methodological quality and topic relevance' (Griffiths and Armour 2012: 4). This may be taken as a warning about the emphasis to be given to any summaries or generalizations within this research field.

References

Andrews, D. L., Mason, D. S. and Silk, M. L. (eds) (2005) *Qualitative Methods in Sports Studies*, Oxford: Berg, 1-13.

Bailey, R., Collins, D., Ford, P., MacNamara, Á., Toms, M. and Pearce, G. (2010) *Participant Development in Sport: An Academic Review*, Leeds: Sports Coach UK.

Bearman, M., Smith, C. D., Carbone, A., Slade, S., Baik, C., Hughes-Warrington, M. and Neumann, D. L. (2012) 'Systematic review methodology in Higher Education', *Higher Education Research and Development*, 31(5): 625–40.

Cushion, C. J. and Lyle, J. (2010) 'Conceptual development in sports coaching', in J. Lyle and C. Cushion (eds) *Sports Coaching: Professionalisation and Practice*, Edinburgh: Churchill Livingstone, 1–14.

Cushion, C. J., Nelson, L. J., Armour, K. M., Lyle, J., Jones, R. L., Sandford, R. and O'Callaghan, C. (2010) *Coach Learning and Development: A Review of Literature*, Leeds: Sports Coach UK.

Duffy, P., Hartley, H., Bales, J., Crespo, M., Dick, F., Vardhan, D., Nordmann, L. and Curado, J. (2011) 'Sport coaching as a 'profession': Challenges and future directions', *International Journal for Coaching Science*, 5(2): 93–123.

Gilbert, W. and Trudel, P. (2004) 'Analysis of coaching science research published from 1970–2001', *Research Quarterly for Exercise and Sport*, 75: 388–99.

Gough, D., Oliver, S. and Thomas, J. (2012) *An Introduction to Systematic Reviews*, London: Sage.

Gratton, C. and Jones, I. (2010) *Research Methods for Sports Studies* (2nd ed.), London: Routledge.

Griffiths, M. and Armour, K. (2012) *Connected Communities: An Analysis of the Capacity of Volunteer Sports Coaches as Community Assets in the Big Society: A Scoping Review*, Connected Communities: Arts and Humanities Research Council.

Higgins, J. P. T. and Green, S. (eds) (2008) *Cochrane Handbook for Systematic Reviews of Interventions: Cochrane Book Series*, The Cochrane Library: John Wiley & Sons.

Jones, R. L., Harris, R. and Miles, A. (2009) 'Mentoring in sports coaching: A review of the literature', *Physical Education and Sport Pedagogy*, 14(3): 267–84.

Keary, E., Byrne, M. and Lawton, A. (2012) 'How to conduct a literature review', *The Irish Psychologist*, 38(9–10): 239–45.

Langan, E., Blake, C. and Lonsdale, C. (2013) 'Systematic review of the effectiveness of interpersonal coach education interventions on athlete outcomes', *Psychology of Sport and Exercise*, 14(1): 37–49.

Levy, Y. and Ellis, T. J. (2006) 'A systems approach to conduct an effective literature review in support of information systems research', *Information Science Journal*, 9: 181–211.

Lyle, J. (2007a) 'A review of the research evidence for the impact of coach education', *International Journal of Coaching Science*, 1(1): 17–34.

——(2007b) *UKCC Impact Study Phase One Report: Definitional, Conceptual and Methodological Review*, Leeds: Sports Coach UK.

——(2009) *Sporting Success, Role Models and Participation: A Policy Related Review*, Research Report No 101, Edinburgh: Scotland

Lyle, J. and Vergeer, I. (2013) 'Recommendations on the methods used to investigate coaches' decision making', in P. Potrac, W. Gilbert, and J. Denison (eds) *Routledge Handbook of Sports Coaching*, London: Routledge, 121–32.

Martindale, R. J. J., Collins, D. and Daubney, J. (2005) 'Talent development: A guide for practice and research within sport', *Quest*, 57(4): 353–75.

North, J. (2013) 'A critical realist approach to theorising coaching practice', in P. Potrac, W. Gilbert and J. Denison (eds) *Routledge Handbook of Sports Coaching*, London: Routledge, 133–44.

O'Donoghue, P. (2010) *Research Methods for Sports Performance Analysis*, London: Routledge.

Pawson, R. and Tilley, N. (1997) *Realistic Evaluation*, London: Sage.

Randolph, J. J. (2009) 'A guide to writing the dissertation literature review', *Practical Assessment, Research & Evaluation*, 14(13), http://lincs.etsmtl.ca/uploads/media/v14n13.pdf.

Rangeon, S., Gilbert, W. and Bruner, M. (2012) 'Mapping the world of coaching science: a citation network analysis', *Journal of Coaching Education*, 5(1): 83–108.

Taylor, W. and Garratt, D. (2008) *The Professionalisation of Sports Coaching in the UK: Issues and Conceptualisation*, Leeds: Sports Coach UK.

Tenenbaum, G. and Driscoll, M. P. (2005) *Methods of Research in Sport Science: Quantitative and Qualitative Approaches*, Oxford: Meyer & Meyer.

Thomas, J. R., Nelson, J. K., Silverman, S. and Silverman, S. J. (2010) *Research Methods in Physical Activity* (6th ed.), Champaign, IL: Human Kinetics.

Tranfield, D., Denyer, D. and Smart, P. (2003) 'Towards a methodology for developing evidence-informed management knowledge by means of systematic review', *British Journal of Management*, 14: 207–22.

Trudel, P. and Gilbert, W. (2006) 'Coaching and coach education', in D. Kirk, M. O'Sullivan and M. McDonald (eds) *Handbook of Research in Physical Education*, London: Sage, 516–39.

Webster, J. and Watson, R. T. (2002) 'Analysing the past to prepare for the future: writing a literature review', *MIS Quarterly*, 26(2): 13–23.

Whittemore, R. and Knafl, K. (2005) 'The integrative review: updated methodology', *Journal of Advanced Nursing*, 52(5): 546–53.

8 The place of theory

Lee Nelson, Paul Potrac, and Ryan Groom

Introduction and overview

Those who attempt to engage in coaching research quickly learn that the academic community holds theory in high regard. Demonstrating a sophisticated understanding and adept application of theory are criteria against which undergraduate dissertations, postgraduate theses, and scholarly research articles are frequently judged. The importance placed on theory by the academic fraternity is captured by Wright (2008), who, in the context of educational research, argued that:

> the quality of educational research rests in large part in its capacity to engage theory, to recognise the situatedness of the research in a contested field of knowledge, and be able to speak to the work of theory in relation to the analysis and explanation of data.
>
> (Wright 2008: 1)

Many coaching scholars, including us, would make a similar claim in relation to the quality of research in sports coaching. The purpose of this chapter is to introduce you, the reader, to not only what theory is, inclusive of its multiple interpretations, but also how theory can, and is, used in coaching investigations. We also share some of our own experiences and evolving thoughts about the application and construction of theory in coaching research. It is hoped that this chapter will help readers to reflect upon the purpose, place, utility, and development of theory.

Defining and conceptualizing the use of theory

Theory is a complex and ambiguous term, which has been used amongst other things to describe models, frameworks, and paradigms (Hammersley 1995; Strauss 1995). Indeed, it has been argued that discussions surrounding theory have not only lacked definitional clarity but also do not consider 'what "level" of theory is relevant for particular research problems and projects' (Wright 2008: 2). Such ambiguity is further compounded by the fact that some research methods scholars choose to distinguish between theory and research paradigms, seeing them as separate but related concepts, whilst others incorporate them together (Kawulich 2009).

When attempting to understand the relationship between theory and research, Bryman (2012) urges researchers to contemplate whether they are referring to what he terms the *deductive* or *inductive* use of theory. He explains that deductive theory use is a process whereby the social scientist attempts to verify theory by creating a working hypothesis that is confirmed or rejected by the research findings. Deductive theory use is most commonly associated with quantitative investigations, where the data of experimental research designs are subjected to statistical analysis. When used in this way, theory becomes a framing device that helps the researcher to construct research questions or hypotheses and formulate appropriate data collection procedures (Creswell 2009).

While theory is the starting point for deductive research, Bryman contends that theory is the outcome of research when applying an inductive approach (Bryman 2012). Here, the social scientist gathers qualitative data that are analyzed to form themes or categories (Creswell 2009). Once this initial stage of analysis has occurred, researchers 'collect further data in order to establish the conditions in which a theory will and will not hold' (Bryman 2012: 26). Inductive theory-building of this nature is often referred to as grounded theory, an approach that was first developed by Glaser and Strauss (1967, 2012).

Although it can be useful to think about the relationship between theory and research in deductive and inductive terms, we also find ourselves agreeing with Bryman's (2012) suggestion that such conceptualizations are not always as 'clear-cut as they are sometimes presented' (Bryman 2012: 27). Here he contends that inductive and deductive strategies might be more appropriately conceptualized as tendencies rather than separate approaches, as inductive logic is sometimes present in deductive analysis and vice versa. Additionally, others have critiqued an inductive understanding of theory use and construction, arguing that theory should inform every aspect of the research process (i.e. setting the problem, identifying participants, development of questions, and how one goes about collecting, analyzing, and presenting findings), as opposed to simply being the product of qualitative investigations (Kawulich 2009).

At this juncture we believe that it is important to give thought towards the relationship between theory use and discussions about the philosophy of science, which is often referred to as the paradigm debate (see Chapter 2). Researchers holding contrasting paradigmatic beliefs often view the place and use of theory in different ways. For the purpose of this chapter, we will consider three contrasting positions; namely positivism, interpretivism, and postructuralism/postmodernism. Each of these holds a distinct set of beliefs about the nature of reality (i.e. what is known as ontology), the nature of knowledge (i.e. what is termed epistemology), and approaches to research (i.e. methodological choices).

Positivists assume that one external social reality exists which is made up of structures and objects with cause-and-effect relationships (i.e. ontology), and that this reality is independent from consciousness (i.e. epistemology). Positivists tend to utilize experimental, scientific, research designs (i.e. methodology) to identify causal understandings. The work of Ronald Smith and Frank Smoll (see Chapter 3) provides an example of positivistic coaching research. Positivists define theory 'as a statement of relationships between abstract concepts that cover a wide range of empirical observations' and consider the objectives of theory to be '*explanation* and *prediction*' (Charmaz 2006: 125–6). Positivist theory 'seeks causes, favors deterministic explanations, and emphasizes generality and universality' (Charmaz 2006: 126).

Conversely, interpretivists assume multiple social realities (i.e. ontology) and that knowledge statements are subjectively created (i.e. epistemology). Interpretivists tend to favor the use of qualitative approaches to research (i.e. methodology) to understand the subjective realities of their participants. The work of Robyn Jones and colleagues (see Chapter 4) is broadly interpretive. Interpretive theory 'calls for the imaginative understanding of the studied phenomenon' and 'emphasizes *understanding* rather than explanation' (Charmaz 2006: 126). Theory of this nature assumes indeterminacy, multiple realities, a link between facts and values, and holds that truth is provisional (Charmaz 2006).

Finally, poststructuralism/postmodernism assume fragmented and contested truths (i.e. ontology), and that the development of certain discourses serve vested and fluctuating positions (i.e. epistemology). As a result, post-structuralists/postmodernists often utilize theorists (e.g. Foucault, Lacan, Derrida) to provide readings of a particular social condition (i.e. methodology). The work of Jim Denison and colleagues (see Chapter 5) is an example of this line of inquiry. The poststructuralist/postmodernist position holds a view of theory that is quite different from that of positivism and interpretivism. Whereas positivist theory seeks prediction and interpretivist theory understanding, Gulson and Parkes (2010) explain that when adopting a poststructuralist stance:

> Theory typically acts as a disruptive force, a deconstructive tactic, a denaturalising strategy, or a diffractive lens through which to view afresh a particular set of problems, or to problematise a phenomena, text, or event that is usually taken-for-granted.
>
> (Gulson and Parkes 2010: 78)

Ball (1995) presents a similar argument when exploring educational theory in light of the work of Foucault and Bourdieu:

> Theory is a vehicle for 'thinking otherwise'; it's a platform for 'outrageous hypotheses' and for 'unleashing criticism' ... Theory is destructive, disruptive and violent. It offers a language for challenge, and modes of thought, other than those articulated for us by dominant others ... The purpose of such theory is to de-familiarize present practices and

categories, to make them seem less self-evident and necessary, and to open up spaces for the invention of new forms of experience.

(Ball 1995: 266)

What should be apparent from the above discussion is that there is no globally accepted definition and conceptualization of theory. Rather, researchers' thoughts about theory are often influenced, be it implicitly or more explicitly, by underpinning philosophical beliefs. Positivists, interpretivists, and post-structuralists/postmodernist each hold contrasting views about the definition, purpose, and use of theory.

Types, breadth, and range of theory

It is also important to recognize that there are different *types* of social theory. For example, Merton (1967) distinguishes between grand (i.e. all-embracing and unified conceptual schemes that operate at a more abstract level and attempt to explain many aspects of social life) and middle-range (i.e. those that operate in a limited domain and range of social life) theories (Denzin 1970, 2009). In their discussion of grounded theory, Glaser and Strauss (1967, 2012) also compare substantive (i.e. an empirical area of inquiry) and formal (i.e. a conceptual area of inquiry) theory; both of which they suggested are middle-range as 'they fall between the "minor working hypotheses" of everyday life and the "all-inclusive" grand theories' (Glaser and Strauss 1967, 2012: 33). Theories also vary in their *breadth* of coverage (Creswell 2009). Neuman (2000) makes a distinction between macro (i.e. cultural systems, social institutions, and whole societies), meso (i.e. communities, organizations, and social movement), and micro (i.e. small slices of time, space, and numbers of people) level theories (Creswell 2009).

Coaching researchers should also give consideration towards the *range* of theories that are available to them. As an area of academic study coaching remains relatively embryonic. Coaching scholars have as a result drawn on theory from a range of established disciplines in an attempt to better understand and theorize coaching and coach education. For example, coaching researchers have utilized the work of theorists from the field of education/learning (e.g. Stephen Ball, Peter Jarvis, Geert Kelchtermans, Nel Noddings, Donald Schön), psychology (e.g. Albert Bandura, Jean Piaget, Carl Rogers, Burrhus Frederic Skinner, Lev Vygotksy), and sociology (e.g. Pierre Bourdieu, Norman Denzin, Michel Foucault, Anthony Giddens, Erving Goffman) literature.

So it would seem that there are a range of disciplines and theories that you could potentially draw on to help ease the growing pains associated with theoretically understanding coaching phenomena (Jones 2006). That said, those engaging in coaching research should be mindful of the fact that diverse *positions* exist within a given discipline. Each of these is invariably underpinned by contrasting theoretical beliefs. For example, Merriam and Caffarella (1991) have identified four categories of learning theories (i.e. behaviorist, cognitivist, humanist, and social and situational), and Haralambos and Holborn (2008) six theoretical perspectives in sociology (i.e. functionalism, Marxism, conflict perspective, feminism, interactionism, and postmodernism). Coaching scholars therefore need to develop an appreciation of the various theoretical positions that exist within the discipline(s) considered relevant to a given research project, where the work of individual theorists are located within such groupings, and how the beliefs of a given perspective fit (or not as the case may be) with their own theoretical understandings and thoughts about the philosophy of science and topic of investigation.

Applied issues and considerations

To demonstrate the various ways in which you might use theory within your own research project, we present examples that evidence different approaches to the application of theory in coaching studies. This is by no means an exhaustive list, but nonetheless we hope that these illustrations will help to bring some of the possible choices, and the above discussions, to life.

Use of theory I: Deductive testing

The first article we wish to consider is a study by Amorose and Anderson-Butcher (2007). We have chosen this article as it provides an example of a quantitative investigation that utilized theory in a deductive way. In this study the authors purposely sought to investigate the relationship between autonomy-supportive coaching and self-determined motivation in high school and college athletes. It is important to note that the hypotheses utilized in this study were derived from Amorose and Anderson-Butcher's reading of Deci and Ryan's self-determination theory (SDT). That is, theory was the starting point for this project. This is evidenced in the following quotation, which has been taken from the closing paragraph of the authors' introduction:

> The second purpose was to test whether the pattern of relationships among the set of variables was similar for different groups of athletes, specifically males vs. females and high school vs. college athletes. Given that Deci and Ryan (1985) and Ryan and Deci (2000, 2002) argue the tenants of SDT are essentially universal, we expected that hypothesized patterns of relationships would be invariant across gender and competitive level.
>
> (Amorose and Anderson-Butcher 2007: 658–9)

In order to test their hypotheses, 581 (263 male, 318 female) high school (n = 335) and college (n = 246) athletes, across a range of sports, were asked to complete a battery of questionnaires (Sports Climate Questionnaire; items previously developed by Amorose; Feelings of Relatedness Scale; Sport Motivation Scale). Data collected from these questionnaires were statistically analyzed and the results highlighted the motivational benefits of autonomy-supportive coaching behaviors. The findings of this study therefore offered empirical support for self-determination theorizing. Of significance here is that theory (i.e., self-determination theory) was the starting point of the study. Theory enabled the authors to establish hypotheses that could be tested. Consistent with the positivist research paradigm a quantitative design was utilized to verify the authors' hypotheses and, in doing so, the claims of the theory.

Use of theory II: Theoretical lens

A study by Garratt *et al.* (2012) is the focus of our next example. It demonstrates how theory can be used to inform all aspects of a qualitative research investigation. In this study the authors specifically sought to critically consider and expose the discursive terrain on which safeguarding and child protection policy had emerged in coaching. To achieve this aim, Garratt *et al.* (2012) drew on the Foucauldian concept of genealogy to trace the emergence and development of various discourses and consider how they have shaped child protection policy in sport, and subjected the coach to certain 'regimes of truth'. In their article the authors' contend that:

> Broader concerns about child welfare and children's rights, coupled with more extensive media reporting of serious cases of child abuse and child death inquiries, have produced a reactionary politics in sport, with arguably serious deleterious consequences for coaching policy and practice ... Thus, while safeguarding policy and practice may have its genesis in the concept of child welfare and child protection, its recent teleology points to on-going fear and confusion.
>
> (Garratt *et al.* 2013: 12–13)

Here, theory not only informed the authors' reading of their data, but, in doing so, a Foucauldian analysis provided a conceptual lens through which they were able to critique the discourse in contemporary safeguarding policy and practices in coaching. Garrett *et al.*'s (2012) use of theory, then, is consistent with a poststructuralist/postmodernist position in that it was used to disrupt, challenge, and problematize existing practices and thinking.

Use of theory III: Analytical framework

The next example is a study (e.g. Chesterfield *et al.* 2010) that purposely sought to investigate coach learners' perceptions and experiences of a football-specific coach education program (the Union of European Football Associations 'A' Licence). It is important to note that this investigation was aligned with the interpretivist research paradigm. In order to gain rich insights about how the coach learners perceived and responded to the content, knowledge, and assessment processes of the course, six participants were identified through purposive sampling. Data were collected through semi-structured interviews that each lasted approximately ninety minutes in duration. Data were subjected to inductive analysis and theory was applied in the following way:

> During the analysis, 'analytical memos' were used to make preliminary connections to various theoretical concepts that might explain the key issues evident. This interpretive process was principally informed and shaped by the concepts of the dialectic of socialisation (Schempp and Graber 1992) and the presentation of the self (Goffman 1959).
>
> (Chesterfield *et al.* 2010: 303)

In this example established social theories were used as sense-making tools to help interpret the findings. More specifically, the work of Schempp and Graber, and Goffman, provided readings that helped the authors to understand why the participant coaches engaged in acts of 'studentship' through the adoption of 'impression management' strategies.

Use of theory IV: Grounded theory

Whereas the previous examples have attempted to verify theory (example 1) and use theory as a guiding framework (example 2) or sense-making tool (example 3), one of our recent papers (Groom *et al.* 2011) presents an attempt to construct a coaching-specific theory. In this respect, we drew on the work of Strauss and Corbin to develop a grounded theory 'to understand the delivery of video-based performance analysis by England national team youth soccer coaches' (Groom *et al.* 2011: 29). To construct our grounded theory we collected data from fourteen of the seventeen England youth soccer coaches (four female, ten male) who were utilizing video-based technology within their practices. Data were collected through semi-structured interviews that each lasted between 30–70 minutes in duration. The analysis of data entailed a six-stage process: (1) interviews were transcribed verbatim and returned to participants for the checking of accuracy, (2) concepts were identified in the data, (3) data were reassembled into categories and related subcategories via the process of axial coding, (4) three categories (i.e. contextual factors, delivery approach, and targeted outcomes) were established, via selective coding, as having analytical power, (5) a delayed literature review was completed to contextualize the findings within the broader literature, and (6) two coaches were asked, through a member-checking process, to consider the grounded theory in relation to real-world scenarios. In this project we felt that it was necessary to generate a substantive coaching-specific theory as no existing theory appeared able to make sense of the phenomenon being investigated in its entirety. The methodological approach that we utilized (i.e. grounded theory) was therefore specifically designed to generate theory from empirical data. This example differs from those presented previously in that theory was constructed rather than drawn on from other disciplines.

Reflections from the field

Having introduced some key concepts and explored examples illustrating how scholars have utilized and generated theory in coaching research, we will now end by sharing some of our own experiences and evolving thoughts about this topic. We hope that what follows might help neophyte researchers to think about theory in a critical way. For those more experienced researchers reading this chapter, we wonder if our thoughts resonate in any way with your own.

A common theme across each of our academic and research endeavors is that a range of emotions often accompanies our reading of theory. We have each experienced frustrations when trying to appreciate the intricacies of a new theoretical framework. This can stem from a number of sources, including the difficulties associated with trying to understand primary texts, discovering that secondary sources often provide contrasting interpretations, and discovering that new understandings can challenge existing beliefs. Although learning about new theory has often proved to be a challenging task, we have found that devoting time to this aspect of our scholarly development has, and continues, to be extremely rewarding and beneficial. We have each derived considerable pleasure from overcoming the intellectual challenges associated with establishing a detailed understanding of a theorist's work, and we have come to appreciate that such learnings have permitted us to think about the social world in new and insightful ways.

As broadly interpretivist researchers we have also come to realize that the use of theory in qualitative investigations is often much messier than is depicted in many introductory research methods texts. While the analysis of data in our early research projects might be considered 'more' inductive in nature, we suspect that this could be attributed to a lack of theoretical understanding as much as anything else. The development of broader and more sophisticated appreciations of social theory, however, has led each of us to interpret our social worlds, and our research findings, through these theoretical lenses. Our theoretical readings have prompted us to ask questions of our social world, and 'how' and 'why' people think, feel, and behave in the ways that they do. It would seem that we are increasingly unable and unwilling to put these frameworks aside for analytical purposes, and, therefore, our qualitative analysis of data, and engagement in qualitative research more broadly, might be more appropriately described as an *iterative*, rather than a purely inductive, process (see Chapter 17). That is, we no longer see the analysis of data as being a clean, detached, and unproblematic process whereby patterns, themes, and categories inductively emerge out of qualitative data. Rather, like Srivastava and Hopwood (2009), it has been our experience that the analysis of data is 'driven by what the inquirer wants to know and how the inquirer interprets what the data are telling her or him according to subscribed theoretical frameworks, subjective perspectives, ontological and epistemological positions, and intuitive field understandings' (Srivastava and Hopwood 2009: 77). As qualitative researchers *we* are the instruments that analyze our data and, as such, we heavily shape the outcome of our analysis.

Nor do we consider the analysis of data to be a distinct and isolated feature of the research process. Rather, qualitative research is, in our experience at least, a reflexive and iterative process comprising cycles of data collection, data analysis, and additional, more focused, collection of data. Here, in an attempt to connect the personal to the social, we not only strive to understand reality from our participants' perspective, but also seek to consider our own readings of their thoughts and experiences and contemplate how such findings might be made sense of through social theory. Tracy (2013) describes such an iterative approach to data analysis as alternating 'between emic, or emergent, readings of the data and an etic use of existing models, explanations, and theories' (Tracy 2013: 184).

The final issue that we would like to discuss is the combining of theory to interpret research findings. As researchers we have experienced instances whereby the combining of theory would seem to provide a more comprehensive understanding of our data. While utilizing multiple theoretical lenses might appear to be a pragmatic approach, we often become anxious about the legitimacy of this exercise. Whereas the combining of theories from a school of thought within a given disciplinary area appears to be academically acceptable, the combining of theory across disciplinary boundaries and/or between schools of thought is considered by many to be an untenable practice. The ability to combine theory (or not) is often dependent on the compatibility of the philosophical foundations of the theories in question. While we find ourselves agreeing with this line of thinking, it has, at times, left us in somewhat of a predicament, as we are unable to ignore aspects of our data set simply because such findings cannot be understood by a given theoretical position.

As we contemplate this issue further we wonder whether theory might be conceptualized as consisting of layers, with a theorist's philosophical beliefs at the core and concepts at the surface. Whereas it might be possible to combine theories at the surface, it perhaps becomes increasingly difficult to do so at a deeper philosophical level. When thinking of theory in this way, we are each able to identify theories that we find ourselves agreeing with at the surface level (or elements of the theory at this level) whilst disagreeing with the theorist's underpinning philosophical beliefs. As a result of such reflection, we wonder whether there is a place for coaching specific theorizing that is not only grounded in empirical research evidence, but also draws on aspects of established theoretical concepts. We certainly see a place for the construction of coaching theory as well as learning from existing social theorizing to better understand the complex, messy, and power-ridden nature of coaching and coach education.

References

Amorose, A. J. and Anderson-Butcher, D. (2007) 'Autonomy-supportive coaching and self-determined motivation in high school and college athletes: A test of self-determination theory', *Psychology of Sport and Exercise*, 8: 654–70.

Ball, S. J. (1995) 'Intellectuals or technicians? The urgent role of theory in educational studies', *British Journal of Educational Studies*, 43(3): 255–71.

Bryman, A. (2012) *Social Research Methods* (4th ed.), Oxford: Oxford University Press.

Charmaz, K. (2006) *Constructing Grounded Theory: A Practical Guide Through Qualitative Analysis*, London: Sage.

Chesterfield, G., Potrac, P. and Jones, R. (2010) 'Studentship and impression management in an advanced soccer coach education award', *Sport, Education, and Society*, 15(3): 299–314.

Creswell, J. W. (2009) *Research Design: Qualitative, Quantitative, and Mixed Methods Approaches* (3rd ed.), London: Sage.

Denzin, N. (1970, 2009) *The Research Act*, London: Transaction.

Garratt, D., Piper, H. and Taylor, B. (2013) '"Safeguarding" sports' coaching: Foucault, genealogy and critique', *Sport, Education and Society*, 18(5), 615–29: DOI:10.1080/13573322.2012.736861.

Glaser, B. G. and Strauss, A. L. (1967, 2012) *The Discovery of Grounded Theory: Strategies for Qualitative Research*, Piscataway, NJ: Transaction.

Goffman, E. (1959) *The Presentation of Self in Everyday Life*, Garden City, NY: Doubleday.

Groom, R., Cushion, C. and Nelson, L. (2011) 'The delivery of video-based performance analysis by England youth soccer coaches: Towards a grounded theory', *Journal of Applied Sport Psychology*, 23(1): 16–32.

Gulson, K. N. and Parkes, R. J. (2010) 'Bringing theory to doctoral research', in P. Thomson and M. Walker (eds) *The Routledge Doctoral Student's Companion*, London: Routledge, 76–84.

Hammersley, M. (1995) 'Theory and Evidence in Qualitative Research', *Quality and Quantity*, 29(1): 55–66.

Haralambos, M. and Holborn, M. (2008) *Sociology: Themes and Perspectives* (7th ed.), London: Collins.

Jones, R. L. (2006) 'How can educational concepts inform sports coaching?', in R. L. Jones (ed.) *The Sports Coach as Educator: Re-conceptualising Sports Coaching*, London: Routledge, 3–13.

Kawulich, B. (2009) 'The role of theory in research', in M. Garner, C. Wagner and B. Kawulich (eds) *Teaching Research Methods in the Social Sciences*, Farnham: Ashgate Publishing, 37–48.

Merriam, S. B. and Caffarella, R. S. (1991) *Learning in Adulthood: A Comprehensive Guide*, London: Jossey-Bass.

Merton, R. K. (1967) *On Theoretical Sociology*, New York: The Free Press.

Neuman, W. L. (2000) *Social Research Methods: Qualitative and Quantitative Approaches* (4th ed.), Boston: Allyn & Bacon.

Schempp, P. and Graber, K. (1992) 'Teaching socialisation from a dialectical perspective: Pre-training through induction', *Journal of Teaching in Physical Education*, 11(4): 329–48.

Srivastava, P. and Hopwood, N. (2009) 'A practical iterative framework for qualitative data analysis', *International Journal of Qualitative Methods*, 8(1): 76–84.

Strauss, A. (1995) 'Notes on the nature and development of general theories', *Qualitative Inquiry*, 1(1): 7–18.

Tracy, S. J. (2013) *Qualitative Research Methods*, Oxford: Wiley-Blackwell.

Wright, J. (2008) 'Reframing quality and impact: The place of theory in education research', *The Australian Educational Researcher*, 35(1): 1–16.

9   Writing and representing research

Ryan Groom, Lee Nelson, Paul Potrac,
and Brett Smith

Introduction and overview

Smith (2010) highlights that among other things research is about 'one person's representation of another' (Smith 2010: 101). Because of this, debates surrounding the legitimacy of alternative representational strategies remain a contemporary and fiercely contested issue in the field of sports coaching (e.g. Gard 2014; Gilbourne *et al.* 2014; Wellard 2014; Gilbourne and Jones 2014). This is often because representational strategies reflect the ontological (the nature of reality) and epistemological (the relationship between the inquirer and the known) paradigmatic assumptions within which researchers operate (Mantzoukas 2004). But aside from issues of ontology and epistemology, which may be found debated in philosophy books, why is representation of practical importance for research? Why should a researcher within sports coaching care about how they represent their findings? The simple answer is that everyone doing research – from an undergraduate writing a research project to a seasoned professor who is going to submit work to a journal for publication – has to write. There are, however, options as to how we can represent our findings.

The aim of this chapter is to critically consider representation in sports coaching research. To achieve this we begin by highlighting a number of key considerations that researchers may wish to take into account in deciding how they will choose to represent their research. Following this, we then provide a contextual analysis of existing writing practices in sports coaching research. The chapter then takes sports coaching into new territory by introducing several representational practices that researchers might use in the future. The final section provides some of our reflections upon our experiences as researchers, project supervisors, examiners, and journal reviewers.

The crisis of representation and legitimization

Two historical moments within the development of qualitative research are pivotal to understanding how representation came to be a central concern of contemporary sports coaching research. First, from the mid-1980s to the early

1990s the *crisis of representation* was evident within writing in the social sciences, following poststructural and postmodernist thinking (see Chapter 5). The *crisis of representation* focused upon how researchers *write, explain*, and *describe* the social world (Denzin and Lincoln 1994). Central to such discussions were thoughts about 'Who is the 'Other'? Can we ever hope to speak authentically of the experience of the Other, or an Other? And if not, how do we create a social science that includes the Other?' (Lincoln and Denzin 2000: 1050). In particular, issues of validity, reliability, and objectivity were considered to be problematic (Denzin and Lincoln 1994, 2000, 2005).

Second, following the *crises of representation*, the ongoing *crises of legitimization* recognized that researchers cannot directly capture the lived experience of research participants (Denzin and Lincoln 2005). Subsequently, questions were increasingly asked about the traditional criteria used to judge the quality of qualitative research (Denzin and Lincoln 1994, 2005). In particular, the concepts of validity, generalizability, and reliability necessitate further critical consideration (Sparkes 1995, 2002), particularly regarding 'the need for connection between the text and the world written about' (Denzin and Lincoln 1994: 11). Thus the duel *crisis of representation* and *legitimization* required a reconsideration of the way in which qualitative studies should be evaluated (Sparkes 1995, 2002; see Chapter 18).

Writing is an analytical process

Following this shift within the evolution of qualitative research, representation was identified to be important because we do not simply 'write up' our research. Indeed, as Richardson (1990) reminds us, 'writing is not simply a true representation of an objective reality, out there, waiting to be seen. Instead, through literary and rhetorical structures, writing creates a particular view of reality' (Richardson 1990: 9). It is extremely rare that our ideas are stored neatly in our head and then we pristinely capture them on the page in one writing session. That is not how writing works; writing is a process, not a substance. When our fingers move across the keyboard or notebook, adding words, deleting sentences, editing paragraphs, expunging lines, recrafting pages, the meaning of our findings come into being and the content of our ideas slowly take form. In other words, writing is a form of analysis (Richardson 1990).

Consideration of audience

We believe it is important for coaching researchers to appreciate the different ways in which they might present their work and grapple with which representational option might best serve their needs. Researchers do not write for themselves. We write to communicate our research to certain audiences. But audiences vary. For example, our audience might be research participants, academics, students, coaches, or other professionals who have a stake in the research. Thus, in terms of communicating research we also need to consider our audiences. This is especially so since different audiences often demand different ways of writing.

Crystallization: Embracing diverse modes of representation

How, though, might researchers be enabled to harness the power of writing as a form of analysis, as well as be empowered to write in different ways so that knowledge can be translated to various audiences effectively and, in turn, our work can have wide impact? One exciting possibility is to engage with crystallization. Building on the work of Richardson (2000), Ellingson (2009) described crystallization as a methodology in which multiple forms of analysis and multiple genres of representation are combined in one of two ways. Integrated crystallization brings together different analyses and forms of representation to produce a single text. This might occur in one book or PhD thesis. For example, a PhD student can subject qualitative data to a narrative analysis and a conversational analysis (cf. Groom 2012; see Chapter 21). He can then in separate chapters represent the results through several realist tales and an ethnographic creative non-fiction. In contrast, there is what Ellingson termed dendritic crystallization. This is the ongoing and dispersed process of making meaning of the same topic (e.g. coaching philosophy or coach–athlete relationships) through multiple forms of analysis and forms of representation to produce a series of related texts. For example, a researcher can first subject her data to a conversational analysis and then 'write up' her work for a journal in the form of a realist tale. Later, they might subject the same data to a narrative analysis and then publish their work in another journal in the form of an ethnographic creative non-fiction. After this, they might examine the same topic again, but through a discourse analysis and represent this work in a different journal in the form of a realist tale (see Chapter 20). Crystal-lization, therefore, opens up possibilities for researchers to examine their data through multiple analytic lenses so that more complex and multi-layered understandings can be revealed. Crystallization also carves out a space for researchers to write differently for different audiences, think critically about the limits of each genre of writing, and engage in discussions about how we can expand our forms of representation further. Another strength of engaging with crystallization is that researchers are pushed to make informed decisions about which genre to use to communicate findings rather than simply choosing a way of representation because it is the 'way we always do things', is novel, or fashionable (Smith 2010; Sparkes and Smith 2013).

Applied issues and considerations

Within this section we will now outline some of the modes of representation that have been utilized within the sports coaching literature to date. It is important to note that the examples provided are merely illustrative of characteristics of alternative representational and writing practices for the purpose of critical reflection and to open a space for dialogue. We finish this section by considering some future possibilities for coaching researchers.

Scientific tales

According to Sparkes (1995) the style of science is the 'style of no style', which is a textual strategy and 'rhetorical device in its own right' (Sparkes 1995: 161). The scientific tale is the dominant tale not only in the natural sciences but also in the social sciences (Sparkes 2002). Scientific tales can be characterized through the impersonal, objective, neutral, form of representation, where 'the tables, the findings, the tested hypotheses, simply speak for themselves and the exercise is simply one of presenting and not writing the findings' (Plummer, cited in Sparkes 2002: 27). Scientific tales follow the familiar format of abstract, introduction, hypothesis, method, results (including tables and figures), discussion, conclusion, and references. Such manuscripts are crafted in the passive, third-person, voice with the aim of persuading the reader of the separation of the researcher from the method, data collection, interpretations, and presented findings (Sparkes 1995, 2002).

It could be suggested that Lorimer and Jowett's (2010) paper, 'Feedback of information in the empathic accuracy of sport coaches', is an example of a scientific tale. In their article the authors present four research-driven hypotheses about coaching efficacy. To test these hypotheses an experimental design was utilized whereby sixty badminton coaches were randomly assigned to either an experimental (i.e. feedback) or control (no feedback) group. The data collected from the participants were statistically analyzed and the findings were presented through tables, charts, and written text. The authors employed a scientific writing style throughout the article, which is perhaps evidenced by the following statement taken from the discussion of findings: 'The third hypothesis was supported by the finding and indicated that coaches' assessment of their perceived empathic accuracy ability had no significant association with their actual empathic accuracy ability' (Lorimer and Jowett 2010: 16). Consistent with the style of a scientific tale then, the writing conventions employed within this paper principally sought to present conclusions that were data and not researcher driven (Sparkes 2002).

Realist tales and modified realist tales

Van Maanen (1988) suggests that realist tales are characterized by the presentation of research in a detected, dispassionate, third-person voice, and that perhaps 'the most striking characteristic of the realist tale is the almost complete absence of the author from segments of the finished text' (Van Maanen 1988: 46). The realist tale is the dominant form of representation within qualitative research. Indeed, this form of writing can be seen in many of the leading journals in sports coaching, where the researcher deploys a neutral voice written in the third person. Here, Sparkes (1995) further highlights that 'once the researcher has finished the job of collecting the data, he or she simply vanishes' (Sparkes 1995: 162).

Bucci *et al.*'s (2012) study of elite ice hockey coaches' perceptions of athlete leadership arguably provides an example of a realist tale. In this article the authors reported that they purposively sampled six elite male ice hockey coaches of high-performance players aged between 16 and 20 years. Each of the coaches participated in semi-structured, open-ended interviews. The data gathered from the interviews were subject to inductive content analysis. In an attempt to enhance, and demonstrate, the trustworthiness of the presented findings, the authors employed a range of strategies. One such strategy was to ask a peer reviewer to examine the accuracy of the authors' thematic analysis. Here, the reviewer was given 25 percent of the meaning units and asked to place these within the already established themes; 80 percent of the meaning units were successfully coded, and after conversations an agreement level of 100 percent was eventually established. In this respect, the authors employed a peer-review process to 'help diminish researcher bias' and to ensure 'that an accurate representation of the coaches' knowledge and experience was formed' (Bucci *et al.* 2012: 248).

In the results section the authors presented findings comprising 69 percent of meaning units taken from the larger data set. Here, the four properties (i.e. selecting an athlete leader, coach–athlete leader relationship, developing athlete leadership, athlete leader responsibilities) acted as subheadings under which an overview of findings, including example verbatim interview extracts, was presented. In this article, the authors adopt a principally detached, third-person, writing style. The approach taken by Bucci *et al.* (2012) is representative of much qualitative coaching research, which has tended to 'construct authority and objectivity through the use of a passive voice' in an attempt to 'distance the disembodied author from the data' (Sparkes 2002: 44).

While a large proportion of qualitative coaching research might be considered realist tales, Purdy *et al.* (2009) employed a variation of a realist tale in their study of an athlete's use of power in an elite men's rowing programme. In this study, Purdy *et al.* (2009) contended that 'authors are ever present throughout articles' and that the author-evacuated nature of realists tales should therefore 'be considered a textual illusion' (Purdy *et al.* 2009: 327). It is in light of such thinking that Purdy *et al.* (2009) acknowledged 'that it is not only the participants' story that the reader gets, but our interpretation of it', which brings with it discussions about whose story is really being told. As such, the authors explain that the findings presented in their article might be more appropriately thought of as 'a modified realist tale' (Purdy *et al.* 2009: 327).

Confessional tales

In comparison to realist tales, confessional tales are highly personalized accounts of the research process. These often follow realist tales in an attempt to expand upon the messy realities of the research process (Sparkes 1995, 2002). In particular, the confessional tale reintroduces the researcher as a person into the research narrative, focusing upon issues such as 'ethics, gender, race, validity, reciprocity, sexuality, voice, empowerment, [and] authorship' (Smyth and Shacklock, cited in Sparkes 2002: 58). Furthermore, Sparkes (2002) highlights that confessional tales 'explicitly problematize and demystify fieldwork or participant observation by revealing what actually happened in the research process from start to finish' (Sparkes 2002: 58). The work of Purdy and Jones (2013) is arguably an example of a confessional tale within sports coaching research. In this article the authors critically reflect on Purdy's role as a female ethnographer in the world of elite male rowing. Here, Purdy and Jones (2013) highlighted that 'the significance of this work is rooted in exploring how the roles we adopt as field researchers are constantly renegotiated in context and the implications of doing so for the subsequent data' (Purdy and Jones 2013: 2).

Laura (Purdy) describes how she employed a number of strategies in an attempt to gain the trust and approval of group members to secure the required data. She reflects upon a conscious mental effort to 'play the role of a researcher', adopting a position of neutrality, whilst being at pains to emphasize that her role was one of understanding rather than being there to judge or spy on the participants (Purdy and Jones 2013). Furthermore, Laura employed a number of overt strategies in her attempts to secure 'buy in' from the coaching staff and athletes. These included appearing helpful by engaging in various tasks, volunteering for activities outside of the coaching programme, helping entertain the coach's children, and participating in frequent 'banter' (humorous social exchanges). While Laura believed that her involvement in the latter in particular helped her to establish a bond with the male rowers, she described how she thought that much of the friendly banter aimed towards her was laced with sexual innuendo and sarcasm. Here, she went on to describe how she felt that she had to pretend that such comments did not bother her if she was to continue to collect data in this setting. The work of Purdy and Jones (2013), then, might be understood as a confessional tale as it resituates the author in the research process by announcing: 'Hear I am. This happened to me and this is how I felt, reacted, and coped. Walk in my shoes for a while' (Sparkes 2002: 59).

Autoethnography and narratives of the self

As opposed to the scientific presentation of the participant or 'other' in the research process, autobiographical writing through autoethnographies and narratives of the self has, in recent years, been increasingly utilized within the social science literature (Sparkes 2002; see Chapter 19). These forms of representation are highly personalized and evocative forms of writing, utilizing dramatic recall, vivid characters and strong metaphors, where authors tell stories about their own lived experiences (Richardson 1994). Typically, autoethnographic work displays multiple layers of consciousness, connecting the personal to the cultural (Ellis and Bouchner 2000). Indeed, Jones (2006) highlighted that the central purpose of such work 'is to tell a different, perhaps a "truer", story about coaches and coaching through illuminating a number of unexamined issues that currently lie undiscovered and undisturbed in the muddy depths of the activity' (Jones 2006: 1017).

Potrac *et al.*'s (2013) recent exploration of the competitive, calculating, and frequently uncaring nature of coaches' working relationships is an example of an autoethnographic coaching text. In this paper, Paul (Potrac) shares with the reader how he not only acquired but also practiced the social rules of high-performance soccer coaching. Here, Paul learnt that in order to survive and advance his coaching career he needed to follow and apply the following rules: (1) 'look after yourself', (2) recognize that 'coaches come and go', (3) 'watch your back', and (4) 'seize any opportunity to promote your position'. Importantly, in order to link the personal to the social, the authors drew on Bauman's work on liquidity as a theoretical lens. In doing so, it was hoped that this autoethnographic sharing would help to develop the notion of coaching as a political activity (Potrac *et al.* 2013).

With a greater emphasis upon personal introspection, rather than (re)situating research back into the broader socio-cultural arena, narratives of the self follow many similar writing practices to autoethnographic work (Sparkes 1995). The work of Toner *et al.* (2012) arguably represents an example of a narrative of the self. In this paper the authors offer an account of John's (Toner's) engagement in shared critical reflection and how this process resulted in his re-storying a narrative experience. More specifically the authors explain how a process of reflection, writing, talking, and sharing with his co-authors led John to alter his position from a victim of bad coaching to a more symbiotic understanding of the relationship between coach and athlete. In this respect, Toner *et al.* (2012) suggest that the reflective writing of a narrative of the self moved John's story from a closed to an open narrative, which 'allowed different perspectives to emerge, perspectives that brought forward new possibilities, and new interpretations' (Toner *et al.* 2012: 74–5). Within his narrative, John utilizes a number of writing conventions to tell his story, including direct recall conversation and short vignettes that invite the reader to experience and inhabit his lived world in more vivid terms.

Poetic and fictionalized representation

According to Sparkes (2002), it has been argued that poetic representation is well placed to retell lived experience and can be an evocative form of communication. To date there are few examples of poetic representation in the sports coaching literature. One example comes from Gilbourne in his 2012 paper 'Contemplations on sport, complexity, ages of being and practice'. In this article, Gilbourne includes a poem titled 'Such a nice lad' to help to capture and express his witnessing and experiencing of hearing about an elite-level sport person who had reportedly committed suicide in the eighteen months leading up the his writing of the article. Here, the work of Gilbourne (2012) demonstrates how the evocative nature of poetic representation is not only cognitively but also emotionally engaging.

Similarly, at the present time, there are relatively few instances of fictionalized representation. One example is Jones' (2007) 'Coaching redefined: an everyday pedagogical endeavour' paper in which the author presents a hypothetical dialogue between an actor representing present-day coaching science and an individual arguing for coaching to redefine itself as an educational endeavor. Responding to Sparkes' (2002) call for greater experimental writing, Jones (2007) employed a dialogue approach in the hope that his readers would 'find it easier to participate in the conversation' that he had constructed when compared to 'what is often perceived to be firm and "safely" enclosed official academic prose' (Jones 2007: 161). Additionally, Jones (2007) hoped that this form of representation had the potential to unearth ideas, clarify muddied thinking, and trigger new ways of understanding.

Future prospects

Having highlighted a range of ways in which sports coaching researchers have represented their work, we now offer some possible directions of travel for the future. Expanding the autoethnographic work in sport coaching, two prospects or directions that may be taken is what is termed meta-autoethnography and duoethnography. Ellis (2009) described meta-autoethnographies as 'occasions in which I revisit my original representation, consider responses, and write an autoethnographic account about autoethnography' (Ellis 2009: 13). For example, having published a sports coaching autoethnography the author might a few years later revisit his or her stories and write a meta-autoethnography in which he or she critically reflects on these earlier stories from their current historical position.

According to Norris *et al.* (2012), duoethnography shares similar assumptions and goals with autoethnography. It is though different in that rather than one person being the author, two or more people work in tandem to dialogically show the interconnections between the personal and the cultural, and to offer stories of exposure and resistance to dominant narratives. For example, a student and his supervisor, or two researchers from different universities, might for certain purposes choose to work together to represent their experiences of the culture of sports coaching through a series of stories that expose the similar, different, interlacing, and conflicting narratives they have witnessed over time.

The visual also holds great potential to represent research findings (Phoenix 2010). Researchers in sport coaching might use film or photographs to represent their research findings. Examples of the use of photography as a research method in sports coaching can be seen in the work of Jones *et al.* (2013) exploring caring and the politics of touch in sports coaching. Furthermore, researchers may generate and analyze data from filmed interviews, participant-driven video diaries, and ethnographic research captured on a camera smart phone. For example, within the wider sport science literature Kluge *et al.* (2010) used film as a mode of representation. Likewise, in her project on aging and physical activity entitled 'Moving Stories', Phoenix (2010) harnessed the power of film to represent findings and communicate her research to diverse audiences (to see the film go to: http://vimeo.com/43182928).

Another example of the use of film as a form of representation can be found in the work of Parsons and Lavery (2012), who used broken dialogue. Theoretically informed by the traditions in narrative inquiry and visual anthropology, broken dialogue is premised on the idea that dialogue possesses features making it unique as a generator of new knowledge and opportunities for social intervention. One of the benefits of using film is that, as Parsons and Lavery note, it is an excellent medium for knowledge transfer and dissemination. It can also be a useful means for representing people's embodied multi-sensory worlds that goes beyond talking about the body or senses on the page to showing these in action through film.

Furthermore, as exemplified in Blodgett *et al.*'s (2011) participatory action research with Aboriginal community members' experiences of physical activity, vignettes can be highly useful to represent data. Vignettes, especially when written in a storied form, can be highly accessible to members of the community. A vignette can enable participants to reflect on a situation or event that they may not have considered before, or which is highly routinized. In so doing, vignettes can generate rich data on topics that are rarely considered or taken for granted, yet remain important to understand. Further, by inviting participants to comment on characters in vignettes, rather than talk directly about their own experiences, sensitive topics can be examined in ways that appear less threatening and distressing to the participant. Also a vignette can be translated into multiple languages, thereby allowing researchers to collect cross-cultural data with relative ease in comparison to many other qualitative methods.

However, researchers need to choose each form of representation in informed, principled, and disciplined ways (Sparkes and Smith 2013). Choosing a form of representation simply because it is novel or personally interests me will not suffice because, as Smith (2010) noted, there is the danger of fetishizing form and elevating style, or panache, over content. A researcher needs to have something worthwhile to say and a specific genre, irrespective of novelty or personal liking, might not be best suited to communicating ones points. Indeed, for Smith, the use of any genre depends on a range of matters including, epistemological and ontological commitments, the nature of the data, the intended purpose for writing up one's research, 'theoretical points wished to be made, what truths can be told, the intended audience, and what, if anything, can the genre of choice say that is of value' (Smith 2010: 103). Likewise, researchers need to respect the training and hard work that is often needed to produce, for example, a good film or musical performance that works as a piece of research. Researchers might not have the skills to represent their work in these ways alone. As such, they may need to collaborate with experts, spend time learning the craft, or recognize that sometimes a way of representing research is beyond them. Indeed, sports coaching research needs to be held up to high and difficult standards (Sparkes and Smith 2013). If it is not, then the field will stagnate and the research produced will be superficial and of limited significance for the coaching community.

Reflections from the field

While the various forms of representation presented in the previous section have been, and remain, available to those engaging in coaching research, it has been our experience that author-evacuated text continues to be the dominant discourse in our discipline. We believe that this might be explained by the fact that discussions about representation have received relatively little attention in the coaching literature and, arguably, the sports sciences more broadly. Rather, during their attendance of research methods modules undergraduate and postgraduate students are often taught the importance of developing an objective and detached academic writing style and conform to the tenets of (post) positivistic research. Thesis guidelines and marking criteria tend to stipulate rigid structural requirements, whereby students have to produce theses containing chapters in a predefined order (i.e. introduction, literature review, methodology, results, discussion, and conclusion). Students' reading of academic journals that are heavily populated with author-evacuated scientific and realist tales further reinforce such messages.

As researchers and supervisors of undergraduate and postgraduate projects we have found that asking our students whether they intend to write themselves into their theses understandably confuses many. Once they have understood the arguments for author presence in academic text, those individuals who decide to build themselves into their work can find the shift from a 'third person' to a 'first person' writing style to be an odd, and sometimes challenging, experience. Our efforts to suggest that personal experiences, in the form of an autoethnography or narrative of the self, can be the legitimate focus of a research thesis have proven to be equally challenging as there appears to be a limited understanding of such genres of representation in many sports science departments. Positivistic research communicated through scientific and realist tales still dominates.

However, let us consider the work of Sir Timothy Hunt, winner of the 2001 Noble Prize in Physiology and Medicine for his work in cellular biology, in which with colleagues he discovered two proteins, cyclin and CDK (cyclin dependent kinase), responsible for cell division. Interestingly, within this work the research team often wrote themselves into the findings and interpretation of this work (e.g. Kobayashi *et al.* 1991; Hunt *et al.* 1992). This highlights the point that representation is a choice, a textual strategy, rather than a specific marker of academic quality in its own right. We could all write ourselves *into* or *out of* our research but the decision to do so, is exactly that; a decision made by the researcher.

References

Blodgett, A. T., Schinke, R. J., Smith, B., Peltier, D. and Pheasant, C. (2011) 'In indigenous word: Exploring vignettes as a narrative strategy for presenting the research voices of Aboriginal community members', *Qualitative Inquiry*, 17(6): 522–33.

Bucci, J., Bloom, G. A., Loughead, T. M. and Caron, J. G. (2012) 'Ice hockey coaches' perceptions of athlete leadership', *Journal of Applied Sport Psychology*, 24(3): 243–59.

Denzin, N. K. and Lincoln, Y. (1994) 'Introduction', in N. Denzin and Y. Lincoln (eds) *The Sage Handbook of Qualitative Research*, Thousand Oaks, CA: Sage, 1–17.

——(2000) 'Introduction', in N. Denzin and Y. Lincoln (eds) *The Sage Handbook of Qualitative Research* (2nd ed.), Thousand Oaks, CA: Sage, 1–28.

——(2005) 'Introduction: The discipline and practice of qualitative research', in N. Denzin and Y. Lincoln (eds) *The Sage Handbook of Qualitative Research* (3rd ed.), Thousand Oaks, CA: Sage, 1–32.

Ellingson, L. L. (2009) *Engaging in Crystallization in Qualitative Research: An Introduction*, Thousand Oaks, CA: Sage.

Ellis, C. (2009) *Revision: Autoethnographic Reflections on Life and Work*, Walnut Creek, CA: Left Coast Press.

Ellis, C. and Bouchner, A. (2000) 'Autoethnography, personal narrative, reflexivity', in N. Denzin and Y. Lincoln (eds) *The Sage Handbook of qualitative research* (2nd ed.), Thousand Oaks, CA: Sage, 733–68.

Gard, M. (2014) 'On the myth of the crisis of representation: A response to Gilbourne, Jones and Spencer', *Sport, Education and Society*, 19(1): 93–98.

Gilbourne, D. (2012) 'Contemplations on sport, complexity, ages of being and practice', *Sports Coaching Review*, 1(1): 4–16.

Gilbourne, D. and Jones, R. L. (2014) 'Further thoughts on the writing of stories: A response to Michael Gard and Ian Wellard', *Sport, Education and Society*, 19(1): 105–111.

Gilbourne, D., Jones, R. L. and Jordan, S. (2014) 'Applied utility and the autoethnographic short story: Persuasions for, and illustrations of, writing critical social science', *Sport, Education and Society*, 19(1): 80–92.

Groom, R. (2012) 'Towards an understanding of the use of video-based performance analysis in the coaching process', unpublished PhD thesis, Loughborough University.

Hunt, T., Luca, F. C. and Ruderman, J. V. (1992) 'The requirements for protein synthesis and degradation, and the control of destruction of cyclins A and B in the meitic and mitotic cell cycles if the clam embryo', *The Journal of Cell Biology*, 116(3): 707–24.

Jones, R. L. (2006) 'Dilemmas, maintaining "face", and paranoia: An average coaching life', *Qualitative Inquiry*, 12(5): 1012–21.

——(2007) 'Coaching redefined: An everyday pedagogical endeavour', *Sport, Education and Society*, 12(2): 159–73.

Jones, R. L., Bailey, J. and Santos, S. (2013) 'Coaching caring and the politics of touch: A visual exploration', *Sport, Education and Society*, 18(5): 648–62.

Kluge, M. A., Grant, B. C., Friend, L. and Glick, L. (2010) 'Seeing is believing: Telling the 'inside' story of a beginning masters athlete through film', *Qualitative Research in Sport and Exercise*, 2(2): 282–92.

Kobayashi, H., Minshull, J., Ford, C., Golsteyn, R., Poon, R. and Hunt, T. (1991) 'On the synthesis and destruction of A- and B-type cyclins during oogenesis meiotic maturation in xenopus lavis', *The Journal of Cell Biology*, 114(4): 755–65.

Lincoln, Y. and Denzin, N. (2000) 'The seventh moment', in N. Denzin and Y. Lincoln (eds) *The Sage Handbook of Qualitative Research* (2nd ed.), Thousand Oaks, CA: Sage.

Lorimer, R. and Jowett, S. (2010) 'Feedback of information in the empathic accuracy of sport coaches', *Psychology of Sport and Exercise*, 11(1): 12–17.

Mantzoukas, S. (2004) 'Issues of representation within qualitative inquiry', *Qualitative Health Research*, 14(7): 994–1007.

Norris, J., Sawyer, R. D. and Lund, D. (eds) (2012) *Duoethnography: Dialogic Methods for Social, Health, and Educational Research*, Walnut Creek: Left Coast Press.

Parsons, J. A. and Lavery, J. V. (2012) 'Broken dialogue: A new research method for controversial health and social issues', *Medical Research Methodology*, 12(92): 1–9.

Phoenix, C. (2010) 'Seeing the world of physical culture: The potential of visual methods for qualitative research in sport and exercise', *Qualitative Research in Sport and Exercise*, 2(2): 93–108.

Potrac, P., Jones, R. L., Gilbourne, D. and Nelson, L. (2013) "Handshakes, BBQs, and bullets": Self-interest, shame and regret in football coaching', *Sports Coaching Review*, 1(2): 79–92.

Purdy, L. and Jones, R. L. (2013) 'Changing personas and evolving identities: The contestation and renegotiation of researcher roles in fieldwork', *Sport, Education and Society*, 18(3): 292–310.

Purdy, L., Jones, R. and Cassidy, T. (2009) 'Negotiation and capital: Athletes' use of power in an elite men's rowing program', *Sport, Education and Society*, 14(3): 321–38.

Richardson, L. (1990) *Writing Strategies: Reaching Diverse Audiences*. Thousand Oaks, CA: Sage.

——(1994) 'Writing', in N. Denzin and Y. Lincoln (eds) *Handbook of Qualitative Research*, Thousand Oaks, CA: Sage, 516–29.

——(2000) 'Writing: A method of inquiry', in N. Denzin and Y. Lincoln (eds) *Handbook of Qualitative Research* (2nd ed.), Thousand Oaks, CA: Sage, 923–48.

Smith, B. (2010) 'Narrative inquiry: Ongoing conversations and questions for sport psychology research', *International Review of Sport Psychology*, 3(1): 87–107.

Sparkes, A. C. (1995) 'Writing people', *Quest*, 15(1), 93–118.

——(2002) *Telling Tales in Sport and Physical Activity: A Qualitative Journey*, Champaign, IL: Human Kinetics.

Sparkes, A. C. and Smith, B. (2013) *Qualitative Research Methods in Sport, Exercise and Health: From Process to Product*, London: Routledge.

Toner, J., Nelson, L., Potrac, P., Gilbourne, D. and Marshall, P. (2012) 'From "blame" to "shame" in a coach–athlete relationship in golf: A tale of shared critical reflection and the re-storying of narrative experience', *Sports Coaching Review*, 1(1): 67–78.

Van Maanen, J. (1988) *Tales of the Field: On Writing Ethnography*, Chicago: University of Chicago Press.

Wellard, I. (2014) 'Starting points and destinations: Negotiating factual and fictional pathways: A response to Gilbourne, Jones and Spencer', *Sport, Education and Society*, 19(1): 99–104.

10 Ethical considerations

Graham McFee

Introduction and overview

Those seeking to complete research into sports coaching must give thought to ethical considerations. One aspect of any research ethics, reflecting responsible conduct of research, embodies the researcher's obligation to report that the research was conducted without fabrication, falsification, or plagiarism, that an adequate 'paper-trail' was maintained (say, in laboratory notebooks or field-notes), and that researchers adhered to the general constraints on sound research from the parent discipline, in line with the topics designated as central by the Office of Research Integrity in the USA (Shamoo and Resnik 2009: v–vi):

(i)   Data Acquisition, Management, Ownership
(ii) Conflict of Interest and Commitment
(iii) Human Subjects
(iv) Animal Welfare
(v)   Research Misconduct
(vi) Publication Practices/Responsible Authorship
(vii) Mentor/Trainee Responsibilities
(viii) Peer Review
(ix) Collaborative and International Science.

Most of these, while important in themselves, lack specific (or distinctive) application to research into sports coaching: all researchers should behave responsibly in these ways. The other chief aspect of research ethics concerns the treatment of research subjects – and, for sports coaching, this typically means *human* subjects, although (of course) there are experiments in sports science using animal subjects.[1] This focus on research subjects is our primary topic here: how should a researcher behave so as to respect the rights of research subjects (and other obligations to them) while still obeying the imperative provided both by the right to investigate a chosen topic (reflecting academic freedom) and the public interest in the outcome of research?

The moral imperative in respect of one's research subjects might be explained by reference to the kinds of *prima facie* obligations one might have in dealing appropriately with other persons: justice, autonomy, respect for persons, non-maleficence (Shamoo and Resnik 2009). These ground much morally appropriate action. Here such moral obligations must be contrasted with *prudential obligations*: moral obligations should be respected as *the right thing to do* in the circumstances – one ought to return the borrowed money, keep one's promise to visit granny, respect the rights of other persons. With prudential obligations, one ought to do whatever it is only in order to avoid the punishment that accrues from failure to do the thing, or to attract the praise that might follow.

Such prudential obligations are typified by legal obligations: if only fear of punishment stops me killing you, my motivation is purely prudential – I have not yet learned that it is wrong to behave in that way. This contrast is fundamental here, since research ethics can degenerate into the proscription of activities, not directly from research-ethical considerations but because they are likely to lead to litigation. The perspective of research ethics concerns right (or conversely, wrong) action in the particular situation, whether or not it might lead to litigation. Indeed, when the concern is with the ethical obligations of the researcher, prudential obligations, such as (say) the legal obligations to data protection, are implicitly set aside. Typically, the ethical imperative here will be more stringent than the legal one. But recognizing this also grants that our concerns here are not merely with how to avoid litigation. That already highlights the flaws in any account of research ethics that rests content with just a completed consent form: what has been called 'tick-box consent' (McNamee *et al.* 2007: 72; McFee 2010: 48, 74).

Very broadly, research into coaching may usefully be divided into two classes, differing importantly from the perspective of research ethics. The first, ideally, takes account of the context of the particular coaching practice – and hence is naturalistic – while the second can be conducted in isolation from the specific coaching context: it might, for instance, be conducted in a laboratory. This first, naturalistic kind seeks to preserve the coaching context, since that is part of its topic. It will be most distinctive of sports coaching as such, since it emphasizes the interpersonal dimension of coach–athlete relations as topics of research inquiry. Therefore the research most characteristic of investigations of sports coaching will be naturalistic in this sense; and for these reasons. But, of course, the knowledge that one is being researched typically impacts that context, to some degree or other. Research *subjects* may tailor their responses or behaviors to those that they imagine the researcher would prefer; or may set out to thwart her. At the least, one cannot guarantee that the *fact* of being researched will not change the behavior of research subjects.[2] Therefore, any data from the behavior (including verbal behavior) of those subjects reflecting that context will not be *safe* (in the legal sense): one cannot *trust* that these data were not altered once the research context was identified. As a result, this characteristic style of research into sports coaching – in wishing to preserve as much naturalism as possible – will not make subjects fully aware of some fundamental dimensions in which they are being researched. In this sense, the research designs will be *covert* research to some degree or other, since there will be things the subjects do not know or to which they have not agreed. Moreover, all (or almost all) research into coaching has, as its object of final scrutiny, *human subjects.*[3] So all will raise complex ethical questions, in addition to the issues for responsible research noted above, since ethical questions typically arise in our interaction with one another.

Understanding such covert research into sports coaching usefully begins from an idealized version of *overt* research. Such an idealization typically begins with some research-based 'horror stories': in my personal 'favorite' (Homan 1991; McFee 2010: 136), research in a family planning clinic involved some of the women being given a placebo, rather than the contraceptive pill, with what the researchers described as 'unexpected consequences' (namely, some of the women became pregnant). The moral to be taken from such cases, a moral seemingly enshrined in the Nuremberg Code of 1947 and the Helsinki Declaration of 2000, is that – in the 'horror story' – the consent of subjects for what was done to them had not been sought. Perhaps, too, this highlights that some research suggestions *should not* (and would not) receive consent. So subjects are viewed as capable of such decisions. Hence the idealization is that the rights of subjects would be safeguarded whenever the *voluntary informed consent* (VIC) of those subjects has been obtained. In effect, this leaves *subjects* responsible for their own behavior: they *agreed* to whatever it was. That seems to absolve the researcher.

This, in turn, allows us to idealize *overt* research designs as those where (full) VIC – understood on this model – is achieved. To understand, we must elaborate both informational and consenting aspects of VIC. Thus, on my account (McFee 2010), subjects should be informed:

- that they are being researched;
- of all aspects of the research protocol;
- of *any* harms or dangers, physical and psychological;
- of the fate of the data – how and where it will be disseminated. And this will include the degree of anonymity provided.

Further, the subject should be in a position to consent (so, not a minor, for instance) and without coercion of any kind. Finally, it must be clear to subjects that their consent can be withdrawn at any time.[4]

Four features of this idealization of (full) VIC are centrally important here:

1. At every level, even short of (full) VIC, the requirement must be substantial, so this is not just 'tick box' consent – in particular, this is part of the subjects' right to withdraw.
2. Responsibility rests with subjects (and subjects' understanding), since they can pull out at any time. Hence *their* standards must be met. Indeed, the

point of the 'horror stories' used to motivate the demand for VIC is just that the responsibility should reside with subjects.

3. Full VIC is the 'gold standard' (assuring the rights of subjects) such that when there is (full) VIC, subjects' rights are safeguarded – but, of course, only *if* (full) VIC in this sense is attainable, and attained.

4. But (full) VIC is not attainable in theory or in practice.

As Onora O'Neill (2003) has urged, it follows from the account of (full) VIC offered that both information and consent must cover *all* those things which, if a particular subject knew them, would lead that subject to withdraw, or not give, consent. For only then could it be a 'gold standard'. Since one cannot guarantee this, even in principle, no research can meet this condition fully.[5] O'Neill's point is that full VIC requires that you must be informed of (and therefore consent to) *anything* that would make you withdraw. But anything which *did* make someone else withdraw *might* make you do so too. So any crazy idea which actually does (or even might) make *any* person withdraw has to be ruled out in every case – as a potential research subject, you have to be informed of them *all*, in any manner of presentation of the points.

VIC need not be given up entirely, of course. In some cases, some weaker version ('best we can get' VIC) will offer some ethical safeguards to research subjects. So: (a) overt research is governed by 'best we can get' VIC – which introduces some covert aspects, as such research (in failing to completely address O'Neill's condition) is not fully overt; typically, researchers introduce realistic restrictions on the scope of O'Neill's condition, drawing on theory. But it follows that some of the responsibility now rests with the researcher; and (b) different kinds/categories of covert research arise as the constraints of (full) VIC are not met. Thus Homan (1991) rightly distinguishes four 'principles' of covertness, three of which are relevant here: *concealment* (not letting subjects know that they are being researched); *misrepresentation* (not letting subjects know the topic or protocol); and *camouflage* (the aim to be invisible in the field one is researching).[6] These indicate different ways of realizing less than 'best you can get' VIC. Although these will all preclude full overtness of that kind, our argument must be that research deploying them can still be performed ethically. Of course, any research with human subjects (indeed, any research at all) must be worthwhile; and the requirement for a degree of worthwhileness may seem intensified when there is the possibility that the rights of other persons – as research subjects – will be infringed or traduced if that research is conducted. But, here, both covert and overt designs require a sound justification: in particular, the convert researcher should not be held to a higher scale here. And this point is fundamental to the justification for research as such.

Applied issues and considerations

As we have seen, the justification for covert designs lies in the preservation of the context to be researched – if the subject was aware of the relevant aspects of the research protocol, he/she might not respond as he/she would otherwise have done. To preserve the context, then, always involves some degree of deception (or something similar) in covert research:[7] the subjects do not know something important for the research design and hence cannot consent to it. As Schrader-Frechette (1994: 8) grants, 'deception for the purposes of ensuring spontaneous reactions may be justified', for only then can one be sure that the subject's responses were not altered by the fact of being researched, or any aspect of it. So, such covert research designs are the only *safe* (in the legal sense) way to pursue this topic. Hence they cannot be a 'competitor' with overt designs; therefore, they cannot be 'second best' to such designs.

Thus there is a justification for preserving that ignorance in one's subjects: if the ignorance were removed, the results would be *unsafe*. And, of course, as we have recognized, a similar pattern of ignorance will also apply in practice for the 'best we can get' VIC – it fails O'Neill's condition (above) precisely in not responding to *all* that might lead, or might have led, the *subject* to withdraw, since there can be no *all*. Instead, in practice, the decision as to the extent of information deemed *relevant* rests with the researcher. In this sense, then, the rights of the subjects are being 'safeguarded' by the researcher. Once this point is granted, it becomes easier to see how a covert researcher too might seek to safeguard aspects of the subject's rights. This is the substance of my 'treat like a friend' condition (McFee 2010: 157): that, as a covert researcher, one should give special regard to the rights of subjects in any respect not involved in the covertness.

The thought, then, is to treat one's research subjects as if they were people one especially cares about; for instance, one's children, or one's friends: that these were the people for whom one would 'go the extra mile'. Adopting such an attitude to one's research subjects affords them an appropriate ethical status. So, of course, there is nothing magic to the term "friends" here,[8] or to any of these others. This is a recipe for *good* (or positive) treatment, to be applied to one's research subjects: they are not to be treated as some 'nameless other' (even when they are). Further, this stance is typically intelligible to most people – they can ask (for instance), "Would I be happy if this happened to my child?" as one way to pose, in a concrete form, the question of how to act ethically. This is the knowledge the typical researcher requires to manage (or, anyway, to *raise*) typical ethical issues for typical research in sport with human subjects. One further feature useful in covert research designs should also be mentioned here. If the subject does nothing he/she would not do anyway, the dangers of the research are thereby minimized: there are lots of kinds of danger that such a research design cannot cause. Thus, if Jill is going to run the marathon anyway, the research design does not place her at additional risk in this respect – at least if we do not ask her to wear such-and-such, or to do so-and-so, that is beyond her normal or routine practice in such a case.

It will help to sketch examples of such research in more detail, thereby emphasizing that not all covert research is covert to the same degree. For instance, as a first example, suppose a coaching intervention took the form of mental skills training, with the team's sports psychologist. An associated research design might investigate which of a number of prompting strategies were most likely to be effective in leading the athletes to complete the assigned mental skills training. Such a research design would be *covert* in that the precise topic under investigation would be kept from those athletes since, if they knew it, that knowledge might alter their behavior. At the least, it would be *unsafe* to assume that the knowledge would not lead the subjects to behave differently. But, in other respects, that design would share features with overt research; the athletes would know they were being researched; and they would trust the coach to ensure that no harm (physical or psychological) came to them. They might even give consent to this. Further, in a favored case, the athletes would know the *range* of journals into which coach and/or sports psychologist would submit papers detailing research of this kind and its outcomes. In particular, they would be confident that academic journals of that sport did not engage in the sorts of exposé characteristic of tabloid journalism. And they might be expected to know the degree of anonymity provided by such journals. These features either *are*, or *parallel*, the features of which overt research aims to inform its subjects. In this case, then, the research design – although naturalistic – is only covert to a small degree.

By contrast, as a second example, a study which aimed at the coaching aspect of the impact of fan behavior on the team might hope to be fully naturalistic, in that it would try – as far as possible – not to disturb the responses of either team-members or fans. For it would aim to *understand* what was going on before trying to modify it (as/if necessary). This naturalism would preclude the researcher from informing the subjects that he/she was indeed a researcher (and hence that research was going on) or the precise character of that research. We can readily imagine that neither team-members nor fans were familiar with academic journals of the sort in which such material would be presented. So a suitable research design based on participant observation, which gave the researcher some plausible role with the team – say, as driver of the team bus – might be fully covert: neither team members nor fans would be informed of any impact of the research; and their consent could not be sought. So, while both research designs are covert, the second might with justice be thought *more* covert.

In defending the second such design against major objections, the researcher will insist that any information given to subjects here (and hence any consent sought) would undermine the research process, making it no longer *safe* to regard the data thereby generated as reliable. Hence only this covert context could provide potentially reliable data. Then, first, the research is worthwhile (let that be granted); and, second, it does not ask of its subjects ranges of behavior different from those which they would have been performing anyway. At most, they would have had a few extra conversations with a well-informed person, who was a good listener. So there is no *extra* threat to their physical or psychological well-being as a result of their being (unknowing) research subjects. In that sense, they continue to take responsibility for their behaviors in this respect, *as they always had*. Moreover, the context of covert research puts the researcher under a powerful obligation to protect the general rights of the subjects. But, as we saw, that obligation *also* exists when, in overt research designs, 'best you can get' VIC is achieved. For here too *some* of what might have caused subjects to withdraw is typically unavailable to them: the O'Neill condition (above) cannot be met, even in principle. And that deficiency is once again rectified by the trust of those subjects in the researcher's good intentions, and by the researcher's principled and theoretically informed decisions in respect of whatever is not made plain to subjects. So the ethical safeguards here depend centrally on the researchers. In this sense, the ethical safeguards in the covert case are of the same kind and degree as those in the overt case.

To summarize our position so far, we can introduce six points for covert research with human subjects:

(a) *That covert research with human subjects should not be held to a higher standard of relevance than overt research* – that both should be justified in terms of the general interest of the investigation, and so on (as above).

(b) *That covert research is never an alternative to overt research*: if a research design permits an area designated for research to be investigated overtly, it follows that, in researching, one cannot be disrupting inappropriately the research environment; and hence that there can be no justification for a covert design. Conversely, if the research is justified in a context where that environment would be disrupted to the degree that the data were no longer 'safe' (in the legal sense), that research cannot be conducted overtly (if it is to remain research).

(c) *That a blanket treatment of 'covert research' is inappropriate*. There are degrees of covertness, reflecting the various aspects around which, in overt research, subjects should be informed and asked to voluntarily consent: that one can sometimes inform subjects of, say, everything except the fine details of the research protocol without compromising their responses. In a context of trust in the researcher, this would safeguard the rights of subjects as much as many overt designs, and in precisely the same manner.

(d) *That the limitations on ethical safeguards for human subjects in overt research must be recognized as theoretical*. Once it is accepted that the research subject can withdraw at any time (that the consent is 'voluntary'), the perspective of the subject becomes critical: in particular, the researcher cannot decide that such-and-such is or is not relevant. As O'Neill (2003) urged (cited above), it follows that both information and consent must cover *all* those things which, if a particular subject knew them, would lead that subject to withdraw, or not give, consent. Since one cannot guarantee this even in principle, no research can meet this condition fully. In practice, then, both covert researcher and overt researcher will be making key decisions.

(e) *That, in practice, both overt and covert research designs must aim to do 'the best the researcher can' to safeguard the moral rights of subjects* (in line with point (d)).

(f) *That discussion concerns the ethical obligations of researchers*, which would normally be more stringent than the legal (or other prudential) obligations, where these diverge.

Recognizing these six points is seeing covert research designs as importantly continuous with overt designs, and as potentially ethically constrained. Given that these are our principles, how should we act in practice? Here, four areas of consideration highlight aspects of the ethical treatment of subjects in covert research (McFee 2010: 155–57):

1. No harm, physical or psychological: expressed like that, this goal cannot strictly be achieved, since it presupposes a finite totality ('all') where there is none. But this aspect of covert research is usually achieved through a combination of the subjects not doing anything 'unusual' or additional (they were going to run the marathon anyway) and their trusting the researcher – and such trust can be built up!
2. Debriefing where possible.
3. No exposé – given treatment appropriate to academic research, not sensationalized into tabloid journalism.
4. 'Treat subjects as friends' (see above).

None of these strategies, of course, ensures the ethical treatment of one's research subjects. However if, by the fourth strategy above, a very positive attitude is adopted to the welfare and well-being of research subjects – as we would of friends – there is a basis here for the trust of subjects. And the point above is: nothing could absolutely guarantee that one's subject's rights were not traduced. This stresses again the *researcher*'s role in determining what is *relevant*; and hence reaffirms the need for the subject to *trust* the researcher. Yet, once that is done, the sanctity of the subject's rights now depends on the researcher (at least in part) – and hence *not* on the judgment of the subjects, as the idealization of (full) VIC assumed. Indeed, it is because the subject is thought to be in a position – in (full) VIC – to safeguard his/her *own* rights that (full) VIC is viewed as the ultimate safeguard of such rights: the *gold standard* of the rights of subjects not being traduced, say, by researchers. The demise of that conception takes with it *any* safeguard to that degree. In particular, it makes clear that in *any* case (theoretical as well as practical) *some* responsibility for the treatment of research subjects will always reside with the researcher. In this sense, the researcher can never simply 'pass back' responsibility for the subjects' rights to the subjects themselves, in the way (full) VIC presupposes. And now the strategies available to the covert researcher can offer some safeguards to research subjects in the context of trust in the researcher's judgment.

Reflections from the field

My experiences of the complex realities of ethical decision-making in the field have been mainly through the supervision of students and participation on ethics committees generally ignorant about covert research. Sometimes, as in the mental training example above, the demands of *covert* research make little impact: this researcher, one of my students, could safely inform the subjects of almost all the protocol, and get their consent to it. Of course, the objections to (full) VIC mean that some responsibility still rested with the researcher – he included only what *he* deemed relevant. Still, such a case involves few messy decisions.

By contrast, when another of my students used modified participant observation techniques to address the recent past of a cricket team, additional issues appeared, even though (again) the subjects were informed that she was a researcher (although, since this fact was not repeated, and she had another role with the team, some subjects may have forgotten). So her listening-in on conversations in the locker-room, to see how players characterized these past events, would not necessarily have been recognized as data collection. After all, the locker-room was a semi-private place, offering team members the expectation of privacy. But these data could only be collected covertly, to ensure their reliability. Interviewing, say, would not have guaranteed the frankness of some of these conversations. However, the researcher ensured that the information gathered was treated sensitively; that only information relevant to the research was recorded (or, if other material was recorded, that the records were destroyed as soon as its irrelevance was recognized – although unexpected material became relevant); and that the final debriefing was clear on this point. Knowing the researcher well and trusting her, team-members agreed that their rights had not been traduced (perhaps because the 'other role' had allowed them to engage with her as a person). And a similar outcome arose, for a similar reason, with another of my students, even though, there, the research was fully covert (the researcher was not 'announced' initially).

A further issue concerned anonymity: since team-members were frequently identified by their playing positions (fundamental to any coaching advantage), identifying the team would mean that players too would be identifiable. Yet, after all, this problem could arise even with (idealized) VIC. The researcher explained to the team where those data would be published (in a thesis, and in articles in learned journals), convincing them that any sensationalized presentation was unlikely – but here no guarantee could be provided. Of course, the issue derived, not from the covert nature of the research as such, but from the frankness of some of the material, which might make it of interest to some tabloid newspapers, given some players' fame (in the case, this did not occur). Team-members were reassured, again based on trust of the researcher.

Moreover, the process of checking with the subjects (the team-members) to ensure the accuracy of the reported histories ultimately generated also allowed those subjects some comment on the data they had provided, both on the preservation of anonymity, and on what might be gleaned were it breached, which increased confidence in the sensitivity of treatment and the reality of concern with subjects' welfare. But it was fundamental that the 'last word' here, the analysis of these data, resided with the researcher: in this sense, the contribution of the others rightly ended with the conclusion of the data-collection phase.

Further, this student felt a clash of roles: the aspiration of a sports coach to *improve* her team (or athlete) conflicted with those of a researcher, even though, as in this case, they were the same person. Since researching the coaching process may well fail, in and of itself, to improve (or to suggest improvements) to either the coaching or the performance of teams, while succeeding as research, research into sports coaching must respect the coach's commitment to the welfare of her team (or athlete), which follows from the coach's role as a *professional* (as doctors and lawyers are professionals: see Koehn 1994). In this case, a sharper separation of responsibilities proved helpful.

By contrast with these endeavors to behave ethically, respecting the rights of subjects, I once attended a meeting on research ethics of a governing body for research into sport (and coaching) in the UK, where the topic was simply how to avoid litigation: in not beginning from the rights of subjects, the discussion never approached research ethics (and my suggestion to this effect was set aside). Moreover, this discussion was made all the more problematic in jointly assuming (falsely) that VIC provided a *gold-standard* for the ethical treatment of research subjects, and that a 'tick-box' version gave genuine VIC.

Notes

1 See note 3 below.
2 On 'Hawthorne effect' (see McFee 2010: 53–4).
3 Animal subjects have a place in, say, physiological research ultimately aimed at sports science (with the central question being, for instance, how to keep the goat on the treadmill); and here the Five Rs (from Shamoo and Resnik 2009: 226–8) form the basis of an ethically sound policy. But animal subjects have little place when our topic is sports *coaching*.
4 Of course, there are practical problems for this idea: that injections (and such like) cannot simply be reversed, and that exposure to high-pressure environments (say, in scuba-research) may require lengthy decompression. The point here is simply that the subject is entitled to begin such processes at any time he/she wishes – again, we might expect these cases to occur less frequently in research into sports *coaching* than into sports science.
5 In the body of the chapter, the focus is on the practical impossibility. To bring out the point about the theoretical impossibility, we can see that the demand for *all* information or for *full* consent presupposes (falsely) that these are finite totalities, such that there is an *all* or a *full* here (McFee 2010: 22–7).
6 The fourth concerns the acquisition of confidential documents.
7 In the USA, this is often called "deceptive research" or "deception research": see McFee (2010: 157–9).
8 When I first discussed these as 'one's friends' (in what became McFee 2010: 155–7), the locution of 'friends' in electronic social networks lacked its present omnipresence. It is important to stress that one's 'facebook friends' are precisely *not* one's friends in my sense – at least typically. Rather, they are at best a kind of pen-pal (and, at worst, almost a kind of stalker).

References

Homan, R. (1991) *The Ethics of Social Research*, London: Longman.

Koehn, D. (1994) *The Ground of Professional Ethics*, London: Routledge.

McFee, G. (2010) *Ethics, Knowledge and Truth in Sports Research: An Epistemology of Sport*, London: Routledge.

McNamee, M., Olivier, S. and Wainwright, P. (2007) *Research Ethics in Exercise, Health and Sports Sciences*, London: Routledge.

O'Neill, O. (2003) *Autonomy and Trust in Bioethics*, Cambridge: Cambridge University Press.

Schrader-Frechette, K. (1994) *Ethics of Scientific Research*, Lanham, MA: Rowman & Littlefield.

Shamoo, A. E. and Resnik, D. B. (2009) *Responsible Conduct of Research* (2nd ed.), Oxford: Oxford University Press.

Part III

Quantitative approaches to coaching research

11 Questionnaires

Daniel Rhind, Louise Davis, and Sophia Jowett

Introduction and overview

While there is merit in the use of qualitative approaches to research, this chapter will primarily focus on the use of quantitative questionnaires. A questionnaire is a research method which usually consists of a series of questions used to collect quantitative and/or qualitative data. Typically questionnaires are administered either in a paper form or electronically. Broadly speaking, questionnaires fall into two categories: surveys and scales (Bryman 2008).

Surveys

Surveys consist of questions used to collect information on related topics that intend to explore and describe the perceptions and experiences of participants (Thomas *et al.* 2010). For example, Sports Coach UK or a National Governing Body may be interested in conducting a survey of their coaches in order to investigate a range of different topics. More specifically, these organizations may require data to analyze the training needs of coaches, or track the development of athletes over time. The data collected can then be used to inform the development of policy, education, and practice relevant to coaching. Surveys tend to be used for exploratory or descriptive research.

Scales

Scales are questionnaires in which responses to a series of questions that have a logical structure among them are combined to obtain an overall score. A key difference between scales and surveys is that the psychometric properties of scales are demonstrated. This includes concepts such as internal reliability and structural validity (see Chapter 14). Furthermore, scales tend to be used to enable inferential statistics to be applied through testing relationships or differences between variables. There are many different types of scales which measure variables relevant to coaching. Some of these scales include likert scales, semantic differential scales, ranking scales, and filter questions. Likert-type scales are often the most commonly used scales in sports coaching research.

They usually allow the participant to indicate the extent to which he/she agrees with a particular statement on a scale anchored from 1 (strongly disagree) to 5 or 7 (strongly agree).

Advantages and disadvantages

It is important to have an understanding of the various advantages and disadvantages of all of the available research methods. This will facilitate informed decisions when designing research studies and allow the researcher to be critical when developing the rationale and justification of the methods being employed. Critical analysis is usually a key skill that will need to be demonstrated in order to achieve the higher-grade boundaries at both the undergraduate and postgraduate levels. Furthermore, being critically aware of the various factors in research design will help to ensure you have considered the multiple variables that can influence our understanding of topics related to sport coaching.

There are a number of benefits which are associated with using questionnaires. These benefits contribute to the popularity of questionnaires being used by undergraduates when conducting their dissertations (Armour and MacDonald 2011). Questionnaires generally involve relatively low costs, in terms of both time and finances. In particular, questionnaires can be administered to a large sample in a short period of time. If the questionnaire is well designed, it can also create data which can be analyzed quickly by the researcher (Gratton and Jones 2009). If a standardized scale is being used, then one can be more confident in making comparisons between different sub-groups of the sample; for example, investigating differences or similarities between athletes from individual and team sports (e.g. Rhind *et al.* 2012). One can also make comparisons between the findings, and the conclusions presented in previous studies that have employed the same questionnaire.

There are also benefits for the participants in the study; the questionnaire can normally be completed at a time and place that best suits them. This ensures that it can be a convenient method, and improve the overall response rate. This can also ensure anonymity and confidentiality at the point of data collection. Although data are normally kept anonymous and confidential when it appears in the final dissertation, research report, or journal paper, participants are not directly providing information to the researcher as they would be for alternative methods (e.g. interviews). This may help to enhance the trustworthiness of the data, but it can also increase the chances of receiving dishonest answers (Atkinson 2012).

There are also a range of possible disadvantages of this method which must be kept in mind when conducting your research. There is a limit to the amount of questions one can ask in a questionnaire. Response rates can begin to significantly decline as the questionnaire increases in length. This can contribute to difficulties in recruiting participants, especially if they have no vested interest in completing the questionnaire. Furthermore, participants can only respond to the questions that are asked of them. There may be some very important issues related to the research question which have not been anticipated. There is a risk that crucial details and data are not captured through a questionnaire (Atkinson 2012).

Data entry can also be very time consuming if a large number of questionnaires have been collected and they require being inputted into a spreadsheet/data analysis program manually. Data collected online via websites designed for the use of questionnaires often convert participants' responses into a format to be used with statistical software packages. Understanding the advantages of questionnaires, and taking steps to mitigate against any potential limitations, will assist you in being better able to design an effective questionnaire-based study.

Reliability and validity

Two key concepts related to the use of questionnaires are reliability and validity (Howitt and Cramer 2009). Reliability is a characteristic of the questionnaire itself and concerns whether or not the questionnaire is a dependable measure of the variable of interest. Reliability can relate to the internal consistency of the questionnaire. For instance, if one is intending to measure a coach's use of conflict-management strategies using the Coach–Athlete Relationship Maintenance Questionnaire (CARM-Q; Rhind and Jowett 2012), the set of items contained within the scale should be associated with one another. Reliability can also be demonstrated over time. For example, if you are interested in investigating coaching philosophies, and you assume that there is no reason for this to significantly change over a period of time, then a questionnaire should highlight consistent findings when administered at two different time points (Howitt and Cramer 2009).

Validity concerns whether a questionnaire actually measures what it claims to measure; in other words, "does it do what it says on the tin." It therefore focuses on how the questionnaire is applied. Validity comes in various forms (Tabachnick and Fidel 1998). For example, one can assess 'face validity', which concerns whether the questionnaire looks as though it measures what it claims to measure. If you are claiming to be investigating a coach's perceptions of a specific training course then the questionnaire should contain questions which clearly address this topic, and avoid questions that are unrelated to the investigation. Validity can also be demonstrated in relation to whether the data collected via a questionnaire are associated with theoretically related data (i.e. concurrent or predictive validity). For example, it is theorized that the use of relationship-maintenance strategies, as assessed by the CARM-Q (Rhind and Jowett 2012), should promote the quality of a coach–athlete relationship, as measured by the Coach–Athlete Relationship Questionnaire (Jowett and Ntoumanis 2004). Rhind and Jowett (2011) investigated this through administering the questionnaires to a sample of 251 coaches and athletes. Statistical support was found for the proposed associations which demonstrated the concurrent validity of the CARM-Q. It is important to note that a questionnaire can be reliable and not valid, but it cannot be valid and not reliable (Thomas *et al.* 2010). Hence, the validity of a questionnaire initially relies on its reliability. One needs to demonstrate a range of different forms of validity when developing a new questionnaire (Rhind and Jowett 2010). For a pre-existing questionnaire, it is important that a review of all the available evidence regarding its reliability and validity is conducted. Additionally, you should ensure that the validity of the questionnaire has been established with the population from which data will be collected. In particular, you may learn that a specific questionnaire is not fit for use with your population of interest (e.g. elite level coach vs. youth coach).

There are a number of questionnaires which could be utilized in coaching research. The specific behaviors of a coach can be assessed through a number of measures including the Coaching Behavior Questionnaire (Williams *et al.* 2003), the Coaching Behavior Scale (Côté *et al.* 1999), the Leadership Scale for Sport (Chelladurai and Saleh 1980), and the Controlling Coach Behavior Scale (Bartholomew *et al.* 2010). Other relevant questionnaires focus on the relationship between a coach and an athlete. These can be used to assess the quality of the relationship (Coach–Athlete Relationship Questionnaire: Jowett and Ntoumanis 2004), how the relationship is maintained (Coach–Athlete Relationship Maintenance Questionnaire; Rhind and Jowett 2012), or attachment styles (Coach–Athlete Attachment Scale; Davis and Jowett 2013). Research may also focus on perceptions of competence (Coach Effectiveness Scale; Feltz *et al.* 1999), athlete satisfaction (Athlete Satisfaction Questionnaire; Riemer and Chelladurai 2002), or group cohesion (Group Environment Questionnaire, Carron *et al.* 1985).

These questionnaires have been used in studies which have significantly developed our understanding of the nature, content, and role of the quality of the coach–athlete relationship in sport (Jowett and Poczwardowski 2007). Lyle (1999) explained that the coach–athlete relationship is at the very heart of coaching and that coaches who fail to acknowledge the importance of this relationship risk hindering their athletes' realization of their full potential. Studies have helped to generate empirical evidence for the importance of considering the emotional (e.g. feelings), cognitive (e.g. thoughts), and behavioral aspects of this relationship (Jowett and Ntoumanis 2004; Davis and Jowett 2010; Rhind and Jowett 2011).

Questionnaires have also helped to highlight the links between the quality of the coach–athlete relationship and a range of other key variables in sport. For instance, Jowett and Chaundy (2004) found that athletes' perceptions of the quality of their coach–athlete relationship were able to predict a significant amount of variance in their perceptions of team cohesion over and above that accounted for by perceptions of their coach's specific behaviors during training. Furthermore, Lorimer and Jowett (2009) have found that relationship quality is associated with both the coach's and athlete's level of empathy. This relates to the extent to which the coach and the athlete have a shared understanding within their relationship and are able to accurately describe how their coach or athlete is feeling, thinking or behaving at a given time.

Applied issues and considerations

The following ten questions will help you to consider all of the key aspects of your research. These have been developed based on our experience of conducting research and supervising student projects. It is important to note, however, that you should, where appropriate, use pre-existing questionnaires which have been shown to be reliable and valid.

What is the research question?

Whenever a research project is being designed, it is critical that one clearly specifies the research question(s) and that there is a strong rationale for the study (see Chapter 7). The clearer (i.e. specific and measurable) the research question, the easier it will be to design a questionnaire that will generate data enabling the researcher to answer the question. It is relatively straightforward to design a useful questionnaire, but it is even easier to design a poor questionnaire. It may be tempting to add in extra questions which appear interesting; however, they will be ultimately useless if the data they generate does not help to achieve the overall aims of the study. Moreover, superfluous questions may be detrimental to the study if they increase the response time.

Who is the target population?

The researcher should identify the population of interest. Does the study aim to represent all coaches (i.e. be generalizable)? Alternatively, maybe the researcher is just interested in coaches with a Level 1 coaching qualification in a particular sport or coaches who are under 21 years old. It is important to have an understanding of the specific inclusion criteria for the participants in the study in order to answer the research question. This will ensure that one can design every element of the questionnaire with the characteristics of the population in mind. This, in turn, will help to enhance the response rates and the quality of the data that will be collected.

Is the questionnaire the most appropriate method?

As illustrated throughout this book, there are a wide range of methods which can be employed when conducting coaching research. Please consider whether your question could better be answered using an alternative method. Ultimately research methods are not '*right*' or '*wrong*' in themselves; however, they can be (in)appropriate to answer the research question(s). If one can benefit from the advantages of questionnaires, whilst mitigating against the potential disadvantages, then this method can be a very useful way of collecting coaching data to enhance our knowledge and understanding of coaching practice.

What topics will be included?

The topics that could be explored using questionnaires are virtually endless, perhaps only limited by intellectual curiosity. The researcher needs to think about which topics relate to the research question(s) and hence merit inclusion in the questionnaire. Moreover, there may be sub-topics or dimensions of the research question, which necessitate, or are best represented, by subscales. For example, the quality of the coach–athlete relationship can be distilled into sub-components identified within the 3C's +1 model, and are measured by the closeness, co-orientation, complementarity, and commitment reported by the coach and the athlete in the CART-Q (Jowett and Ntoumanis 2004; Jowett 2009). Additionally, it is customary to include a demographics section to collect data on variables such as the participant's gender, age, qualifications, experience, current role, number of hours per week spent coaching etc. This information may be particularly useful for grouping your participants and subsequent analyses. For example, you may want to explore the potential relationship between how many hours a week a coach spends with their athlete(s) and the coach's perception of his/her commitment to the athlete(s).

What response formats will be used?

Once the researcher has decided the topics to be investigated and the questions to be asked, it is important that the ways in which the participants will respond are considered. In general, you can ask either open or closed questions. Open questions are unrestricted and allow participants to freely expand. However, it is important to note that open questions are more likely to be difficult to quantify as they gather information that is not in numerical form. For example, a simple open question could ask 'Why did you first get into coaching?' This facilitates a flexible approach to exploring your research question, but these types of questions are more associated with qualitative studies.

In contrast, closed questions are more easily quantifiable and therefore are associated with quantitative research. Closed questions involve participants selecting a response from predetermined options which are dictated by the researcher. Researchers use closed questions when they have a clear idea of all of the potential responses. These questions can be dichotomous (e.g. are you male or female?), nominal (e.g. what types of sport do you coach: individual, team or both?), ordinal (e.g. how satisfied are you with the training you have received: 1 = very unsatisfied, 2 = unsatisfied, 3 = neither unsatisfied or satisfied, 4 = satisfied, and 5 = very satisfied), and ranking (e.g. please rank the following in order of how important they are in facilitating your development as a coach: coaching courses, books, websites, other coaches, players). Closed questions benefit from being quick and simple to complete, and more readily facilitate comparisons between participants. However, they inevitably limit the range of possible responses which may result in the researcher not collecting important data.

Have potential biases been considered?

Potential biases can have an influence at all stages of the research process, including the design of the specific questions. It is important to reflect on the content of the questionnaire to mitigate the impact of any such biases. More specifically, leading questions should be avoided as they will prime the participants to respond in a socially desirable manner. For example, 'Questioning techniques are very important during training, to what extent do you use questioning?' This leads the participant to potentially rate their use of questioning higher than they may normally have done (Howitt and Cramer 2009). The researcher should also avoid ambiguous or double-barreled questions such as 'How important are the use of praise and feedback during training?' You can see that two different questions are being asked simultaneously; hence participants will not know which aspect of the question they are responding to when they indicate their score. Similarly, researchers would be making assumptions about what the participant was thinking when responding to this poorly worded question. Double negative statements should also be avoided. For example, 'I don't not trust my athlete' or more subtly but potentially equally confusing, 'my athlete doesn't mistrust me.' Finally, it is recommended that you do not rely on hypothetical scenarios as coaches may not be able to accurately anticipate how they would behave in situations of which they have little or no experience.

Has the layout of the questionnaire been considered?

A clear and accessible layout to the questionnaire will help to promote a participant's engagement with the questions. The questionnaire should therefore have a logical layout which is simple for the participant to complete. This can be achieved through employing each of the following techniques. Overall you should consider the use of colors, lines, and fonts to ensure that the questionnaire is well formatted and legible. Do not try to squeeze lots of questions on one page to reduce the overall length of the questionnaire. If a page is full of text then this can be off-putting for participants. You should also ensure that there is sufficient space for participants to respond to any open questions.

You should think about the use of signposting. In other words, include a clear introduction at the beginning of each section to highlight to the participant the purpose and nature of each section. Furthermore, begin with the more straightforward questions which are easier to complete. The more challenging questions can be placed towards the end of the questionnaire. A clear numbering strategy should be used throughout the questionnaire. This can facilitate the use of filtering. This is used in cases in which it is not necessary for all participants to complete all of the sections. For example, 'If you have completed safe-guarding training in the past six months please complete this section, if not, please go to section 5'.

Has the questionnaire been piloted?

It is good practice to try to include participants at each stage of a research project, and not only at the data-collection stage. However, piloting is most often used once an initial version of the questionnaire has been created. Therefore, once a draft version of the questionnaire has been created, it is important to conduct some piloting to test its suitability. This could be done using a variety of approaches. One could administer the questionnaire to a participant in the same format as that which will be used. You could also administer the questionnaire through an interview style approach to clarify participants' understanding of each question and to ensure that the questions are interpreted in the way in which they were intended. The researcher could also use a focus-group approach such that s/he invites the feedback of a group of coaches. Appropriate adjustments should then be made based on this pilot testing.

How will the questionnaire be administered?

Questionnaires were typically administered in a paper-and-pen format. Thanks to to developments in technology, there are now a wide range of different ways in which a questionnaire can be administered. Each has its own benefits and drawbacks. The selection of the most appropriate should be made based on a consideration of the nature of the research topics and the characteristics of the participants.

The most direct form of administration will be face to face. The participants can then either complete the questionnaire and hand it back to the researcher or return it via post at a time which best suits them. This approach enables the researcher to answer any questions that participants have whilst retaining some control over who is completing the questionnaire. The questionnaire could be posted to potential participants with a stamped addressed envelope. This clearly involves additional resources and it is often difficult to generate high response rates using this approach. An alternative approach is to administer the questionnaire over the telephone. This also allows the researcher to check participant understanding. However, it can be labor intensive.

A questionnaire can be placed on a website with links to the page being e-mailed out to potential participants. This has the benefit of being relatively cost effective as the link can be sent out to large numbers of people. If set up correctly, it can help to avoid having to enter the data by hand if the computer automatically produces the data in a spreadsheet format. One can easily track whether or not a person has completed the questionnaire and send out reminder messages to any non-responders. As social media become an ever present part of daily life, it should also be embraced and utilized by researchers conducting coaching research.

How will the data be analyzed?

This is a question that we ask to all of our undergraduate students before they even begin data collection. However, this section does not aim to provide you with information on the specific types of statistical analysis; instead we aim to outline the steps you will need to consider in order to analyze your data.

First, data analysis should be considered at the planning stage of a research project. This can help to ensure that all of the data collected is relevant to your research question and that any potential problems can be identified prior to the data being collected; realizing there are problems with the data after collection often results in it being too late to rescue the project. Second, you should familiarize yourself with the types of data you could collect. For example, are your data nominal or ordinal? These types of data are likely to be collected through questionnaires and will allow you to run both descriptive and inferential statistics. Third, you should consider what type of statistical package you may want to use to organize and analyze your data. For example, many students often use either Microsoft Excel or the Statistical Package for Social Sciences (SPSS) for developing a spreadsheet that records all of the data collected. This then leads you to your fourth step: considering how you will input your data. For example, once you have collected your data you will then need to define it using data labels in appropriate columns. Labels should succinctly reflect questionnaire items and/or computed subscales so that appropriate variables can be identified for analysis. Data entry can range from typing in all of the data manually or exporting the data from online questionnaires (e.g. surveymonkey) into the statistical program. Fifth, once you have inputted your data you should consider how you will handle missing values. Not all participants will answer every question and sometimes you may forget to input a value. You should double check any missing values against your questionnaires. If missing values are apparent, it is important that you do not just assume your participants' response and add in any value; consult your supervisor for advice on the best approach to take.

Finally, the statistical analysis undertaken should be appropriate for the research question/hypothesis. Statistical analysis can range from being quite simple to complex. In many research projects descriptive statistics (e.g. means, standard deviations, and frequencies) are conducted first to check the data for errors and to provide an initial overview of the results. Inferential statistics (e.g. correlations, regressions, ANOVA) are then considered to explore the data further. How will you report your quantitative data?

First, you should organize your results section in accordance with your research question and/or hypotheses. Second, it is best practice to present descriptive statistics for all of the main variables outlined in the research question. Often, tables are very helpful for understanding quantitative data and facilitate the presentation of means, standard deviation, range, and distribution. When presenting a table, a brief paragraph that interprets the data is necessary. However, it is important to remember that a potential explanation outlining why/how the results may have occurred should be reserved for the discussion section. Once the descriptive statistics have been presented, the next step is to present the results for any inferential statistics. For each type of inferential statistic (e.g. correlations, t-tests, ANOVAs, Chi-square and regression) there are certain formats that should be used when reporting both significant and non-significant findings (Howitt and Cramer 2009). Again, tables and figures are very useful for presenting the results that arise from inferential statistics, and a clear statement identifying 'what' is evident in the analysis. Identifying 'why' should be left for the discussion, where you can interpret the findings in relation to the theoretical and practical underpinning.

Reflections from the field

When planning questionnaire research, we have witnessed the importance of the piloting stage to check participants' understanding. For example, in the Rhind and Jowett (2010) study we were developing a new version of a questionnaire to measure the quality of the coach–athlete relationship. As part of this, a large pool of items was developed. The piloting phase of this study highlighted that certain questions were unclear. For example, 'During training, my athlete is antagonistic'. Many participants were confused about the meaning of this question and hence it was removed. Similarly, the phrase 'My coach … ' also caused confusion as some athletes reported having numerous coaches (e.g. a club coach, a regional coach, and a national coach). As such, we needed to be very clear with regard to whom we were referring.

In relation to administration, you can begin to question your choice of method when you are standing in the freezing cold waiting for a training session to finish, clutching a box of questionnaires and pens. This is unlikely to be helped by the players' unenthusiastic response when they are subsequently invited to complete a questionnaire. This highlights the need for an approach which has the philosophy of conducting research *with* rather than *on* participants. Involving participants in the study allows them to develop a sense of ownership and to better appreciate the purpose of the research.

Once you are sitting in front of a pile of completed questionnaires, the excitement of reaching one's response target can be short lived as the realities of deciphering handwriting and entering page after page of data hits home. The prospect of analyzing your data to address your research question(s) can help to spur you on. Although we have painted a rather negative picture, this needs to be balanced with the rewards of this approach. We have been contacted by coaches, athletes, sport psychologists, and parents who have all thanked us for our research as it has helped to enhance the performance and well-being of people in their lives. This makes the challenges of undertaking such research worthwhile and demonstrates that questionnaires can be used to facilitate real changes within the world of coaching.

References

Armour, C. and MacDonald, D. (2011) *Research Methods in Physical Education and Youth Sport*, London: Routledge.

Atkinson, M. (2012) *Key Concepts in Sport and Exercise Research Methods*, London: Sage.

Bartholomew, K. J., Ntoumanis, N. and Thogersen-Ntoumani, C. (2010) 'The controlling interpersonal style in a coaching relationship', *Journal of Sport and Exercise Psychology*, 32: 193–216.

Bryman, A. (2008) *Social Research Methods*, Oxford: Oxford University Press.

Carron, A. V., Brawley, L. R. and Widmeyer, M. V. (1985) 'The development of an instrument to measure cohesion in sports teams: The group environment questionnaire', *Journal of Sport Psychology*, 7: 244–66.

Chelladurai, P. and Saleh, S. D (1980) 'Dimensions of leader behavior in sports: development of a leadership scale', *Journal of Sport Psychology*, 2: 34–45.

Côté, J., Yardley, J., Hay, J., Sedgwick, W. and Baker, J. (1999) 'An exploratory examination of the coach behaviour scale for sport', *Avante*, 5: 82–92.

Davis, L. and Jowett, S. (2010) 'Investigating the interpersonal dynamics between coaches and athletes based on fundamental principles of attachment theory', *Journal of Clinical Sport Psychology*, 4: 112–32.

——(2013) 'Measuring attachment styles within the coach-athlete relationship context: Development and validation of the coach-athlete ttachment scale (CAAS)', Manuscript under review.

Feltz, D. L., Chase, M. A., Moritz, M. E. and Sullivan, P. J. (1999) 'A conceptual model of coaching efficacy: Preliminary investigation and instrument development', *Journal of Educational Psychology*, 91: 765–76.

Gratton, C. and Jones, I. (2009) *Research Methods for Sports Studies*, London: Routledge.

Howitt, D. and Cramer, D. (2009) *Research Methods in Psychology*, London: Prentice Hall.

Jowett, S. (2009) 'Validating coach-athlete relationship measures with the nomological network', *Measurement in Physical Education and Exercise Science*, 13: 1–18.

Jowett, S. and Chaundy, V. (2004) 'An investigation into the impact of coach leadership and coach–athlete relationship on group cohesion', *Group Dynamics: Theory, Research and Practice*, 8: 302–11.

Jowett, S. and Ntoumanis, N. (2004) 'The coach–athlete relationship questionnaire (CART-Q): Development and initial validation', *Scandinavian Journal of Medicine and Science in Sports*, 14: 245–57.

Jowett, S. and Poczwardowski, A. (2007) 'Understanding the coach–athlete relationship', in S. Jowett and D. Lavallee (eds) *Social Psychology in Sport*, Champaign, IL: Human Kinetics.

Lorimer, R. and Jowett, S. (2009) 'Empathic accuracy, meta-perspective, and satisfaction in the coach-athlete relationship', *Journal of Applied Sport Psychology*, 21: 201–12.

Lyle, J. (1999) 'Coaching philosophy and coaching behaviour', in N. Cross and J. Lyle (eds) *The Coaching Process: Principles and Practice for Sport*, Oxford: Butterworth-Heineman, 25–46.

Rhind, D. J. A. and Jowett, S. (2010) 'Initial evidence for the criterion-related and structural validity of the long versions of the direct and meta-perspectives of the coach–athlete relationship questionnaire', *European Journal of Sport Science*, 10: 359–70.

——(2011) 'Linking maintenance strategies to the quality of coach–athlete relationships', *International Journal of Sport Psychology*, 42: 1–14.

——(2012) 'Development of the coach–athlete relationship maintenance questionnaire (CARM-Q)', *International Journal of Sports Science and Coaching*, 7 (1): 121–38.

Rhind, D. J. A., Jowett, S. and Yang, X. (2012) 'A comparison of athletes' perceptions of the coach–athlete relationship who participate in team and individual sports', *Journal of Sport Behavior*, 35: 433–41.

Riemer, H. A. and Chelladurai, P. (2002) *Manual for the Athlete Satisfaction Questionnaire (ASQ)*, Regina, Saskatchewan: University of Regina.

Tabachnick, B. G. and Fidel, L. S. (1998) *Using Multivariate Statistics* (3rd ed.), New York: HarperCollins.

Thomas, J., Nelson, J. and Silverman, S. (2010) *Research Methods in Physical Activity*, Champagne, IL: Human Kinetics.

Williams, J. M., Jerome, G. J., Kenow, L. J., Rogers, T., Sartain, T. A. and Darland, G. (2003) 'Factor structure of the coaching behaviour questionnaire and its relationship to athlete variables', *The Sport Psychologist*, 17: 16–34.

12 Systematic observation

Gareth Morgan, Bob Muir, and Andy Abraham

Introduction and overview

The role of the coach is to create meaningful learning and development experiences that bring about the guided improvement of participants relative to their needs, motives, stage of development, and sporting context (ICCE 2012). In an attempt to achieve this objective, coaches employ behavioral strategies aimed at facilitating the technical, tactical, physical, psychological, and social development of athletes (Muir *et al.* 2011a). One means of examining coaching behaviors is through the utilization of systematic observation instruments. According to More and Franks (2004: 245):

> Systematic observation permits a trained observer to use a set of guide-lines and procedures to observe, record, and analyse observable events and behaviours, with the assumption that other observers using the same observation instrument, and viewing the same sequence of events, would agree with the recorded data.

In this respect, systematic observation instruments provide a method of objectively quantifying coaching behavior.

The use of systematic observation to study coaching behavior has been a prominent research methodology for nearly four decades. Half of the studies published in coaching science between 1970 and 2001 included a focus on describing coaches' behavior (Gilbert and Trudel 2004). Consequently, a considerable amount of systematic observation coaching literature exists, in a variety of sports, indicating its suitability and prevalence as a method to explore the behavior of coaches in practice and competition settings (e.g. Tharp and Gallimore 1976; Claxton 1988; Bloom *et al.* 1999; Cushion and Jones 2001; Potrac *et al.* 2002; Horton *et al.* 2005; Smith and Cushion 2006; Partington and Cushion 2013).

The initial interest in analyzing coach behavior was to generate a better understanding of what 'expert' coaches do. Research of this nature was based on the premise that the identification of those behaviors that 'expert' coaches use would assist the construction of training interventions designed to develop the effectiveness of neophyte coaches. Certainly, the accumulation of data emerging from these studies has begun to provide a useful database against which coaches' behavior can be considered (Potrac *et al.* 2007). Indeed, studies that explored the behaviors exhibited by 'successful' coaches such as John Wooden (Tharp and Gallimore 1976), Jerry Tarkanian (Bloom *et al.* 1999), and Pat Summitt (Becker and Wrisberg 2008) provided detailed descriptions of the frequencies and volume (e.g. rate per minute and percentage of overall behaviors) of discrete behaviors exhibited during practice sessions.

To date, systematic observation has been used to make comparisons between different coaching populations. For example, researchers have observed coaches working in different sports (e.g. Horton *et al.* 2005), male and female coaches in the same sport (e.g. Lacy and Goldston 1990), different types of practice activities in the same sport (e.g. Ford *et al.* 2010) and across sports (e.g. Harvey *et al.* 2013), competitive levels within the same sport (e.g. Cushion and Jones 2001), and differing levels of success (win/loss record) (e.g. Claxton 1988) and experience (e.g. Jones *et al.* 1997). Inquiries have also been concerned with an exploration of the quantity or quality of coaching behaviors directed toward high and low expectancy participants (e.g. Becker and Wrisberg 2008) and the stability of coaches' behaviors over time (e.g. Harvey *et al.* in press).

While the findings of studies that have employed systematic observation instruments have helped to advance understanding about coaching behavior, scholars have identified some of the limitations associated with this methodology. For example, Abraham and Collins (1998) highlighted the problematic nature of this approach, pointing to the often-implicit behaviorist assumptions that underpin research in this area. Central to the argument made is that descriptions of coaches' behavioral strategies are often devoid of other contextual information (e.g. the learning objectives being worked towards and how the practice activities are structured). Calls have also been made to supplement descriptive accounts of behavior with more interpretive methods of enquiry to establish an understanding of the cognitive processes underlying them (Potrac *et al.* 2000, 2002; Smith and Cushion 2006). In this respect, it has been argued that continued investigation into not only 'what' coaches do, but also the underlying knowledge structures and cognitive processes that determine 'why' and 'how' they do it, will provide useful information for the development of coach education programs, and 'generate theory that is true to the complex realities of sports coaching' (Smith and Cushion 2006: 356).

Applied issues and considerations

Having given thought towards what systematic observation is and why it can be a useful means of studying coaching behavior, we will now outline some of the practical issues that coaching researchers are advised to consider when utilizing this approach.

Selecting a tool and evidencing its validity

When choosing to use a systematic observation tool, it is probable that researchers interested in this mode of data collection will encounter the two most popular systematic observation instruments used for analysis in sports coaching research: the Coach Behavior Assessment System (CBAS) (Smith *et al.* 1977) and the Arizona State University Observation Instrument (ASUOI) (Lacy and Darst 1984). When we set out to engage in an early study of coach behavior, we considered both instruments in order to ascertain the tool that offered the highest level of face and ecological validity. This test initially entailed an assessment of the rigor of the behavioral categories included in the instruments in order to query whether the component features of the tool accurately described the true nature of the behaviors to be observed (Brewer and Jones 2002) and if they applied to coaches working within the context under investigation (i.e. English youth soccer).

The first key observation from this process was that there was quite a high frequency of behaviors that could not be adequately coded by the existing categories. For instance, when the coach questioned his players on an aspect of team play, no corresponding category could be identified within the CBAS. The 'questioning' classification within the ASUOI, however, satisfied the coding of this behavior. While the ASUOI accommodated 'uncodable' behaviors that did not obviously fit within any of the other behavioral categories, it was felt that this category was used too regularly during this initial assessment process. It was also noted how the ASUOI provided greater opportunity for collecting detail during instructional moments. The level of detail required in a systematic observation instrument is obviously dependent on the researcher's objectives.

More recently, Cushion *et al.* (2012) drew on advancements in computer analysis software to develop the Coach Analysis and Intervention System (CAIS). The CAIS enables a trained observer to capture different types of behavior (i.e. management, feedback, instruction, questioning, physical behaviors, verbal/non verbal), to whom the behavior is directed (recipient[s]), when it occurred (timing – pre, post, concurrent), and its content (i.e. technical, tactical, other) in relation to the context (i.e. training or competition state). Importantly, the system permits the coding of multiple behaviors simultaneously, recognizing that coaches often execute combinations of behaviors within a single 'coaching moment' (i.e. verbal reinforcement whilst providing a physical demonstration). Moreover, it has the capacity to locate behavior within the practice or competition setting, thus providing a means to explore differences in coaching behavior as a consequence of context. Whilst the CAIS would therefore appear to be an obvious choice for those engaging in systematic observation, it does come at a complexity cost. As Cushion *et al.* (2012) have acknowledged, accurate observations of coaches' practice will only be achieved following thorough behavioral definition familiarization and training in the actual use of the tool (with the large number of dimensions and behavioral categories incorporated within the instrument making this more challenging than those instruments that have been reviewed herein). As such, coaching researchers are advised to give consideration towards which tool they are going to utilize and the reasons for selecting a particular instrument.

Reliability checks

Coaching researchers also need to ensure that systematic observation instruments are used in a consistent way; that is, researchers need to demonstrate that their data are reliable. Here, thought should be given to inter-observer and intra-observer agreement. *Inter*-observer agreement occurs when one observer's records of an event are compared with those of a second observer who is trained and competent in using the instrument (Cushion and Jones 2001; Darst *et al.* 1989). Siedentop (1976) has set an acceptable level of inter-observer agreement at 85 percent, as a minimum standard for data reliability. Like systematic observation itself, this process of attaining inter-observer agreement can be conducted via the observation of live practices *in situ* or by reviewing footage of pre-recorded practices.

Following an education period to help familiarize those participating in the agreement checks with the behavioral definitions of the observation tool's categories, participants are individually shown video footage of an agreed number of coaching episodes, in which a specified coaching behavior is highlighted for coding. These video clips should be randomly compiled and displayed in a manner that enables coders to clearly ascertain the specific behavior they are being asked to identify. Each participant must then view the selection of behaviors and categorize them by choosing one of the coding options available from the observation instrument. Inter-observer agreement can be regarded as being achieved when Siedentop's agreement level of 85 percent is consistently reached by each of the observers partaking in the coding process.

Achieving *intra*-observer agreement requires an observer to observe the same events twice (or more) at different points in time (Van der Mars 1989). Once again, the attainment of satisfactory agreement levels (again, Siedentop 1976 suggests 85 percent) is crucial to the credibility of the data, with intra-observer checks protecting against observer drift (i.e. a scenario wherein the same coder views a sequence of events for the second time at a later point in time, but categorizes the observed behaviors differently second time round). To conduct this test, any researchers involved in the coding of data should observe and categorize the behaviors being displayed in a video-recorded coaching session. Following this, a minimum fourteen-day period should be allowed to elapse (so as to avoid memory influencing the scored data; Darst *et al.* 1989) before the researcher re-scores the same session. The data should then be compared to check the re-test reliability coefficients between the behavioral records of the same coaching session. To maintain intra-observer reliability, researchers should repeat this process throughout the data analysis process so as to ensure a consistency of data coding.

Live vs. video recording

Prior to committing to a systematic observation of coaches' behaviors, researchers must choose whether to code the behaviors in real time (at the side of the actual practice environment) or whether to video-record the coaches' practice and code the behaviors afterwards. Having trialed both modes, we can offer a series of guiding points.

Early attempts to code *in situ* revealed occasions on which instances of coach behavior went uncoded simply because the time spent physically recording a previous behavior had prevented the researcher from clearly witnessing the subsequent behavior(s). Furthermore, instances occurred whereby the researcher was aware of verbal coach–athlete interaction, however, due to a combination of the researcher's physical distance from the coach and players, and the low volume of verbal communication, could not interpret the comments made. In live observations, the researcher is often obliged to follow the coach (which can be highly intrusive) in an attempt to gain a clear and accurate understanding of the coach's verbal behaviors (Darst *et al.* 1989). Therefore, a more effective method might be to transmit the verbal communications of the coach directly to the video camera. The advantages to the use of video recording are many. The record of events can be reviewed over and over again – a crucial feature of this procedure in allowing opportunities for clarifying uncertainties about the coding of behaviors. Furthermore, with recorded footage of coaching behaviors digitally stored, researchers have the benefit of being able to return to the recorded footage for different types of analyses. That said, not all coaching researchers will have access to such technology. Additionally, some coaches may not permit you to video and audio record their sessions, preferring that you code live instead. Although capturing a permanent record of events has numerous advantages, it is perhaps important to acknowledge that the presence of a video recorder can increase the change of subject reactivity (Darst *et al.* 1989).

Reflections from the field

While we tend to advocate the use of video capture when systematically observing coaches, and supported the use of video when seeking to achieve inter-observer reliability, the use of technology is not without its issues. For example, despite our having employed video footage when training others to use systematic observation instruments we have experienced a number of difficulties. Here, we recall one example where each of the participants in our training program viewed the selection of behaviors and were asked to simply categorize the behavior they had just seen, choosing one of the coding options available from the observation instrument. Following three reliability checks with participants, it was apparent that Siedentop's (1976) criterion for inter-observer agreement (agreement exceeding 85 percent) was not being reached. After the reliability tests had been completed, we went through each of the clips with the participants to inform them whether agreement/disagreement had occurred. Particular interest was paid to the specific clips in which disagreement had occurred. Speaking with each of the participants the consensus was that it was difficult to identify isolated, discrete, behaviors. Rather, they felt that many of the video clips contained several different coaching behaviors. The reliable coding of coaching behavior is, therefore, far from a straight and simplistic process.

When trying to develop an in-depth understanding of a coach's practice, a logical rule of thumb is that the more you observe them, the more accurate the picture. Hence, researchers seeking to study the behaviors of a coach are advised to schedule several observations in order to increase the meaningfulness of their data. While the organization of such scheduling can be relatively easily achieved, conducting multiple observations does throw up challenges relating to the consistency of variables associated with the practices of the coach. This issue was most prevalent for us within a study of professional football coaches; confounding variables within this study included factors associated with the nature of the practices, the number of players participating in the practices, and the consistency of people participating in each of the observed practices. For instance, while specified sessions were agreed up front with the coaches participating within the study, the reality of gathering data on the agreed session dates entailed a mixture of observing practices that might be regarded as 'typical': some that were completely focused upon preparing the players for a specific, forthcoming fixture; others that were predominantly oriented towards physical development; and others still that comprised a series of relatively uninterrupted games. Logically, coaches' behaviors within such disparate practices vary greatly, so limited conclusions can be drawn from such differing examples.

Likewise, when observing coaches that work with squads of players that support a 1st team/reserve team – such as a youth team or, indeed, a reserve team – practices can be compromised by a lack of numbers involved in the practice. When investigating the practice behaviors of a number of Under 18s coaches (at a number of different professional soccer clubs), the coaches admitted that it was common for their players to be called to train with the first team squad, therefore preventing them from training with the Under 18 group. Furthermore, the coaches indicated that this instruction to train with another squad would often occur immediately prior to the Under 18s coaches' planned session time, and sometimes even *during* the session! Also, the coaches referred to how it was possible that some of their players might be involved in reserve team fixtures the night before observed sessions. This too would result in the non-participation of players within the observed sessions. Having witnessed each of the identified issues during a study we conducted, the gathering of telling data from practices that often included very few numbers was a significant challenge.

It is in light of such practical research experiences that we consider coaching to be a strategic, political, social, and pedagogical endeavor; as such, accessing insights into the coach–athlete dynamics of a coaching context (reflecting the strategic, political, and social activities likely to be impacting on the coach's behaviors at an individual-by-individual level) is integral to the authentic understanding of that coach's practice. If participants are only attending sporadically, then the quality of insights afforded by such a context are somewhat compromised. While observing coaches' practice within a youth academy environment, a persistent problem encountered related to this very matter. Feedback from the coaches revealed that it is considered a normal activity for players to move up and down between different age groups according to coaches' beliefs on what is best for the players' development or, occasionally, the need of a particular squad. Irrespective of the reasoning, the issue remains that the non-attendance of players during repeated observations can skew the data gathered in that context. Indeed, we have come to realize that while systematic observation instruments can provide useful insights into the behavioral strategies that coaches employ, like any research method this approach has certain limitations.

That said, despite such limitations, we have found it useful to integrate systematic observation into the education of sports coaches. In this respect, we believe that a clear starting point for meaningful coach development is to enable coaches to generate a better understanding of the relationship between their purpose, their perspectives and practice through audio and video feedback. For the last three years we have been using systematic observation combined with more interpretive methods as a platform for one-to-one coach development with national age group and Olympic coaches in rugby league, hockey, and sailing. Coaches have been encouraged to explore coded audio and video footage of their coaching and highlight key moments and dilemmas using the Coaching Practice Planning and Reflective Framework (Muir *et al.* 2011a) in preparation for in-depth reflective conversations with a facilitator. Indeed, we believe that such an approach can help coaches to explore the congruence between their coaching objectives, the structure of their learning activities, behavioral strategies, and ultimately the implications for participant engagement and learning (Muir *et al.* 2011a, 2011b). We think that systematic observation can play a key role in such work.

References

Abraham, A. and Collins, D. (1998) 'Examining and extending research in coach development', *Quest*, 50: 59–79.

Becker, A. J. and Wrisberg, C. A. (2008) 'Effective coaching in action: Observations of legendary collegiate basketball coach Pat Summitt', *The Sport Psychologist*, 22: 197–211.

Bloom, G. A., Crompton, R. and Anderson, J. E. (1999) 'A systematic observation study of the teaching behaviours of an expert basketball coach', *The Sport Psychologist*, 13: 157–70.

Brewer, C. and Jones, R. L. (2002) 'A five-stage process for establishing contextually valid systematic observation instruments: The case of rugby union', *The Sport Psychologist*, 16(2): 139–61.

Claxton, P. (1988) 'A systematic observation of more and less successful high school tennis coaches', *Journal of Teaching in Physical Education*, 7: 302–10.

Cushion, C. and Jones, R. L. (2001) 'A systematic observation of professional top-level youth soccer coaches', *Journal of Sport Behavior*, 24(4): 1–23.

Cushion, C., Harvey, S., Muir, B. and Nelson, L. (2012) 'Developing the coach analysis and intervention system (CAIS): Establishing validity and reliability of a computerised systematic observation instrument', *Journal of Sport Sciences*, 30(2): 201–16.

Darst, P. W., Zakrajsek, D. B. and Mancini, V. H. (1989) *Analyzing Physical Education and Sport Instruction* (2nd ed.), Champaign, IL: Human Kinetics.

Ford, P. R., Yates, I. and Williams, M. A. (2010) 'An analysis of practice activities and instructional behaviours used by youth soccer coaches during practice: Exploring the link between science and application', *Journal of Sport Sciences*, 28(5): 483–95.

Gilbert, W. and Trudel, P. (2004) 'Analysis of coaching science research published from 1970–2001', *Research Quarterly for Exercise and Sport*, 75: 388–99.

Harvey, S., Cushion, C., Cope, E. and Muir, B. (2013) 'A season long investigation into coaching behaviours as a function of practice state: The case of three collegiate coaches'. *Sports Coaching Review*, 2(1): 13–32.

Horton, S., Baker, J. and Deakin, J. (2005) 'Experts in action: A systematic observation of 5 national team coaches', *International Journal of Sport Psychology*, 36: 299–319.

International Council for Coaching Excellence and the Association of Summer Olympic International Federations (2012), *International Sport Coaching Framework (version 1.1)*, Champaign, IL: Human Kinetics.

Jones, D. F., Housner, L. D. and Kornspan, A. S. (1997) 'Interactive decision making and behaviour of experienced and inexperienced basketball coaches during practice', *Journal of Teaching in Physical Education*, 16(4): 454–68.

Lacy, A. C. and Darst, P. W. (1984) 'Evolution of a systematic observation system: The a.s.u. coaching observation instrument', *Journal of Teaching in Physical Education*, 3(3): 59–67.

Lacy, A. C. and Goldston, P. D. (1990) 'Behavior analysis of male and female coaches in high school girls' basketball', *Journal of Sport Behavior*, 13: 29–39.

More, K. and Franks, I. (2004) 'Measuring coaching effectiveness', in. M. Hughes and I. M. Franks (eds) *Notational Analysis of Sport: Systems for better Coaching and Performance in Sport* (2nd ed.), London: Routledge, 243–56.

Muir, B., Morgan, G. and Abraham, A. (2011a) *Player learning: Implications for Structuring Practice Activities and Coach Behaviour*, London: Football Association.

Muir, B., Morgan, G., Abraham, A. and Morley, D. (2011b) 'Developmentally appropriate approaches to coaching children', in. I. Stafford (ed.) *Coaching Children in Sport*, London: Routledge, 17–37.

Partington, M. and Cushion, C. (2013) 'Performance during performance: Using Goffman to understand the behaviours of elite youth football coaches during games', *Sports Coaching Review*, 1(2): 93–105.

Potrac, P., Brewer, C., Jones, R., Armour, K. and Hoff, J. (2000) 'Toward an holistic understanding of the coaching process', *Quest*, 52(2): 186–99.

Potrac, P., Jones, R. L. and Armour, K. (2002) "It's about getting respect': The coaching behaviours of a top-level English football coach', *Sport, Education and Society*, 7(2): 183–202.

Potrac, P., Jones, R. L. and Cushion, C. J. (2007) 'Understanding power and the coach's role in professional English soccer: A preliminary investigation of coach behaviour', *Soccer and Society*, 8: 33–49.

Siedentop, D. (1976) *Developing Teaching Skills in Physical Education*, Boston: Houghton-Mifflin.

Smith, M. and Cushion, C. J. (2006) 'An investigation of the in-game behaviours of professional, top-level youth soccer coaches', *Journal of Sport Sciences*, 24: 355–66.

Smith, R. E., Smoll, F. L. and Hunt, E. B. (1977) 'A system for the behavioural assessment of athletic coaches', *Research Quarterly*, 48: 401–7.

Tharp, R. G. and Gallimore, R. (1976) 'What a coach can teach a teacher', *Psychology Today*, 9: 75–8.

Van der Mars, H. (1989) 'Systematic observation: An introduction', in P. W. Darst, D. B. Zakrajsek and V. H. Mancini (eds) *Analyzing Physical Education and Sport Instruction* (2nd ed.), Champaign, IL: Human Kinetics, 53–80.

13 Analysis of quantitative data

Adrian Midgley and Bryna Chrismas

Introduction and overview

Much research in the science of sports coaching involves the analysis and interpretation of quantitative data. Quantitative data can be defined as data that are generated from the measurement of phenomena that result in numeric values. In sports coaching, examples of research that generate quantitative data are the use of questionnaires to investigate the passion for coaching and the coach–athlete relationship (Lafrenière *et al.* 2011), and the use of observational instruments to investigate the practice activities and instructional behaviors used by soccer coaches (Ford *et al.* 2010). These particular methods of research were covered in Chapters 11 and 12 of this book. This chapter will introduce the reader to basic concepts in applied statistics applicable to the analysis of quantitative data derived from sports coaching research. Problems often encountered by sports coaching researchers when analyzing data, often not covered in books on quantitative data analysis, also will be discussed. Such problems include corrective strategies for meeting statistical assumptions and dealing with missing data. Owing to limited space, this chapter does not provide a 'cookbook' of how to perform specific statistical tests, but introduces general statistical principles that readers will be able to apply to most quantitative research that they conduct. References have been provided within the text so that the reader can further explore the topics being discussed. Where possible, references have been provided that are accessible to readers with limited knowledge of mathematics and applied statistics.

Summarizing sample data

When you look at data that have been collected from sports coaching research it is usually extremely difficult to distinguish characteristics of that data, such as relationships and differences between variables, or other patterns that might have occurred. The main purpose of applied statistics is to examine and summarize the variability in data so that its main characteristics can be discerned and explained in a clear and concise manner. Descriptive statistics summarize the variability in the characteristics of the sample of people from which you have collected the data. These characteristics usually include such variables as age, height, and body mass, as well as other variables of specific interest to the researcher, such as the effect of coach education on self-efficacy (Malete and Feltz 2000), type of coaching behavior adopted (Myers *et al.* 2005), or the perceived self-efficacy and emotional state of athletes (Meijen *et al.* 2013). Sample data are typically described using two statistics: a statistic that describes the 'average' person (central tendency) and a statistic that describes the variability (dispersion) around this average. The mean and standard deviation (SD) are the most often used descriptive statistics because they use all the data in their calculation and possess properties that allow us to clearly describe the characteristics of a sample. When interpreting the mean and standard deviation, the usual approach is to add and subtract two standard deviations to and from the mean, as this range encompasses approximately 95 percent of the values in the sample. Knight *et al.* (2013), for example, investigated the personal and situational factors influencing coaches' perceptions of stress. Stress was measured using a 10-item Perceived Stress Scale that ranges from 0 to 50. The mean (SD) reported stress of the coaches was 15.1 (6.7), meaning that 95 percent of the coaches' stress scores were between 1.7 and 28.5, and 5 percent of the scores were either lower or higher than this range.

Extrapolating to the population

During research, the primary focus is typically not the results from the sample that were observed or tested, but the broader population from which the sample was taken. Where descriptive statistics summarize the characteristics of sample data, inferential statistics make probabilistic statements about the population based on the sample of people that was taken from the population (Hopkins 2006). Inferential statistics also typically involve building a statistical model from the sample data, where the model is an estimate of the characteristics of the population. An important assumption of inferential statistics is that the sample is representative of the population from which the sample was taken. Such a sample is known as an unbiased sample (Vincent 1999). From a practical perspective, obtaining an unbiased sample is a major challenge since sports coaching research typically uses convenience samples rather than random samples, the latter of which are desirable for obtaining an unbiased sample. A random sample is where each person in the population has an equal chance of being selected for the sample and subsequent engagement in the research, whereas a convenience sample usually includes people who have volunteered to participate in the research and are included as long as they fit the research inclusion criteria (Newell *et al.* 2010), such as being a particular gender, playing a particular sport, or competing at a particular level.

In traditional statistical inference, the main aim is to reject the null hypothesis by providing sufficient statistical evidence to declare the null hypothesis untenable. The null hypothesis always describes the state of no relationship or difference existing in the population with respect to the variables of interest (Fallowfield *et al.* 2005). The statistical tests that are performed generate a significance probability (usually referred to as the p value), which represents the probability that data as least as extreme as that observed in the sample would occur if the null hypothesis was true (McConway *et al.* 1999). A small p value is therefore a statement of surprise. For example, Figure 13.1a shows the relationship between Banister's TRIMP and Edward's TRIMP in a sample of people who participated in a study conducted by Scott *et al.* (2013). A TRIMP is a measure of training load that coaches often use to monitor their athletes' training. Figure 13.1b shows the scatter of data points if there was no relationship between Banister's TRIMP and Edward's TRIMP in the population from which the sample was taken. In this research example the p value was less than 0.001, indicating that there is less than a 0.1 percent probability that a relationship at least as strong as that observed in Figure 13.1a would have occurred in the sample if there had been no relationship in the population, as represented by Figure 13.1b. By convention, a p value that is below 0.05 is typically regarded as being statistically significant – that is, there is sufficient statistical evidence to suggest that a relationship or difference does exist in the population. This approach to statistical analysis, known as null hypothesis significance testing, predominates in sports coaching research, as well as in other scientific disciplines, but has received widespread criticism (e.g. Sterne and Smith 2001). Consequently, alternative statistical approaches such as Bayesian statistics (Goodman 2001) and magnitude-based inferences (Batterham and Hopkins 2006) have been recommended. The main feature of the Bayesian approach is that the analysis takes into account the researcher's prior beliefs about the phenomenon under investigation, which are updated once the data are collected. Magnitude-based inferences focus on the size of the experimental effect and a qualitative description of whether the

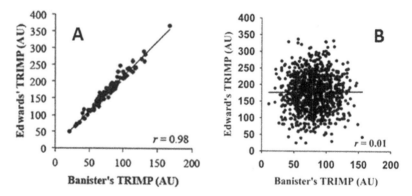

Figure 13.1 A scatterplot of the observed relationship between Banister's TRIMP and Edward's TRIMP in a sample of research participants (A) and a scatterplot representing no relationship in the population from which the sample was taken (B). The data for (B) was randomly generated by statistical analysis software. Figure 13.1A is reprinted from Scott *et al.* (2013) with permission.

effect is trivial, beneficial, or harmful. Although these alternative approaches are valid, they are not yet mainstream practice and researchers should consider this issue if considering using them.

Applied issues and considerations

Statistical procedures should be identified when formulating the research questions and establishing the study design. Sports coaching researchers can find themselves in a position where they conduct some research and the data cannot be appropriately analyzed using inferential statistics because the analyses were not identified when designing the study. This is particularly evident with questionnaire-based studies where open questions are used, or more than one answer can be provided for a question. In these instances a purely descriptive or qualitative approach is forced upon the researcher.

Although specific statistical analyses should be identified at the design stage of sports coaching research, conducting analyses is often an iterative process because when the researcher obtains the data, the statistical analyses that were initially proposed are sometimes found to be inappropriate. The appropriateness of a particular statistical analysis is typically evaluated in stages 1 and 3 of the three key stages of the analysis. These three key stages are applicable (and desirable) during conducting almost all statistical analyses and are introduced in the following sub-sections.

Stage 1 of the analysis: Exploratory data analysis

Exploratory data analysis (EDA) allows researchers to evaluate whether there are any associations between variables, or differences in the spread of data between groups, or across time, and helps identify an appropriate statistical test. Any errors or unexpected results also can be identified. Exploratory data analysis also is used to check some assumptions of inferential statistical tests. Although descriptive statistics can be used, graphical methods predominate in EDA. The importance of EDA has been clearly demonstrated by Anscombe (1973), who used four sets of data that had the same mean, standard deviation, and correlation (a measure of the strength and direction of a relationship between two continuous variables). Although the four data sets have the same mean, standard deviation, and correlation, Figure 13.2 shows that the patterns of the data are different and a Pearson correlation would only be an appropriate statistical test for the X1 and Y1 data, as the Pearson correlation assumes a linear relationship between the two variables being correlated. Although X3 and Y3 demonstrate a linear relationship, conducting a Pearson correlation, or any other statistical test, on this data would not be appropriate, as these data exhibit perfect linearity except for one data point. A practical example of this is where the weekly wages of sports coaches are correlated with their monthly wages. One is a linear transformation of the other, so perfect linearity would be expected and not informative.

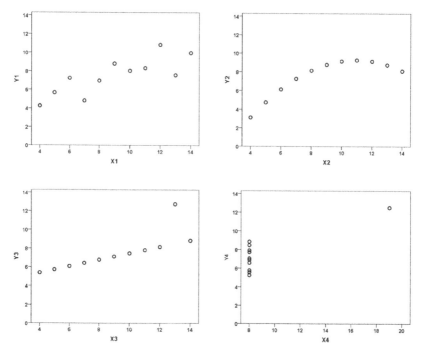

Figure 13.2 Scatterplots showing the relationships in four sets of bivariate data. Each X variable has a mean of 9.00 and a standard deviation of 3.32 and each Y variable has a mean of 7.50 and a standard deviation of 2.03. The Pearson correlation for each of the four data sets is 0.82.

Stage 2 of the analysis: Choosing and conducting the statistical test

The statistical test is typically chosen based on the initial findings of the EDA. Identifying an appropriate statistical test to analyze data is sometimes a challenge for sports coaching researchers. Table 13.1 shows common statistical tests used in sports coaching research, the type of data that the tests are used to analyze, the statistical assumptions of the tests, and non-parametric equivalents. Examples from the sports coaching research literature also are provided to place each statistical test into context. Further examples are provided in the next section.

Stage 3 of the analysis: Diagnostics

Diagnostics are used to check that the statistical test is a useful one with respect to the accuracy of the results. In our introduction to this chapter we stated that the main purpose of applied statistics is to examine and summarize the variability in data. Accurate statistical summaries and associated inferences

Table 13.1 Statistical tests that are common in sports coaching research, the type of data that they are used to analyze, a research example from sports coaching research, statistical assumptions that need to be formally evaluated during the analysis, and each test's non-parametric equivalent. See the table footnote for a glossary of terms used in the table

Parametric Test	Analysis	Research example	Analysis assumptions	Non-parametric equivalent
Not applicable	Association between two categorical variables	Association between categories of coaching comments and different sports (Walters et al. 2012)	Lowest expected frequency in each cell is at least five.	Chi-square test for independence
Pearson correlation	Relationship between two continuously distributed variables	The relationship between coaching behaviors and competitive anxiety in Golestan Province Fustal super league players (Bai et al. 2013)	Data normally distributed. Linearity between variables.	Spearman signed rank test
Linear regression	Relationship(s) between a continuously distributed variable and one or more other continuously distributed or categorical variables	Relationships between competitive success in NBA basketball after a change in coach and variables such as the number of previous games coached and the number of previous games won by the coach before the change (Martinez and Caudill 2013)	Residuals normally distributed around a mean of zero and with constant variance. Linearity between variables.	Passing-Bablok regression
Independent t test	Comparing two means from different groups of participants, each measured once	Mean difference between the age at the end of the professional career of a group of judo coaches and a group of coaches from other sports (Sindik and Rendulic 2012)	Data normally distributed. Equality of variances.	Mann–Whitney U test
Dependent t test	Comparing two means from one group of participants, each measured twice	Mean differences in perceived competence before and after manipulated feedback during a physical education task (Mouratidis et al. 2008)	Differences normally distributed.	Wilcoxon signed rank test

Table 13.1 (continued)

Parametric Test	Analysis	Research example	Analysis assumptions	Non-parametric equivalent
Between-subjects one-way ANOVA	Comparing means from three or more different groups of participants, each measured once	Mean differences in the perceived value of knowledge of coaching methodology in coaches categorized as experienced, less experienced, or more experienced (Marques dos Santos et al. 2010)	Residuals normally distributed around a mean of zero and with constant variance.*	Kruskal–Wallis test
Repeated measures one-way ANOVA	Comparing means from one group of participants, each measured on three or more occasions	Mean differences in the heart rate response of cricketers during seven overs of a simulated batting work bout (Christie et al. 2008)	Residuals normally distributed around a mean of zero and with constant variance. Sphericity.	Friedman test

*When run under the general linear model. *Glossary of Terms*: **categorical variable** = a variable where values are grouped into categories, such as whether a person is male or female, or the type of sport someone plays; **continuously distributed variable** = a variable that typically consists of measurements (e.g. distance covered by a football player during a competitive match); **equality of variance** = where the variability in data from different groups (e.g. the ages of players in different sports teams) are similar; **residual** = the difference between an observed value and the value predicted by a statistical model; **sphericity** = equality of variance of the differences between each pair of values.

about the population, however, can be achieved only if the statistical assumptions of the tests have been met. Diagnostics mostly focus on checking whether statistical assumptions have been met. Most of the statistical tests used by sports coaching researchers are based on the normal model and, therefore, checking the normality assumption should be an extremely common procedure in sports coaching research. Figure 13.3a shows a histogram, which is a graphical procedure for showing whether data have been derived from a normally distributed population. The data are clearly normally distributed because the bars follow the shape of the normal curve (the curved black line). Figure 13.3b shows right-skewed data, which is an example of non-normality. You can see from this graph that there are more younger people than older people and this is the cause of the skewness. Other graphical methods for evaluating whether data are normally distributed are shown in Figures 13.3c–d. Figure 13.3c shows a box plot, where normality is evident when the graph is symmetrical around the horizontal line (representing the median value) that is located inside the box. Box plots are also particularly useful for identifying outliers – shown on the graph as small circles. Outliers

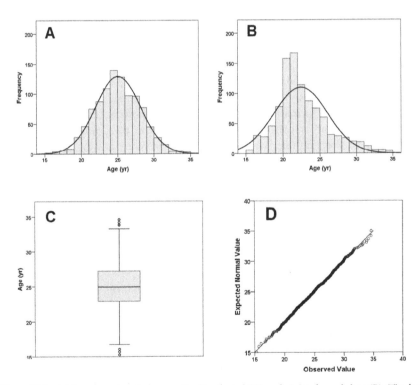

Figure 13.3 A histogram showing normally distributed (A) and right-skewed data (B). The box plot (C) and quantile–quantile plot (D) are other graphical methods for assessing whether data are normally distributed.

are extreme values that are not representative of the rest of the data and can cause inaccurate results. Figure 13.3d shows a quantile–quantile (Q–Q) plot, where evidence of normality is when data points are close to the diagonal line, known as the line of identity. These plots are particularly useful for evaluating normality when the sample size is small. There are many formal inferential statistical tests to evaluate normality, such as the Shapiro Wilk and Kolmogorov–Smirnov tests used in SPSS. We recommend that these tests are not used, however, because the decision whether data are normally distributed is largely dependent on sample size (see Newell *et al.* 2010: 134 for further information). When performing ANOVA and regression under the general linear model, it is the residuals (the differences between the observed and modeled values) that need to be normally distributed, not the observed data, and this is always evaluated after running the statistical test during model diagnostics.

When statistical assumptions are not met there are two approaches that are typically used to address the issue. The first is to use non-parametric statistics that have fewer assumptions (if any) about the distribution of the data. These are sometimes referred to as assumption-free statistics (O'Donoghue 2012). An issue with non-parametric statistics is that they are generally less powerful than their parametric counterparts (Thomas *et al.* 2011). That is, they are less likely to reject the null hypothesis and, therefore, parametric tests are typically preferred as the first choice. Another issue is that there are no non-parametric equivalents of some of the more complex parametric statistical tests. The second approach is to transform the data and use a parametric test. Data transformations are mathematical manipulations of data that are often used to correct violations of statistical assumptions. A strategy to correct skewness, for example, is to choose a data transformation from the ladder of powers (Figure 13.4). The transformation that is chosen is dependent on the direction and extent of the skewness. For example, right-skewness is common in data collected from people and is often corrected by natural log transformation. The log transformation reduces the size of the higher numbers more than it does the lower numbers, thereby 'pulling in' the skewed data. Strategies for evaluating and dealing with violations of other statistical assumptions, such as those shown in Table 13.1, can be found in Field (2013).

Missing data

A common problem experienced during sports coaching research is that of missing data. Missing data are often encountered due to research participants not completing all aspects of the research, or due to some technical problem with equipment that is being used to collect the data. Most statistical analysis software packages will omit participants from an analysis if they have any missing data and is known as listwise deletion. In extreme cases, researchers have a number of research participants with a full set of data that is insufficient for the statistical analysis to be completed. Fortunately, there are modern statistical methods that can handle missing data without listwise deletion that

Name	Transformation
Cube	Y^3
Square	Y^2
Observed data	Y^1
Square root	$\sqrt{Y}$
Logarithm	$Log(Y)$
Reciprocal root	$1/\sqrt{Y}$
Reciprocal	$1/Y$
Reciprocal square	$1/Y^2$

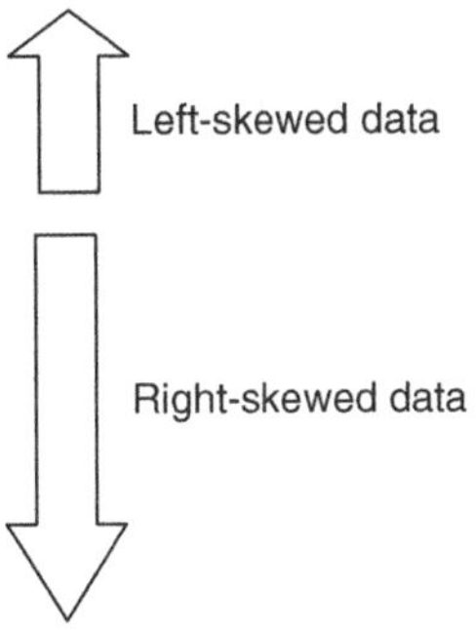

Left-skewed data

Right-skewed data

Figure 13.4 The ladder of powers. When data are left skewed you need to pick a transformation
that is up the ladder of powers and move down the ladder of powers when data are
right skewed.

are typically based on a mathematical procedure called maximum likelihood
estimation. An example is linear mixed modeling (West *et al.* 2007). Another
approach to dealing with missing data is known as imputation. Imputation is
where the statistical analysis software inserts values where there are missing
values based on some mathematical criterion. Simple imputation methods,
such as mean imputation, have been criticized and should not be used (Enders
2010), although they may be considered an acceptable strategy for undergraduate sports coaching research. Multiple imputation is the recommended
method for published research (Enders 2010).

Reporting the results

Once accurate and meaningful statistical results have been obtained, the next
step is to effectively communicate the results. The most important consideration in effective communication is that the results are reported within
the context of the research topic and should not rely solely on the formal
statistical values. When comparing the mean years of experience of two
groups of sports coaches, for example, it would not be sufficient to state that
the results are statistically significant and $t = 2.7$ and $p = 0.018$, as this does
not inform the reader of which group had, on average, the most coaching
experience, how big the difference was (known as the effect size), and whether
from a practical perspective the difference is meaningful. Another important
strategy is to always report the most important findings first and to ensure
they have prominence in your results section. The most important findings
are typically related to the main aims of the study. Readers are directed to
the following textbooks for further guidance on reporting the results of
statistical analyses that can easily be applied to sports coaching research:

American Psychological Association (2009), Lang and Secic (1997), and Pallant (2010).

Reflections from the field

The applied statistical techniques covered in this chapter have been employed in published research to analyze quantitative data in the science of sports coaching. Questionnaires, interviews, and observational analyses are methods of data collection consistently utilized within research. Both a mixed method approach (Potrac *et al.* 2002) and a purely quantitative method (Millar *et al.* 2011) have been employed to interpret and disseminate research findings obtained using these methods. Although qualitative analysis can be useful to explicate the meaning of quantitative research in sports coaching, it may be more intuitive for researchers to use quantitative methods of analysis. Furthermore, this section will demonstrate that in some areas of research the data collection dictates the use of quantitative analysis.

Quantitative analysis of data derived from questionnaires can use descriptive statistics to report specific information on the sample from which the data were derived. For example, a study by Smith *et al.* (2007) examined the mean and standard deviation levels of anxiety in youth sports players. Additionally, absolute frequency and percentage statistics have been derived from questionnaires to show the type of verbal feedback provided by a coach during a handball match (Guzman and Calpe-Gomez 2012), percentage of time spent in 'Training form' activities and 'Playing form' activities during soccer training sessions (Ford *et al.* 2010), and the patterns of coach behaviors in youth soccer (Cushion *et al.* 2012a). Providing percentage statistics for the patterns of coaching behavior across different levels of sports enables researchers to observe the variation in instruction provided (Cushion *et al.* 2012a). Performance analysis is ubiquitous in the science of sports coaching, and global positioning systems (GPS) analysis is a popular monitoring technique used to obtain player statistics during training and competition in certain sports. This type of data collection dictates the use of quantitative statistics. Descriptive statistics have been used to report the average performance statistics derived from GPS during soccer (Stolen *et al.* 2005), rugby (Austin and Kelly 2013), and Australian football (Gray and Jenkins 2010). Furthermore, descriptive statistics have been obtained for the number of collisions (Gabbett 2013), temporal patterns of acceleration and deceleration (Akenhead *et al.* 2013), and training load (Scott *et al.* 2013). These data are used by coaches, physiotherapists, and sport scientists for numerous reasons, including setting the intensity of training programs, monitoring recovery, and predicting injury risk. The importance of using appropriate descriptive statistics for the accurate description of these applications cannot be overstated.

Pearson's chi-squared test has been used to examine the association between how often participants participated in sport and the participants' future expectations in terms of their employment and personal aspirations

(Gisladottir *et al.* 2013). Additionally, Kendall Tau-c (a non-parametric equivalent of the Pearson correlation) was calculated to investigate whether there was any relationship between these variables (Gisladottir *et al.* 2013). The authors rationalized the use of Kendall's Tau-c by stating that their data were ordinal (ranks) rather than continuously distributed; assumed by the more commonly used Pearson correlation. This highlights the importance of checking the assumptions of tests when conducting statistical analyses.

Regression has been utilized in sports coaching research to examine relationships between continuously distributed variables. Multiple linear regression has been employed to investigate the contribution of athletes' perceptions of coach leadership and coach–athlete relationship measures of cohesion (Jowett and Chaundy 2004). Multiple regression also has been applied to examine how much variation in sports club participation could be explained by body image, mental and physical condition, and parents' socio-economic status (Gisladottir *et al.* 2013). Deciding on which regression model is the best fit is an important consideration for researchers, and should be determined by looking at the R^2 change value. A statistically significant R^2 change indicates that a greater amount of variability in the outcome variable can be explained by using the model with the higher R^2. Subsequently, this would allow researchers to identify the most important predictors of the outcome variable. There are many different methods of regression modeling such as forced entry, stepwise, and hierarchical regression and choosing the appropriate method can be challenging for sports coaching researchers. The reader is directed to Field (2013) for guidance on this issue.

Traditional statistical inference tests, including t-tests and ANOVAs, have been used to investigate differences between coaching and performance variables. If several t-tests are conducted, however, it is important to be aware of the type I error rate. The type I error rate refers to the probability of finding a significant difference, when there is no difference in the population. The probability of obtaining a type I error increases with the number of comparisons performed. Subsequently, a correction factor must be used to control this error rate. A study conducted by Austin and Kelly (2013) used a between-subjects one-way ANOVA to examine the differences in distance covered between playing positions in professional rugby league matches. Additionally, the effect of either positive or negative coaches' feedback following a professional rugby game on levels of testosterone and cortisol, and subsequent performance, were analyzed using a repeated measures one-way ANOVA (Crewther and Cook 2012). In both of these studies *post hoc* Bonferroni corrections were applied to control the type I error rate when locating statistically significant paired differences. In our experience, researchers are often confused as to which correction to choose from the many that are typically available in statistical analysis software. Different *post hoc* corrections are used in different circumstances, such as how much control you want over the type I error rate, or whether or not there are an equal number of participants in each group. Further information on this topic can be found in Field (2013).

As with any area of research, determining the reliability and validity of measurement tools used within sport coaching research is critical (see Chapter 14). The validity and reliability of the Coach Analysis and Intervention System (CAIS), for example, was measured using content validity, face validity and intra- and interobserver reliability checks to establish agreement levels between coaches (Cushion *et al.* 2012b). Correlation statistics were used to establish observer agreement, and a two-way ANOVA conducted to show there were no statistically significant differences between observers and coaching sessions (Cushion *et al.* 2012b). The latter of these statistical tests demonstrated that differences in the coding of the CAIS were not due to individual variation.

In our experience, the accurate analysis of data and subsequent reporting of research findings is something that requires much time and careful attention to detail. We have observed many times fundamental flaws in statistical analyses and reporting of results. One example is the reporting of the mean and standard deviation for data that are clearly not normally distributed. A more serious error is not taking into account the fact that more than one data point in a correlation or regression analysis has been derived from each person (Wilkinson and Akenhead 2013). Such errors result in poor scientific communication and reflect poorly on the discipline of sports coaching science. Probably the worst case scenario would be where sports coaches alter their practice based on flawed data analysis and reporting. The design, ethical approval, and data collection of research takes substantial time and effort, and readers are encouraged to apply the same rigor to their statistical analyses and reporting of results. Where possible, we encourage consultation with statisticians and other suitably competent people to help with experimental design, data analyses, and reporting of statistical results.

References

Akenhead, R., Hayes, P. R., Thompson, K. G. and French, D. (2013) 'Diminutions of acceleration and deceleration output during professional football match play', *Journal of Science and Medicine in Sport*, 16: 556–61.

American Psychological Association (2009) *Publication Manual of the American Psychological Association* (6th ed.), Washington, DC: American Psychological Association.

Anscombe, F. J. (1973) 'Graphs in statistical analysis', *The American Statistician*, 27: 17–21.

Austin, D. J. and Kelly, S. J. (2013) 'Positional differences in professional rugby league match play through the use of global positioning systems', *Journal of Strength and Conditioning Research*, 27: 14–19.

Bai, N., Sheikh, M., Rad, L. S. and Anzehaie, Z. H. (2013) 'The relationship between coaching behaviors and competitive anxiety in Golestan Province Futsal super league players', *European Journal of Experimental Biology*, 3: 383–6.

Batterham, A. M. and Hopkins, W. G. (2006) 'Making meaningful inferences about magnitudes', *International Journal of Sports Physiology and Performance*, 1: 50–57.

Christie, C. J., Todd, A. I. and King, G. A. (2008) 'Selected physiological responses during batting in a simulated cricket work bout: a pilot study', *Journal of Science and Medicine in Sport*, 11: 581–4.

Crewther, B. T. and Cook, C. J. (2012) 'Effects of different post-match recovery interventions on subsequent athlete hormonal state and game performance', *Physiology and Behaviour*, 106: 471–5.

Cushion, C., Ford, P. R. and Williams, M. (2012a) 'Coach behaviours and practice structures in youth soccer: Implications for talent development', *Journal of Sport Sciences*, 30: 1631–41.

Cushion, C., Harvey, S., Muir, B. and Nelson, L. (2012b) 'Developing the Coach Analysis and Intervention System (CAIS): Establishing validity and reliability of a computerised systematic observation instrument', *Journal of Sports Sciences*, 30: 201–16.

Enders, C. K. (2010) *Applied Missing Data Analysis*, New York: The Guilford Press.

Fallowfield, J. L., Hale, B. J. and Wilkinson, D. M. (2005) *Using Statistics in Sport and Exercise Science Research*, Chichester: Lotus Publishing.

Field, A. (2013) *Discovering Statistics using IBM SPSS Statistics*, London: Sage.

Ford, P. R., Yates, I. and Williams, M. (2010) 'An analysis of practice activities and instructional behaviours used by youth soccer coaches during practice: exploring the link between science and application', *Journal of Sports Sciences*, 28: 483–95.

Gabbett, T. J. (2013) 'Influence of playing standard on the physical demands of junior rugby league tournament match-play', *Journal of Science and Medicine in Sport*: http://dx.doi.org/10.1016/j.jsams.2013.03.013.

Gisladottir, T. L., Matthiasdottir, A. and Kristjansdottir, H. (2013) 'The effect of adolescents' sports clubs participation on self-reported mental and physical conditions and future expectations', *Journal of Sports Sciences*, 31: 1139–45.

Goodman, S. N. (2001) 'Of p-values and Bayes: a modest proposal', *Epidemiology*, 12: 295–7.

Gray, A. J. and Jenkins, D. G. (2010) 'Match analysis and the physiological demands of Australian Football', *Sports Medicine*, 40: 347–60.

Guzman, J. F. and Calpe-Gomez, V. (2012) 'Preliminary study of coach verbal behaviour according to game actions', *Journal of Human Sport and Exercise*, 7: 376–82.

Hopkins, W. G. (2006) 'Estimating sample size for magnitude-based inferences', *Sportscience*, 10: 63–70.

Jowett, S. and Chaundy, V. (2004) 'An investigation into the impact of coach leadership and coach–athlete relationship on group cohesion', *Group Dynamics: Theory, Research, and Practice*, 8: 302–11.

Knight, C. J., Reade, I. L., Selzler, A. M. and Rodgers, W.M. (2013) 'Personal and situational factors influencing coaches' perceptions of stress', *Journal of Sports Sciences*, 31: 1054–63.

Lafrenière, M. A. K., Jowett, S., Vallerand, R. J. and Carbonneau, N. (2011) 'Passion for coaching and the quality of the coach–athlete relationship: the mediating role of coaching behaviors', *Psychology of Sport and Exercise*, 12: 144–52.

Lang, T. A. and Secic, M. (1997) *How to Report Statistics in Medicine: Annotated Guidelines for Authors, Editors, and Reviewers*, Philadelphia, PA: American College of Physicians.

Malete, L. and Feltz, D. L. (2000) 'The effect of a coaching education program on coaching efficacy', *The Sport Psychologist*, 14: 410–17.

Marques dos Santos, S. F., Mesquita, I. M. R., dos Santos Graca, A. B. and Rosado, A. F. B. (2010) 'What coaches value about coaching knowledge: a comparative study across a range of domains', *International Journal of Applied Sports Sciences*, 22: 96–112.

McConway, K. J., Jones, M. C. and Taylor, P. C. (1999) *Statistical Modelling using GENSTAT*, London: Arnold.

Meijen, C., Jones, M. V., McCarthy, P. J., Sheffield, D. and Allen, M. S. (2013) 'Cognitive and affective components of challenge and threat states', *Journal of Sports Sciences*, 31: 847–55.

Millar, S. K., Oldham, A. R. H. and Donovan, M. (2011) 'Coaches self-awareness of timing, nature and intent of verbal instructions to athletes', *International Journal of Sports Science and Coaching*, 6: 503–13.

Martinez, J. A. and Caudill, S. B. (2013) 'Does midseason change of coach improve team performance? Evidence from the NBA', *Journal of Sport Management*, 27: 108–13.

Mouratidis, A., Vansteenkiste, M., Lens, W. and Sideridis, G. (2008) 'The motivating role of positive feedback in sport and physical education: evidence for a motivating model', *Journal of Sport and Exercise Psychology*, 30: 240–68.

Myers, N. D., Vargas-Tonsing, T. M. and Feltz, D. L. (2005) 'Coaching efficacy in inter-collegiate coaches: sources, coaching behaviour, and team variables', *Psychology of Sport and Exercise*, 6: 129–43.

Newell, J., Aitchison, T. and Grant, S. (2010) *Statistics for Sports and Exercise Science: A Practical Approach*, Harlow, UK: Pearson Education Limited.

O'Donoghue, P. (2012) *Statistics for Sport and Exercise Studies: An Introduction*, Abingdon: Routledge.

Pallant, J. (2010) *SPSS Survival Manual* (4th ed.), Maidenhead, UK: Open University Press.

Potrac. P., Jones, R. and Armour, K. (2002) '"It's all about getting respect": The coaching behaviours of an expert English soccer coach', *Sport, Education and Society*, 7: 183–202.

Scott, B. R., Lockie, R. G., Knight, T. J., Clark, A. C., Xanne, A. K. and Jonge de, J. (2013) 'A comparison of methods to quantify the in-season training load of professional soccer players', *International Journal of Sports Physiology and Performance*, 8: 195–202.

Sindik, J. and Rendulic, D. (2012) 'Life satisfaction and general life experience in judo and other sport coaches', *Sport Science*, 5: 53–8.

Smith, R. E., Smoll, F. L. and Cumming, S. P. (2007) 'Effects of a motivational climate intervention for coaches on young athletes sport performance anxiety', *Journal of Sport and Exercise Psychology*, 29: 39–59.

Sterne, J. A. C. and Smith, G. D. (2001) 'Sifting the evidence – what's wrong with significance tests?', *British Medical Journal*, 322: 226–31.

Stolen, T., Chamari, K., Castagna, C. and Wisloff, U. (2005) 'Physiology of soccer', *Sports Medicine*, 35: 5–36.

Thomas, J. R., Nelson, J. K. and Silverman, S. J. (2011) *Research Methods in Physical Activity*, Champaign, IL: Human Kinetics.

Vincent, W. J. (1999) *Statistics in Kinesiology*, Champaign, IL: Human Kinetics.

Walters, S. R., Schluter, P. J., Oldham, A. R. H., Thomson, R. W. and Payne, D. (2012) 'Then sideline behaviour of coaches at children's team sports games', *Psychology of Sport and Exercise*, 13: 208–15.

West, B. T., Welch, K. B. and Gałecki, A. T. (2007) *Linear Mixed Models: A Practical Guide using Statistical Software*, Boca Raton, FL: Chapman and Hall/CRC.

Wilkinson, M. and Akenhead, R. (2013) 'Violation of statistical assumptions in a recent publication?', *International Journal of Sports Medicine*, 34(3): 28.

14 Judging quantitative research

John Toner and Aidan Moran

Introduction and overview

Learning how to judge the quality of published research is an important step in your development as a quantitative researcher for a number of reasons. First, you need to learn how to read and use research reports so that you can identify sources of useful information that can help inform your own research project. Second, to ensure that these sources are providing you with valid and reliable information, you will need to learn how to critically evaluate the degree of care with which a study was performed and how to recognize erroneous assumptions made by other researchers. Acquiring these skills should help you avoid making mistakes that are likely to decrease the trust that readers can place in your findings. With this in mind, the present chapter aims to provide students with some guidelines and recommendations on how to assess the quality of published quantitative research in the field of sports coaching. We have organized the chapter as follows. In the first section of the chapter we outline the most important practical issues that researchers typically encounter when engaging in this form of research. In the second section, we give some practical tips on how to evaluate quantitative research studies in sports coaching. Finally, the first author relates some of his experiences learning to read and evaluate quantitative research papers.

There are a number of essential steps in conducting any piece of quantitative research, and when judging the quality of any paper or report you should pay careful attention to how the researcher(s) has executed each stage of this process. Unfortunately, space constraints prevent us from providing a detailed account of each step. For a comprehensive account of this process see Dunn (2009), Kumar (2010), and Locke *et al.* (1998). Instead, the following section will address how the quality of a research paper or project may be compromised by mistakes that researcher(s) can make when formulating their *research question*, devising their *research design*, *interpreting data*, and discussing the *practical significance* of their findings.

One of your first tasks when judging the quality of a quantitative research paper is to examine the *research question*(s) to gain an idea of the specific aims and objectives of the study. Quantitative research studies are usually driven by the desire to test hypotheses from specific theories. Typically, the aims of a paper are clearly stated as testable hypotheses – towards the end of a paper's introduction. Writing your research questions as hypotheses has three key advantages. First, it reminds readers of exactly what you are trying to find out. Second, it serves as a bridge between other peoples' work (which is reviewed in the introductory section of the paper) and what you plan to do. Finally, explaining your research question in a non-technical way allows the reader to judge the quality, relevance, and potential significance of your work. Remember that the reader should be left with a very clear impression of how answering the stated research question(s) will add something *new* to what is already known in this particular field of inquiry. In fact, many research studies will seek to address a gap in our understanding by identifying a problem that has remained unresolved.

In order to determine whether the study has the potential to develop our understanding, you should consider some of the following questions. Is there a clear theoretical justification for the generation of the hypotheses? Does the research question investigate specific issues that have yet to be addressed by previous researchers in this field? Do the authors provide a rationale for predicting that the results of their study may deviate from those of earlier publications? Finally, does the research generate and develop ideas, rather than merely test them? If you find that a study fails to address most of these questions then it is doubtful whether you can place much confidence in its ability to make a telling and worthwhile contribution to the body of literature.

After considering the research question, you should determine whether the study has adopted an appropriate *research design* (e.g. survey, questionnaire) (see Cozby 2012). The quality of any study depends heavily on the *validity* of the methods used to collect data. Therefore, researchers will often consider validity with regard to two different aspects of their investigations. First, *internal validity* is concerned with the extent to which the research study has been designed so that it truly deals with what is being examined. In other words, has it been designed to yield truthful results and does the data gathered match the research question? For example, if you wished to explore the role coaches' passion for coaching plays in influencing athletes' perceptions of the *quality* of the coach–athlete relationship, you would need to select a method of inquiry that actually measures the relationship between these variables. In this case, you would gather objective data by administering a questionnaire that explored coaches' passion for coaching and another questionnaire that measured athletes' perception of the *quality* of the coach–athlete relationship. Once they had been administered and subsequently analyzed, you could then examine the relationship between these two variables. Second, *external validity* is concerned with the extent to which findings can be *generalized* to settings other than that in which the data were obtained. In other words, the issue here is the degree to which your results apply *beyond* the specific context in which your study was conducted. For example, you should be wary of any study that has examined one group of people (e.g. elite young athletes) but applied their results and conclusions to a different group (e.g. sedentary adults). Issues which may severely compromise the external validity of a study's findings include an insufficient sample size and inappropriate sampling method, and problems with the instrumentation or measurements used to collect the data (see next section for a detailed discussion). However, if there are issues with a study's external validity you would hope to see the quantitative researcher outline the limitations of the study and explain how these findings may not be valid for another group of people.

Having analyzed the data and presented the results, most researchers try to provide an *interpretation* of their findings. In evaluating this part of a published study you should pay careful attention to whether the researcher makes unjustified claims about 'causation' (i.e. that one variable is directly responsible for a change in another variable). This issue is important given the prevalence of correlational designs within the sports science literature. To explain, a cursory look within prominent sports science journals (e.g. *Psychology of Sport and Exercise*) indicates that much of the recent quantitative research in sports coaching has relied heavily on self-report (e.g. questionnaires) measures of psychological traits, states, and behavior. For example, self-report measures have been used to investigate how coaches' passion for coaching may influence athletes' perceptions of the quality of the coach–athlete relationship (Lafrenière *et al.* 2011) and to examine the temporal relationships between athletes' perceptions of coach-autonomy support, basic need satisfaction, and indices of well-being and ill-being (Adie *et al.* 2012). Many of these studies have adopted research designs that are correlational in nature. That is, they examine the *relationship* between different variables. Although these designs are useful, they have certain limitations. For example, when evaluating findings from *correlational* research you should be mindful that a significant correlation between two or more variables does *not* mean that one of those variables *caused* the other(s). Ideally, researchers should use a methodological approach which employs multiple strategies to support a causal relationship including the use of cross-sectional and longitudinal methods to examine the proposed pattern of correlations between the variables. This could be followed by a more robust test of causative effects using carefully controlled and randomized experimental methods (see Hagger and Chatzisarantis 2009 for a detailed explanation).

The final step in the research process requires the quantitative researcher to make a judgment about the *practical significance* of their findings. One of the potential issues that may arise here is when researchers claim that a statistically significant effect represents the true nature of that effect in the population. However, significant findings are likely to be biased according to the size of the sample in which the effect was tested. For example, a study employing a small sample size has less chance of finding a statistically significant effect, which may result in an effect that actually exists in the population going unobserved. Although we outline the importance of a large sample size in the next section it is necessary to note that even though a very large sample size may result in the detection of a statistically significant effect, it may also result in small, relatively unsubstantial effects being detected as significant when, in fact, they are relatively inconsequential (Hagger and Chatzisarantis 2009). Consequently, when judging the true effect of a statistical finding you should pay close attention to *effect size* statistics. So, rather than relying solely on statistical significance testing researchers will often report effect size statistics like Cohen's *d* (see Cohen 1988 for rules of thumb regarding the magnitude of effect sizes). These effect sizes are informative because they emphasize the size of the difference between two groups rather than confounding this with sample size.

To provide further evidence concerning the meaningfulness of their results a researcher may also supply the reader with what is known as confidence intervals for effect sizes (CI; Ivarsson *et al.* 2013). CI describes the interval where most (90 percent or 95 percent) of the participants in a study are located for a specific variable (Thompson 2002). While recommending the importance of reporting effect sizes you should note that erroneous assumptions can also be made regarding the genuine significance of a large effect size. To explain, if you examined the total number of successfully completed passes in a soccer match, and found that Team A completed 600 passes while Team B completed 400, you would likely find a statistically significant difference between the two teams on this measure, and a large effect size. However, if Team A ended up losing the match then the practical significance of this latter finding would be called into question. In this case, you should report the statistically significant finding but be careful not to overstate its meaningfulness or practical significance.

Applied issues and considerations

Having considered some of the key concepts that underpin quantitative research, the next section outlines a number of important issues you may need to consider when conducting your own quantitative research in sports coaching. Here we focus on two important features of the research process (i.e. *sampling* and the *validity/reliability* of measurements) and seek to provide some guidelines on how you may enhance the generalizability of your research findings.

Sampling size and sampling method

It would be extremely difficult for any investigator to measure every possible example of the phenomenon which is under investigation. Instead, in accordance with standard scientific practice, the researcher selects a *sample* of subjects from the target population. In attempting to increase the *generalizability* of their findings, investigators try to ensure that this sample is an accurate representation of the wider target audience to whom the research might apply. The size of the sample is an important issue here and may have a significant bearing on how comfortable a reader may be with the suggestion that it truly represents the target population. In terms of your own research, readers may place very little trust in the meaningfulness of your findings if you have conducted your test with a small sample. An additional issue relates to the need for the sample size to be large enough to detect a statistically meaningful result. Indeed, the smaller the sample size the less likely you are to find a statistically meaningful effect, which might mean an effect that truly exists in the population goes undetected. Consequently, statistical operations known as *power tests* are often used by researchers as a means of providing a rational basis for their sample sizes (see Murphy *et al.* 2009 for a simple and general model of statistical power analysis). Having described the power test, you may wish to provide a statement in the methods section which explains that your study's sample size has been chosen in order to have sufficient power to detect a meaningful result at a certain level of statistical significance. Following these steps should enhance the reader's confidence in the external validity/ generalizability of your findings.

However, the size is not the only factor influencing the adequacy of a study's sample and may, in fact, be one of the least problematic issues. Indeed, you will also need to ensure that your *sampling method* has avoided any forms of recruitment or sampling *bias*. A sample is deemed to be biased if certain members are underrepresented or overrepresented relative to others in that population. To ensure you avoid bias in your own research you will need to become familiar with two different categories of sampling methods: probability sampling and non-probability sampling. Probability sampling (also known as random sampling) is any sampling procedure in which each member of a target population has an equal chance of being chosen. In fact, random sampling will often be employed to avoid selection bias. Non-probability sampling (e.g. convenience sampling) is a sampling strategy in which the probability of an individual being chosen is unknown. Through engagement with the literature you may be surprised to learn that much of the recent quantitative research in sports coaching has actually employed convenience sampling (e.g. solely recruiting university athletes). Researchers may justify this approach by arguing that the population of athletes participating in competition is inherently heterogeneous (possessing non-uniform characteristics) and that their convenience sampling strategy merely reflects this reality. If you are concerned that this form of convenience sampling may severely compromise the generalizability of your findings then you may wish to use a cross-section of ages which could be generalized to a wider population (Felton and Jowett 2013). Ideally, you should provide a rationale for the use of non-probability sampling and, when utilized, outline and acknowledge the limitations of this process. Regardless of the sampling method utilized, you should provide a clear explanation of how you recruited your subjects and how you sought to avoid sampling bias (see Kumar 2010 for further advice on sampling methods).

Another goal of the recruitment process is to create a sample in a manner which ensures that extraneous variables (i.e. variables whose effects are not of interest to the researcher) are unable to influence the findings. For example, if a researcher is studying the influence of different instructional approaches (e.g. guided discovery learning, explicit learning) on motor skill acquisition amongst novice learners, he or she would probably want to select subjects who have no previous experience of performing that particular skill (e.g. passing a basketball). As such, the criteria used to determine whether potential participants are truly 'novice' performers will be an important consideration. Consequently, sports science researchers will often describe their sample explicitly in terms of demographic descriptors, including, amongst other factors, the participants' age-range, gender, skill level, years playing/competitive experience. Ultimately, the reader should be left with a very clear impression of who is qualified (i.e. inclusion criteria) or not qualified (i.e. exclusion criteria) to be members of the sample.

Validity and reliability

Having identified an appropriate sample size and sampling method, you should now ensure that your data will be collected using measurements that are both *valid* and *reliable* in nature. Using a valid and reliable measure is essential in avoiding measurement error which, in this instance, refers to the discrepancy between respondents' attributes and their measurement responses. First, you should take account of the *validity* of the measurement you intend to use. Here, validity refers to the extent to which the measurement captures what it claims to measure. Importantly, you will need to ensure that your chosen methods/instruments conform to acceptable criteria of validity in order to be confident that the effects you test reflect the true effect in that population (Hagger and Chatzisarantis 2009). In this regard, you should be mindful of six types of validity when considering the adequacy of instruments/measurement: face, convergent, concurrent, discriminant, predictive, and nomological validity (see Table 14.1). For a comprehensive account of these types of validity please see Hagger and Chatzisarantis (2009). While each of these preceding forms of validity can be considered a separate component of overall validity, it is important to ensure that each of them has met acceptable criteria. In doing so, you seek to provide converging evidence for the acceptability and relevance of the measurement being used and to increase a reader's trust in the generalizability of your findings.

Another question that you need to ask about any instrumentation is whether it collects data in a *reliable* manner. Take, as an everyday example, reliability issues we may encounter when using household equipment such as a bathroom scales. If you were to weigh yourself with these scales and get three completely different readings, your instrument doubtless has a problem with reliability. On the other hand, it might show three identical readings (perfect reliability), but each of these may be incorrect (an issue of validity) because your scales do not tell the truth, that is, it is consistent but also consistently misleading. Indeed, our bathroom scales may produce reliable readings and yet not be a valid indicator of one's weight. However, we may be confident that if it provides valid readings then it is also reliable, as reliability is an integral component of validity. In summarizing this issue Locke *et al.* (1998:119) remind us that 'you cannot tell the truth unless you are consistent, but you can be consistent and not tell the truth'.

Table 14.1 Forms of validity (based on Hagger and Chatzisarantis, 2009)

Category	Definition	Example
Face validity	'Expert' judgments of the extent to which a self-report measure captures all aspects of the construct	Important in the early development of a self-report measure to ensure that items have content that is representative of the construct under investigation, and that they have meaning to the participants
Convergent validity	Offers information on whether or not different self-report measures or items on a scale correlate with each other	The athlete burnout questionnaire (ABQ) and the Maslach burnout general inventory survey (MBI-GS) display acceptable convergent validity as matching subscales are highly correlated (see Cresswell and Eklund 2006)
Concurrent validity	Reveals the extent to which a measure of a specific construct correlates with similar or alternative measures of the same construct	Hagger and Chatzisarantis (2009) suggest that in a sport and exercise setting we would expect to see a strong correlation between measures of physical self-concept and global self-esteem
Discriminant validity	Indicates whether the self-report measure of a given construct can be discriminated from theoretically unrelated constructs	The ABQ and MBI-GS scales show an adequate discrimination between the concepts of burnout and depression (see Cresswell and Eklund 2006)
Predictive validity	Informs the researcher whether or not an indicator predicts future events that are logically related to that construct	In establishing the predictive validity of the CART-Q, Jowett and Ntoumanis (2004) found that the measurement could predict the association between the closeness, co-orientation, and complementarity that exists within a coach–athlete relationship and the athlete's level of interpersonal satisfaction
Nomological validity	Indicates whether or not the construct of interest is part of a pattern of effects proposed by theory (Hagger and Chatzisarantis 2009).	Lonsdale *et al.* (2008) found that subscale scores on the behavioral regulation in sport questionnaire were correlated in the expected pattern with scores derived from measures of behavioral consequences.

If you intend to use an existing instrument (i.e. a published measure) in your research then you must describe the established *validity* and *reliability* scores obtained from past use of the instrument. Your goal here is to provide the reader with evidence from which to draw meaningful and useful inferences from scores on the instruments. In most cases it should be relatively straightforward to find instruments that have been heavily tested for *reliability* and *validity*. Indeed, authors often provide descriptions of such verifications in the methodology section of their research reports. Here it is possible to find figures that outline how close the measurement tools come to theoretically perfect validity and reliability (Locke *et al.* 1998). For example, the measurement of reliability which is typically provided by authors is called a reliability coefficient. These coefficients range from 1.00 (the highest score) to 0.00 (the lowest score). In fact, we would hope to see reliability coefficients of 0.9 and above for professionally developed instruments. So, the closer to 1.00 the coefficient, the more confident we can be regarding the ability of an instrument to collect data in a reliable manner. Depending on the nature of the data (i.e. nominal, ordinal, interval/ratio) you may also refer to previously reported measures of internal consistency (i.e. are the items' responses consistent across constructs?) or test–retest correlations (i.e. are scores stable between the first and second occasion of the instrument being administered?).

However, before using measures that have been developed and validated by other researchers it is important to evaluate whether the previous validity tests are appropriate and applicable to the context in which you intend to apply the measure (Hagger and Chatzisarantis 2009). That is, unless the previous validation tests were conducted in a similar context and with a sample with similar characteristics to that which is the focus of your investigation, then it would be dangerous to assume that the measure is valid for your study. For example, it would be inappropriate to apply measures that have been developed in researching adults to research involving children. As such, it is wise not to assume that instruments/measures may translate directly across contexts (Hagger and Chatzisarantis 2009). Instead, the researcher should evaluate previous tests of validity of self-report measures and determine whether these tests were conducted in a similar context and with a similar sample so one can more confidently generalize their findings to the target population. If researchers have any doubt over this matter then they should conduct their own tests of validity, an issue we will now consider.

Indeed, this issue is particularly pertinent if you intend to design a new instrument *or* if you wish to put together an instrument using components from several different measurements. If the latter example applies, you should indicate whether you have received permission to use any part of these instruments. If the instrument has been modified or combines components from several instruments then it is important to bear in mind that the original validity and reliability is unlikely to hold for the new instrument (see previous paragraph). In this case, the researcher must re-establish validity and reliability through a rigorous pilot testing process (for more details on this process see Moran *et al.* 2008). If you intend to proceed with this course of action then you should provide a rationale and outline plans for your pilot testing. This testing will help establish the content validity of the instrument in addition to improving the questions and format of the scale.

Reflections from the field

Learning to read and evaluate research papers is a skill, and like any other skill, it requires training, practice, and experience to master. Indeed, when I first started to read primary sources (e.g. journal articles) I found them almost incomprehensible. In particular, I remember feeling daunted by the vocabulary, concepts, and specialized jargon that ran throughout each section of the reports. But persistence pays off and eventually I developed an iterative strategy for reading scientific reports. This strategy involved skimming through the paper to find out roughly what it said, then looking up key topics or concepts in other sources (e.g. textbooks, reference books), before finally returning to the document with a new perspective to bear on the material. As you can imagine, this was a hugely difficult, frustrating, and time-consuming process. Initially, I found it extremely hard to make sense of the methodologies and research techniques presented in research reports – and by the way, that might still be the case for many researchers as they struggle to understand technical aspects of the results sections of empirical papers in specialized journals. However, I began to realize that there were a number of practical strategies I could use to improve my understanding of the material published in papers. One such strategy involved having resources at hand (e.g. research methods textbooks) to help me get to grips with certain terms relating to methodological, statistical, and analytical procedures. In addition, I found that on occasion it was easier to understand specific theoretical frameworks by reading review papers or book chapters in student textbooks. I found these sources a useful starting point as they provided an overview of a specific topic by introducing concepts in clear and easy-to-understand language because they summarized data and findings from a specific body of research.

Having developed a basic understanding of methodological and analytical procedures I learnt that there were a number of relatively simple indicators I could use to critically evaluate the degree of care with which a study was performed and with which the subsequent report was prepared. I took an important step at this stage by accessing books which could provide me with clear guidelines as to how I could go about this latter process. These texts reassured me that it was possible to glean useful information from research reports without possessing a wealth of technical knowledge or advanced training in research design and procedures. Reading books by authors such as Locke *et al.* (1998) helped me realize that I could develop my range of critical skills by learning to ask a series of basic questions at specific points in research reports where errors are most likely to occur. This approach meant that without deliberately trying to do so, I was becoming a critical reader of research by doing little more than asking some rather common-sense questions. For example, I learnt to ask whether or not a study fits into what is already known in a given field of inquiry and to ask what the reported results really mean. Eventually, I learnt to ask these questions as a matter of routine while I read my way through each report.

My own experiences in learning how to judge the quality of quantitative research studies were extremely challenging so I can easily understand why many undergraduate students may be completely overawed by their initial encounters with scientific reports. It is, however, worth bearing three important points in mind. For those new to coaching research, *first* you should remember that even scientists who are highly familiar with a specific research area might need to engage in multiple readings of a paper to reach an in-depth understanding of its findings and their significance. If experienced scientists occasionally struggle then there is no reason why you should get frustrated if you find it difficult to understand a research paper upon first reading. *Second*, at the undergraduate level you are not expected to be an expert on a wide range of theories or research techniques within a specific area of inquiry. Instead, your initial goal is to learn *how* to read and use research reports and *how* to identify sources of useful information that can help inform your own research project. If you can learn how to identify erroneous assumptions that may severely compromise the trust you can place in a study's findings then you will have made impressive progress indeed (see also Lilienfeld *et al.* 2010). Finally, remember, there is no such thing as a difficult skill – only an unpracticed one (Moran 2012). With these ideas in mind, we hope that you tackle the world of research with increased enthusiasm, and apply these lessons not only to your reading of scientific journal articles but also to the completion and write-up of your own research projects.

Reference

Adie, J. W., Duda, J. L. and Ntoumanis, N. (2012) 'Perceived coach-autonomy support, basic need satisfaction and the well- and ill-being of elite youth soccer players: A longitudinal investigation', *Psychology of Sport and Exercise*, 13: 51–9.

Cohen, J. (1988) *Statistical Power Analysis for the Behavioural Sciences* (2nd ed.), Hillsdale, NJ: Erlbaum.

Cozby, P. (2012) *Methods in Behavioural Research* (11th ed.), London: McGraw-Hill.

Cresswell, S. L. and Eklund, R. C. (2006) 'The convergent and divergent validity of burnout measures in sport: A multitrait-multimethod analysis', *Journal of Sports Sciences*, 24: 209–20.

Dunn, D. S. (2009) *The Practical Researcher: A Student Guide to Conducting Psychological Research* (2nd ed.), Chichester: Wiley Blackwell.

Felton, L. and Jowett, S. (2013) 'The mediating role of social environmental factors in the associations between attachment styles and basic needs satisfaction', *Journal of Sports Sciences*, 31: 618–28.

Hagger, M. S. and Chatzisarantis, N. L. D. (2009) 'Assumptions in research in sport and exercise psychology', *Psychology of Sport and Exercise*, 10: 511–19.

Ivarsson, I., Andersen, M. B., Johnson, U. and Lindwall, M. (2013) 'To adjust or not adjust: Nonparametric effect sizes, confidence intervals, and real-world meaning', *Psychology of Sport and Exercise*, 1: 97–102.

Jowett, S. and Ntoumanis, N. (2004) 'The coach–athlete relationship questionnaire (Cart-Q): Development and initial validation', *Scandinavian Journal of Medicine and Science in Sport*, 14: 245–57.

Kumar, R. (2010) *Research Methodology: A Step-by-Step Guide for Beginners*, London: Sage.

Lafrenière, M.-A. K., Jowett, S., Vallerand, R. J. and Carbonneau. N. (2011) 'Passion for coaching and the quality of the coach-athlete relationship: The mediating role of coaching behaviours', *Psychology of Sport and Exercise*, 12: 144–52.

Lilienfeld, S. O., Lynn, S. J., Namy, L. L. and Woolf, N. J. (2010) *Psychology: A Framework for Everyday Thinking*, New York: Pearson.

Locke, L. F., Silverman, S. J. and Spirduso, W. W. (1998) *Reading and Understanding Research*, California: Sage.

Lonsdale, C., Hodge, K. and Rose, E. A. (2008) 'The development of the behavioural regulation in sport questionnaire (BRSQ): Instrument development and initial validity evidence', *Journal of Sport and Exercise Psychology*, 30: 323–35.

Moran, A. (2012) *Sport and Exercise Psychology: A Critical Introduction* (2nd ed.), London: Routledge.

Moran, A., Guerin, S., Kirby, K. and Macintyre, T. (2008) *The Development and Validation of a Doping Attitudes and Behaviour Scale: Final Report to World Anti-Doping Agency*, Dublin: UCD, School of Psychology.

Murphy, K. R., Myors, B. and Wolach, A. (2009) *Statistical Power Analysis: A Simple and General Model for Traditional and Modern Hypotheses Tests* (3rd ed.), London: Routledge.

Thompson, B. (2002) 'What future quantitative social science research could look like: Confidence intervals for effect sizes', *Educational researcher*, 31: 25–32.

Part IV

Qualitative approaches to coaching research

15 Interviews

Laura Purdy

Introduction and overview

Research in sports coaching has traditionally been conducted from a bio-scientific perspective; recently, however, the dominance of this perspective has been challenged, resulting in the emergence of alternate methodologies and methods. As such, one method which has grown in popularity is the interview. Interviews have become increasingly utilized in research in sports coaching as they have potential for understanding and gaining a 'rich' insight into a person's perspective. Such a method has enabled researchers in sports coaching to develop a better understanding of *what* coaches do and *why*, *how* they interpret their work and their role, as well as how athletes and other key stakeholders (e.g. managers, agents, sport science support) understand the coaching process. On the surface interviewing appears to be relatively straightforward; however it is more than asking a few questions and receiving answers. Rather, by granting insight into people's opinions, feelings, emotions, experience, and the meaning they make of their experience, interviews are interactive and situation specific, possibly leading to unexpected as well as contradictory data that are produced and not simply collected. Therefore, the purpose of this chapter is to explore the multiple uses of interviews in coaching research.

Structured, semi-structured, and unstructured interviews

The way we use and design interviews is influenced by the nature of the study, the requirements of the methodology as well as the research question. Once these have been established, decisions can be made regarding aspects of interviews, that is, form, type, and frequency. A good starting point is to decide the *form* of interview that you will use to collect data; this chapter will focus on structured, semi-structured, and unstructured interviews. While these three forms have benefits and consequences, one might be more appropriate than another to employ in your data collection. For example, if your project requires a focused agenda, you may wish to use a structured interview approach. This form of interview consists of predetermined questions which do not change throughout the course of the study. That is, you would use the same questions in the same sequence for each participant (for an example of work using structured interviews see Gilbert *et al.* 2009). Building on this approach, you could also provide a prearranged list of possible answers from which the participant selects. In contrast, if you are looking for flexibility with the interview questions, semi-structured interviews might be more appropriate. Semi-structured interviews include pre-determined questions but also possess the flexibility for you to explore additional areas which may emerge throughout the discussion. Here, you would use an 'interview guide' (i.e. a plan for the interview) that outlines the main topics/questions of conversation. The phrasing of questions and the order in which the questions are asked are adaptable, allowing you to react to issues that emerge during the interview and not restrict the interview to a fixed agenda (for examples of studies employing semi-structured interviews, see Norman 2008; Rynne *et al.* 2010; Nash *et al.* 2011). Even more flexible is the unstructured interview. In this case, you would have some key areas to discuss, but the interview would be more spontaneous than the previous forms, with the emphasis placed on the natural flow of the interaction and the knowledge and experience of the researcher and participant.

When looking at research in coaching, one-to-one semi-structured interviews are popular; however, more than one approach can be used in data collection. For example, you could employ semi-structured interviews at the start of a project to obtain introductory information from the participants and for you to begin generating a rapport. As the project progresses, you could then use unstructured interviews to build on the information gathered in the introductory interviews as well as respond to new areas of interest which are gleaned from observations of training sessions or discussions with others (for examples see: Cushion and Jones 2006; Purdy and Jones 2011).

One-to-one interviews

A popular method in sports coaching research, one-to-one semi-structured interviews allow for an in-depth examination of an individual's attitudes, opinions, beliefs, and values with respect to a particular phenomenon. Given that their aim is to explore topics in depth, these interviews are time consuming, so studies using these interviews usually involve few participants. In a review of some recent publications which focused on sports coaches, the number of participants ranged from one person to twelve and ranged in duration from 45 to 135 minutes (for examples see: Norman 2008; Debanne and Fontayne 2009; Olusoga *et al.* 2009). There are several issues for you to consider before embarking on interviews. For example, if you are interested in interviewing elite women coaches, you would be limited to a small sample. You will also need to consider if you have access to these potential participants or to a 'gatekeeper' who can help you gain access. You may wish to start your data collection with a small number of participants and, if new information is still emerging following these conversations, you may need to recruit more participants until you feel that you have reached a saturation point (i.e. when 'new' information is not emerging) or if resources (i.e. time, money) dictate that you stop. Furthermore, depending on the type of project you are undertaking, you may wish to interview participants more than once to follow up on comments raised in the introductory interview or to explore additional areas.

Focus group interviews

In addition to one-to-one interviews, focus groups or 'group interviews' are also useful in data collection, either as the main method or in pilot studies, for instance, to explore ideas that you will be investigating further using another approach. While the form of the interview is the same (i.e. structured, semi-structured, or unstructured), focus groups involve a number of participants who provide a wide range of ideas, experiences, and understandings that you may not be able to 'capture' in individual interviews. Another difference results from the interaction that occurs within the focus group, as what is said in focus group interviews might differ from what is said in individual interviews. Hearing others discuss issues might spark new ideas, allowing the group to become more than 'a sum of its parts' (Krueger and Casey 2009: 19).

Similar to one-to-one interviews, focus groups can be structured, semi-structured, and unstructured. Focus groups should be considered if you are looking for a variety of ideas or feelings people have about a subject, exploratory studies in a new domain, and an understanding of differences in perspectives (i.e. athletes/players and coaches). In contrast, some suggest that focus groups are not appropriate if discussing sensitive information (i.e. it could be harmful to someone if shared). This has been disputed as, in some cases, group interviews have been useful in exploring sensitive topics (e.g. Frith 2000). The main concern for you, the researcher, is if sensitive information is to be discussed in a group setting, confidentiality cannot be guaranteed. Therefore, it is useful to remind the participants verbally and in writing (e.g. on the consent form) that it is important to respect the privacy of the other participants by not disclosing the information shared in the group with others.

In recent research involving coaches, focus groups have ranged in duration from 30 to 90 minutes and in size from three to twelve (for examples see: Gould *et al.* 2008; Knight and Harwood 2009). When considering how many participants to include in each group, consider the following: the size of the group should be small enough so that all participants have the opportunity to share their thoughts, yet the group should also be large enough for a variety of perspectives to emerge. In this way, too few participants might hamper sustaining a discussion while too large a group number might be difficult to facilitate. Despite size, some groups may be hard to engage while others might be highly involved. To account for this, your role in the focus group could be similar to that of facilitator or moderator in guiding the discussion and encouraging a variety of viewpoints on the topics (Kvale and Brinkmann 2009). In addition to creating an atmosphere where participants feel that they can express their viewpoint, you can intervene if some participants are dominating the discussion or others are not contributing.

In addition to the size of the focus group, as a researcher you will need to decide how many focus groups to employ in your study. As with one-to-one interviews, you may decide to conduct three to four focus groups and, if new information is still emerging following the first few group interviews, you may need to conduct additional groups until you feel that you have reached a saturation point. In a review of some recent publications which involved sports coaches, focus groups ranged from five to seventeen (for examples see: Wiersma and Sherman 2005; Gould *et al.* 2008; Knight and Harwood 2009). However, in the case of an undergraduate project, the number of focus groups may be less than five as the data collection is often small-scale and largely influenced by time and budget.

Communication technologies

While interviews have primarily been face-to-face, telephone and communication technologies such as Skype are also being used. The choice to use telephone or Skype is usually due to limited resources (i.e. access, time, expenses), making face-to-face interviews impossible. While telephone interviews/focus groups are widely exercised, there are mixed responses to their use. Concerns have been raised relating to the lack of visual cues such as the participant's body language and level of engagement in the process, which may impact the depth and quality of the information that is shared. Some of the limitations of telephone interviews can be overcome by using virtual communication technologies such as Skype. Skype interviews are gaining in popularity due to ease of use, low cost, video option, and ease of recording. For useful tips for facilitating focus groups via telephone or Skype see Krueger and Casey (2009).

Applied issues and considerations

Developing questions

Interview questions are usually designed in light of the literature that you have read about the topic. Here, the literature will assist you in deciding the themes and/or areas that you would like to discuss with the participants. When developing interview questions, it is worth noting that most interviews begin with introductory questions or icebreakers which are aimed at providing background information as well as helping the participant and the interviewer become familiar with the process. This is followed by the easiest questions, gradually increasing the difficulty as the interview progresses. This approach is underpinned by the belief that, over the course of an interview, a rapport develops between the participant and yourself, resulting in the participant being less reluctant to answer (the importance of rapport will be discussed later in the chapter). In addition to considering the order of the questions, it is advisable to use open-ended questions as much as possible. In contrast to closed questions (i.e. those that elicit a yes/no response), these will provide the participant with flexibility to decide the direction of his/her response. For example, 'Tell me about what you expect from yourself when coaching in a high performance environment'. Follow up questions such as 'You mentioned that your behaviour changes very close to competition, could you tell me a bit more about that?', or 'could you give me an example of this', will encourage the participant to continue the conversation. Another useful way to probe for more information is by staying silent. Often silence will prompt the participant to expand upon their line of thinking. Rather than feeling as though you have to fill every lapse in conversation with a question or comment, your silence may encourage the participant to elaborate.

As mentioned previously in relation to semi-structured and unstructured interviews, sometimes participants raise topics that may not directly relate to your research. Here you will need to use your judgment whether you will intervene and ask a question that will redirect the participant to the topic. While tangents could provide new avenues of exploration, sometimes after the interview you will look at the transcript and think 'there is nothing relevant!' Whilst it may feel as though you wasted time (yours and the participant's) by doing the interview, it may be useful to revisit the data at a later date. This could lead to a new theme/section/discussion/project that you had not previously considered.

In preparing for one-to-one or focus group interviews, you will need to consider how many questions you will ask in the course of the conversation/discussion. In semi-structured interviews and focus groups, the aim is to gain an in-depth insight in the topic. As such, you might only draw upon 8–10 questions, but you will need to ask follow-up questions in an effort to probe for more information. The key for the researcher is to listen to the responses and respond with an appropriate question, whether it is a follow-up question which probes for more information or one that moves the discussion to a new area. In developing your research questions, try to avoid wording that may be overly complicated, questions that may contain more than one question, or those lead the participant to the response. For examples and assistance in developing questions, see Kvale (2007), Krueger and Casey (2009), Kvale and Brinkmann (2009) and King and Horrocks (2010).

When developing your interview questions, it is important to consider 'who' will be participating in the interview. That is, if interviewing children, you will need to prepare questions which are age appropriate. In all cases it is always useful to conduct a pilot, or practice, interview as testing the questions might draw attention to issues which you may not have considered. Here, pilot interviews will help you to refine your questions and identify any flaws or problematic areas with the interview which you can rectify before beginning collecting data. It is useful to conduct pilot interviews with people who are similar to the participants in your study.

Where to conduct an interview/focus group?

The context and setting of the interview is also deserving of your consideration as different settings may change the dynamics, direction, and content of the interview (Sin 2003; Manderson *et al.* 2006). While focus groups may be limited to certain venues due to size and resource requirements (i.e. large tables, video cameras), when conducting individual interviews it is worth asking the participant whether he or she has a preferred location for the interview. For instance, conducting an interview in a coffee shop might provide a more 'neutral', less formal setting; however, due to confidentiality issues arising from the interview being held in public, it might limit what information is discussed. Furthermore, if recording the interview, the background noise generated in the coffee shop may distort the conversation. In contrast, a formal environment, such as the researcher's office, may impact upon the participant's ease with the process. This may result in the participant being reluctant to share too much information (for an example, see 'Reflections from the field', later in this chapter). An interview conducted in the participant's home might result in the participant being more comfortable, but it is important that you check with your university regarding the safety procedures in place should you wish to conduct a one-to-one interview off-campus.

Recording interviews/focus groups

To ensure a complete and accurate record of the data, it is common practice for researchers to record interviews/focus groups (with the participant's consent). Recording the interview would enable you to concentrate on the topic and dynamics of the interview and also provides an opportunity for you to review and re-listen to the dialogue (Kvale and Brinkmann 2009). The recordings can then be transcribed (i.e. the oral interview is converted into text). Although audio recordings are the most popular method of recording interviews and focus groups, video recording can be very useful in focus groups to help identify speakers and allow an analysis of interpersonal interaction. Digital recording equipment is popular as files are easily downloadable, although video recordings might limit where group interviews can be conducted. Also, the prospect of being videoed might not appeal to all participants and they may not want to be recorded. In this case, you could ask if each participant is comfortable being recorded via dictaphone instead; however, if the participant is still uncomfortable with the prospect of being recorded, the next option is for you to keep a written record of the key points that are said throughout the conversation. A summary of points can then be presented to the participant to check for accuracy.

When recording interviews/focus groups, it is important to consider how an audio or video recording device may impact upon the interview process. To help the participant feel more at ease with the recording device, it is useful for you to make him/her aware of the confidentiality of their participation, and what will happen to the recordings (i.e. where the recordings will be stored, who will have access to the recordings and their transcripts, how the transcripts will be anonymized, participant access to their transcript) (King and Horrocks 2010; see Chapters 20 and 21). At this point, it is also useful for you to show the participant how to stop the recording, either physically or by informing you if s/he would prefer to discuss something 'off the record' (Amis 2005). Another method to help the participant feel more at ease with the process is to give the recording device to the participant to place in a location (i.e. on a table) where he or she feels most comfortable. While the emphasis here has been on making the participant feel at ease, it is worth noting that you also might be quite nervous for the first few interviews, but the nerves tend to subside with practice.

Following the recording of the interview/focus groups is the process of transcribing. As mentioned previously, transcribing involves making a written record of the oral or video interview/focus group. To structure an interview transcript, it is useful to have the participant's name or pseudonym, the topic, date, and place (Minichiello *et al.* 1992). Some people prefer to double space the text so there is room to make notes/comments during the analysis. Most interviews are transcribed verbatim, which includes 'the actual words spoken by your informants, however repetitive, slangy or ungrammatical' (Riley 1990: 25). This includes pauses, hesitations, silences, laughter, 'ums' and 'ahs', and remarks such as, 'you know' and 'like' which not only bring you closer to the data, but are also important should you be employing discourse or conversation analysis (King and Horrocks 2010).

While the quality of voice recognition software has been improving, it is difficult to find a program that is able to accurately capture the entire conversation. The traditional approach of manually transcribing an interview is time consuming; one hour of interview can take you approximately five hours to transcribe. A combination of voice recognition software and traditional transcribing might be less time consuming as the software could create the scaffolding of the interview, leaving you to listen to the recording in order to review, edit, and add the missing information. After the transcript is created, in the case of a one-to-one interview, it is given to the participant to not only confirm the accuracy of the conversation but also to confirm the transcribed words 'capture' the meaning of what was expressed. At this point, the participant may also edit aspects that, with hindsight, he/she does not wish to reveal. Returning the transcript to the participant is an important step as it recognizes that the interview transcript is the property of the participant and affords him/her the right to negotiate what information is made public (King and Horrocks 2010).

Ethical issues

While ownership of the data is one issue, interviews are shrouded in ethical issues (see Chapter 10). For example, during the course of the interviews, sensitive topics may have emerged. Here it is important to consider issues of confidentiality in relation to people/institutions that may have been mentioned. This can be done by removing names or masking the information in the transcript which might reveal the identity of the interviewee (Kvale and Brinkmann 2009). In addition to sensitive topics, the occupation, sport or club name might reveal the identity of the participant. In this case pseudonyms (i.e. an alternate name) can be used or the information can be excluded to ensure the participant's anonymity. Another ethical issue that emerges following the interview arises from returning the interview transcript to the participant. The issues here are twofold: first, some may experience a shock when receiving the transcript as the oral discussion may not appear as 'polished' as a written piece of work (Kvale and Brinkmann 2009). In this case you could provide a letter with the transcript explaining the differences between oral and written expression. The second ethical issue with returning the transcript to the participant relates to the issue of 'burden'. Often the interview transcripts are quite lengthy and asking someone to read and confirm the accuracy of forty pages of text could be considered to be burdensome. Alternatively, providing a summary of the main areas of conversation might not give the participant a big enough picture of the data. It is worth consulting the participant regarding the preferred method.

Reflections from the field

As a researcher, it is important to consider how your gender, age, ethnic background, occupation, socioeconomic status, and appearance impact upon the direction and content of the interview. This reflexivity is essential as ignoring social differences neglects the fact that the respective social roles always shape the interview process (DiCicco-Bloom and Crabtree 2006). For example, when conducting research in an elite rowing program, I needed to consider how being the only female in a men's program, being of a similar age to the participants, and being from another country may have impacted upon the data (see Purdy and Jones 2013).

   In addition to my gender, age, and nationality, my familiarity with the context has also impacted upon the data to which I have been privy. Having previous experience in rowing programs may have afforded me some leverage. For example, in an interview with a top-level coach, I noticed that the participant was quite guarded in his comments. He was providing limited responses to the questions and did not appear to be comfortable with the topic of discussion. Sensing his discomfort, I changed the topic of conversation, taking time to ask him about some current issues that were relevant to his role within the sport. I believe that the change in topic allowed us to share some 'common ground', developing a rapport which resulted in a more relaxed conversation. Following our initial discussion about the sport and various political issues that were impacting upon it at the time, the participant became more relaxed and candid in his discussion. Rather than the short, elusive response that he had started with, he provided more explanation, illustrations leading to 'richer' data. Consequently, the interview became informative and useful in terms of the wider project. Whilst in this case, being an 'insider' in the context helped, some would argue that over-familiarity may be problematic. As such, one concern is that during the interview you might skip over things that you assume everyone knows and not probe for in-depth explanations regarding the topic. Also, because you are an insider, participants may be hesitant to comment about specific people or incidents. At the start of the interview, it is useful to remind the participant about anonymity/confidentiality and what will happen to the data. I have also found it helpful to remind the participant that my role is not to 'judge' them, rather to get a better understanding of the topic in question.

In contrast to being an 'insider' in the process, being an 'outsider' has also been useful, as participants may feel they can 'offload' their thoughts on the topic as speaking to someone who is not involved in the area may provide a sense of security. The important message here is to reflect on the interview process, consider how your background, position, and knowledge of the area impacts upon the data. Such reflections will enable you to be more in tune with the 'realities' of the experience and will provide you with a richer understanding of the research process.

References

Amis, J. (2005) 'Interviewing for case study research', in: D. L. Andrews, D. S. Mason and M. L. Silk (eds) *Qualitative Methods in Sports Studies*, Oxford: Berg, 104–38.

Cushion, C. and Jones, R. L. (2006) 'Power, discourse and symbolic violence in professional youth soccer: The case of Albion football club', *Sociology of Sport Journal*, 23: 142–61.

Debanne, T. and Fontayne, P. (2009) 'A study of a successful experienced elite handball coach's cognitive process in competitive situations', *International Journal of Sports Science & Coaching*, 4(1): 1–16.

DiCicco-Bloom, B. and Crabtree, B. F. (2006) 'The qualitative research interview', *Medical Education*, 40(4): 314–21.

Frith, H. (2000) 'Focusing on sex: using focus groups in sex research', *Sexualities*, 3(3): 275–97.

Gilbert, W., Lichtenwaldt, L., Gilbert, J., Zelezny, L. and Côté, J. (2009) 'Development profiles of successful high school coaches', *International Journal of Sports Science & Coaching*, 4(3): 415–31.

Gould, D., Lauer, L., Rolo, C., Jannes, C. and Pennisi, N. (2008) 'The role of parents in tennis success: Focus group interviews with junior coaches', *The Sport Psychologist*, 22: 18–37.

King, N. and Horrocks, C. (2010) *Interviews in Qualitative Research*, London: Sage.

Knight, C. J. and Harwood, C. G. (2009) 'Exploring parent-related coaching stressors in British tennis: A developmental investigation', *International Journal of Sports Science & Coaching*, 4(4): 545–65.

Krueger, R. A. and Casey, M. A. (2009) *Focus Groups: A Practical Guide for Applied Research* (4th ed.), London: Sage.

Kvale, S. (2007) *Doing Interviews*, London: Sage.

Kvale, S. and Brinkmann, S. (2009) *Interviews* (2nd ed.), London: Sage.

Manderson, L., Bennett, E. and Andajani-Sutjahjo, S. (2006) 'The social dynamics of the interview: Age, class and gender', *Qualitative Health Research*, 16: 1317–34.

Minichiello, C. V., Aroni, R., Timewell, E. and Alexander, L. (1992) *In-depth Interviewing: Researching People*, London: Longman Cheshire.

Nash, C. S., Sproule, J. and Horton, P. (2011) 'Excellence in coaching: The art and skill of elite practitioners', *Research Quarterly for Exercise and Sport*, 82(2), 229: 38.

Norman, L. (2008) 'The UK coaching system is failing women coaches', *International Journal of Sports Science & Coaching*, 3(4): 447–67.

Olusoga, P., Butt, J., Hays, K. and Maynard, I. W. (2009) 'Career development of expert coaches', *Journal of Applied Sport Psychology*, 21: 442–59.

Purdy, L. and Jones, R. L. (2011) 'Choppy waters: Elite rowers' perceptions of coaching', *Sociology of Sport Journal*, 28(3): 329–46.

——(2013) 'Changing personas and evolving identities: The contestation and re-negotiation of researcher roles in field work', *Sport, Education and Society*, 18(3): 292–310.

Riley, J. (1990) *Getting the Most from your Data: A Handbook of Practical Ideas on how to Analyse your Qualitative Data*, Bristol: Technical and Educative Services Ltd.

Rynne, S. B., Mallett, C. J. and Tinning, R. (2010) 'Workplace learning of high performance sports coaches', *Sport, Education and Society*, 15(3): 315–30.

Sin, C. (2003) 'Interviewing in "place": The socio-spatial construction of interview data', Area, 35(3): 305–12.

Wiersma, L. D. and Sherman, C. P. (2005) 'Volunteer youth sport coaches' perspectives of coaching education/certification and parental codes of conduct', *Research Quarterly for Exercise and Sport*, 76(3): 324–38.

16 Ethnography

Christopher Cushion

Introduction and overview

Bourdieu insisted that we should 'encounter the social' (Bourdieu 2000: 50), rather than reassemble the social, and in completing the 'sociological picture' should move closer to the site of social practice and production (Bourdieu 2004; Turnbull and Antalffy 2009). Encountering coaching in this way has led to the recognition that it is a complex social phenomenon, and more than a benign linear process (Cushion and Jones 2012). In developing a more sophisticated understanding of coaching as a problematic social process, more interpretive approaches and methodologies have been adopted. However, there remains a quantitative monopoly on the study of sport, with much policy decided on survey data, and the most cited research in coaching undertaken with quantitative positivist methodologies. That said, coaching research has without doubt grasped and applied qualitative methods (see Chapters 15, 19, 20, 21). However, there is an over-reliance on a singular methodological perspective (Culver *et al.* 2003), with interviewing appearing to be the foundation of qualitative research in coaching. Typically interviews are 'one-off' and are usually structured in some way (Culver *et al.* 2003). There are obvious limitations to these methods, not least that one-off interviews cannot provide a complete examination of the topic of interest, suggesting a need for more methodological diversity (Krane and Baird 2005).

While there maybe more qualitative methods used to research coaching, there is significantly less detailed study of the particularities of coaching, and little attention paid to the social and cultural aspects of experiences in coaching (MacPhail 2004; Cushion and Jones 2012). Therefore, the purpose of this chapter is to explore some of the assumptions and methods employed in ethnography and examine its use in sport-related research and specifically in coaching-related studies. The aim is to understand something of ethnography's utility in researching coaching and offer a remedy to qualitative, but arguably 'thin', one-off cross-sectional interview research. The few coaching specific studies are referred to, but throughout the chapter will examine my perspectives and experiences of researching coaching within an ethnographic framework.

What is ethnography?

Ethnography can be understood as a 'picture of a way of life of some identifiable group of people' (Wolcott 1990: 188), which involves an ongoing attempt to place specific encounters, events, and understandings into a fuller, more meaningful context (Tedlock 2000). Ethnography is described as an umbrella term (Krane and Baird 2005), as a tool (MacPhail 2004), and as both a process and a product (Wolcott 1990; Tedlock 2000) because ethnographers' lives are embedded within their field experiences. Indeed, this insider's perspective 'is instrumental to understanding and accurately describing situations and behaviours ... and is crucial to an understanding of why people think and act in the different ways they do' (Fetterman 1989: 30).

Arguably, it is all of these things, but however described there are a number of basic constituents of ethnography (Hammersley and Atkinson 1983; Lincoln and Guba 1985). The aim of ethnography is to understand the culture of a particular group from the perspective of the group members (Wolcott 1995; Tedlock 2000) and as a result requires the researcher to be immersed within the context over a prolonged period of time. As such it is a field-based methodology. Such immersion enables the capturing of routine everyday activity of participants, the hierarchies involved, understanding the meaning of activities from the participants' point of view, and going beyond thin surface appearances to produce 'thick' description (Wolcott 1990; MacPhail 2004). Regular, in-depth, and prolonged contact with a context and its people is an expectation of ethnography, providing the researcher with the recognition of routine and repeating practices, cyclical or seasonal processes, and the complex patterning of social practice (MacPhail 2004).

A key assumption therefore is that by entering into close and relatively prolonged interaction with coaches and athletes in their every-day lives (becoming an insider), I can understand the beliefs, motivations, and behaviors of the participants better than by using any other approach. Indeed, this insider's perspective 'is instrumental to understanding and accurately describing situations and behaviours ... and is crucial to an understanding of why people think and act in the different ways they do' (Fetterman 1989: 30). To understand highly distinctive cultural realities requires looking at them from the inside, thus representing reality structured in all its layers of social meaning (Woods 1986). Time in a context also enables me to build rapport with participants and to grasp an understanding of language and similar experiences (Cushion and Jones 2006, 2012). These descriptions of ethnography offer more than one-off interviewing for producing a 'sociological picture' *of* coaching but its application *to* coaching remains limited to a handful of studies.

Why ethnography?

Despite its growth coaching research still pays insufficient attention to coaches' and athletes' thoughts and feelings, and has not captured the subtlety and scope of the coaching process in specific contexts, nor of the impact of context on practice. Moreover, when investigating coaching I want to ensure that the data obtained avoids reducing complex social responses and behaviors to a maze of statistical calculations. This means that my paradigmatic assumptions inform my methodological choices. As a result, within an interpretive or critical paradigm informing my assumptions about coaching I am looking for a naturalistic methodology to produce, not only the kind of insight that I'm looking for, but add to existing knowledge about the coaching process *in context*. The coaching environment is so complex that a single-method approach can only yield limited and sometimes misleading data. Therefore, a combination of methods produces a more comprehensive understanding. Intuitively, it makes sense to look at the coaching process and the practical coaching context from differing perspectives, not only methodologically, but also from the perspective of the chief 'members', namely the coaches, the athletes, and other 'stake holders'. Utilizing ethnography to this end means 'different roles within a setting can be explored in order to get access to different kinds of data, as well as to acquire some sense of the various kinds of bias characteristic of each' (Hammersley and Atkinson 1983: 97).

Ethnographic research in sport

A number of studies have been conducted in sporting situations utilizing ethnography and these include, for example, Wacquant (1992, 1995) (boxing), Bolin (1997) (bodybuilding), Klein (1997) (baseball), Bricknell (1999) (sailing), Sands (1999) (American football), MacPhail (2004) (athletics). Despite its obvious utility as a methodology, ethnography has had only limited applications to coaching. This could be for a number of reasons, for example the access required for ethnography can be problematic to achieve, particularly in performance or elite sport contexts. Ethnography by definition is long-itudinal and therefore time consuming, and this may not fit demands to produce 'quick fix' research and data. Ethnography's relative absence could also reflect the disciplinary informed focus of researchers investigating coaching and its related issues where ethnography is not an established, understood, or even accepted methodology. Lastly, ethnography aligns readily with assumptions that coaching is a subjective, social, and constructed phenomenon. These assumptions run counter to an objective, singular, and unproblematic stance taken by many that place coaching exclusively within the individual and therefore have a prescriptive set of methods for researching it.

Ethnographic sports research includes topics such as examining talent development (Christensen *et al.* 2011), experiences in youth sport (MacPhail *et al.* 2003), the coaching process and social reproduction (Cushion and Jones 2006, 2012), and the coach–athlete relationship (Poczwardowski *et al.* 2002). However, only Cushion and Jones identify coaching as the 'dependent variable' within their work. Again, this reflects something of the issues that impact the use of ethnography as a methodology. That said, ethnography has uncovered detail about coaching that would not have been found by other means. For example, MacPhail (2004) identified coaching practices that were deemed to be time wasting or detrimental to the development of athletes and was 'shocked with the level of prominence of similar incidents reoccurring' (MacPhail 2004: 243). While Poczwardowski *et al.* (2002) demonstrated that coaches and players both inherit and personally author their own coaching contexts, highlighting the problematic and individualistic nature of the relationships involved. Poczwardowski *et al.* (2002) support the notion that the coaching process, rather than being simplistic and cyclical, comprises a set of reciprocal interactions between the athlete, coach, and context; a notion further developed by Cushion and Jones (2006, 2012), who demonstrate coaching's contribution to the production and reproduction of social structures within a social and political milieu.

Applied issues and considerations

Ethnography employs multiple methods, such as participant observation and interviewing, but can also include text, photographs, or questionnaire data (Krane and Baird 2005). Through these multiple methods researchers attempt to identify individual meaning to everyday activities (LeCompte and Schensul 1999). Thus extensive fieldwork and intense familiarity with a setting results in a comprehensive, descriptively detailed, conceptually framed understanding of a social group (Krane and Baird 2005; Lofland 1996; Tedlock 2000). Within an ethnographic framework, I have typically used participant observation, individual semi-structured and unstructured interviews, focus group interviews, and document analysis. Through utilizing ethnography I have come to believe that it is impossible to understand coaching as the complex interaction of coach, athlete, and context without an understanding of the social norms and culture that encompass them.

Fieldwork remains the central methodology in ethnography and involves some form of observation. Participant observation is 'an omnibus field strategy' (Patton 1990: 206) in that it 'simultaneously combines interviewing of respondents and informants, direct participation observation and introspection' (Denzin 1978: 183). Indeed, Adler and Adler (1994: 389) characterize observation as 'the *fundamental*[1] base of all research methods in the social and behavioural sciences' (Adler and Adler 1994: 389). While Lofland and Lofland (1984) define participant observation as 'the process in which an investigator establishes a many-sided and relatively long-term relationship with a human association in its natural setting for the purposes of developing a scientific understanding of that association' (Lofland and Lofland 1984: 12). There is simply no substitute for direct experience through participant observation, therefore the importance of the researcher's self as 'human instrument' (Lincoln and Guba 1985) is consistently highlighted throughout the literature (Hammersley and Atkinson 1983).

As the research instrument I am trying to describe the setting observed, the activities that take place in that setting, the people that participate in those activities, and the meanings of what was observed from the perspective of those observed. Direct personal contact with, and observations of coaches, players, and stakeholders in context has several advantages. First, I am better able to understand the context within which the coaching process operates. Understanding the context and its inherent processes is essential to gaining a holistic perspective. Second, observational fieldwork also offers me the opportunity to see things that may routinely escape conscious awareness among participants. In addition, direct observation allows me to learn things about the coaching process, as well as coach and player behaviors, that participants may have been unwilling to talk about, or contradict in interview[2] (Cushion and Jones 2012).

When engaging in ethnography in full-time coaching contexts I have tried to be involved for a season including training sessions and games and pre-season. Typically, I observe between two and four days of each week, largely depending on the games, training and other schedules. A distinguishing feature of an observational strategy is that, to some extent, I am a participant in the setting being studied. The extent of participation is a continuum that varies from complete immersion as a full participant to complete separation from the setting as a spectator (Patton 1990). There is a great deal of variation along the continuum between these two extremes and the extent of participation can change over time. In investigating coaching I never actively coached, my participation usually involves assisting in organizational matters, for example, placing out markers for the boundaries of practices and assisting the coach with the organization of equipment. More often than not I am an observer (see Christensen *et al.* 2011 as an example of more active participation in the coaching context).

During observations I produce comprehensive written field-notes from observation and transcripts from audio taped sources. All field-notes are descriptive, dated, and record key items such as: where the observation took place, who was present, what the physical setting was, what social interactions occurred, and what activities took place. Subject to agreement on gaining access, I openly take extensive notes of the events at which I am present. Immediately following those sessions I go back over the notes to fill in any missing detail and check on the comprehensiveness of the observation. Often, usually during the evening following observation, I find myself recalling instances or events or linking these with remarks made. I always have a notebook on hand to continually add detail to observations. Thus, it is the field observations that provide the focus and basis for further data collection and additional methods. Taken together, these diverse sources of information and data give a fuller picture of the wider context of the coaching process.

Patton (1990) suggests that it is impossible to expect to have the same degree of closeness to, or distance from, each group or faction within the research setting. I have found that during the course of projects my relationship with coaches often changes. I would suggest that this is often very much a two-way process. Other stakeholders react to my presence to varying degrees, with some for example taking an active interest in my work to showing no interest. Initially, in a coaching context I have concerns over relational rejection. In the words of Gans (1982) I often lack 'the personal security to banish rejection fears to feel free to observe fully and to take in as much data as possible' (Gans 1982: 58). As a result, initially, I am very neutral when asked for an opinion, but later on in the fieldwork, once assured that my view is genuinely being sought and not some kind of test, I feel happier expressing an opinion about a given situation. In the early stages of the fieldwork I generally agree or remain non-committal, and, in some instances keep negative opinions to myself, in effect withholding the truth (see also MacPhail 2004). Of course this presents ethical issues both professional and personal (Hammersley and Atkinson 1983). But as I am a researcher seeking to secure long-term acceptance in a context, the long-term research interests take precedence over such issues. Indeed, I am aware of the gate-keeping power and potential of informants; they could demolish my research plans if I overstep the relational bounds in play.

It has been agreed that an observer's presence, after a while, ceases to be novel enough to be disruptive (Angrosino and Mays de Perez 2000). Certainly, I aim to be able to move around the context and interact with respondents who learn that I am someone who can be 'trusted'. Indeed, improved relationships often means that my opinion is asked more and more, and this adds to the development of a good rapport. Acceptance in a context can manifest itself in different ways. My coaching experience enables me to be well versed in the complexity and details of the sub-cultural language and 'shop talk' and, therefore, can be included in the range of discussions between the coaches. My own biographical experiences of the coaching culture can stimulate and increase the feeling of insider relational resonance (Hobbs 1988; Parker 1996). It is upon this basis of mutual commonality that I try to build more meaningful relationships with coaches.

In developing relationships in the field I have frequently and actively cultivated what Patton (1990) describes as a key informant. The key informant is used as a source of information about what I, as the observer, am unable to experience, as well as a source of explanation for events that I have actually witnessed. Selected carefully the key informants can be particularly knowledgeable and articulate and provide insight useful in helping understanding of events. Further, they can yield information regarding activity to which I do not have direct access. I am, however, ever mindful that the information obtained from a key informant represents his or her perception, rather than any objective truth. As a result, data from the key informant are clearly specified as such in field-notes.

Hammersley and Atkinson (1995) note that there may be a danger of 'over-rapport'. They describe this at two levels. First, an over-identification with one group preventing social mobility, such that relationships, within a setting, become impaired. This has happened to me to a certain extent, my relationship with coaches resulting in me having some distance from players. This distance has tended to evolve rather than being any conscious decision on my part. This has been due to my association with the coaches as 'one of them'. Attempting to cultivate good relations with the coaches, inevitably, means that I associate with them the most (talking with them, eating with them, and so on). This positions me squarely in the 'staff camp'. My symbolic behavior, and arguably, in the players' eyes, over-rapport with the coaches, can impact on the players' attitudes toward me. The second and perhaps more serious level of 'over-rapport' is where in the field I could over-identify with the respondents' perspectives and miss or misunderstand what is being observed. This would mean my biased view becoming a prejudiced one. I have dealt with this in a number of ways, essentially a combination of methodological rigor and trying to maintain a more or less marginal position. Because of my biography I am, perhaps, over sensitive to the dangers of 'over-rapport'. I think carefully about my relationship with respondents, sometimes turning down offers to spend time with them away from coaching sessions. I try to maintain a relationship poised between stranger and friend (Everhart 1977).

As the examples suggest, these issues are not abstract theoretical concerns, but real, practical issues concerning my role in the research process. It is important to note that reflexivity is one of the central elements of ethnographic activity and signifies the researcher's part in the social world being investigated and that 'subjects' responses to the presence of the researcher and the researchers response to the context, are as valuable as any other aspect of the study' (Hodgson 2000: 3). So while this can be viewed as a strength, research conducted through ethnography depends largely upon the interpretations and assumptions of the researcher, and familiar settings may present problems in suspending preconceptions (Hammersley and Atkinson 1983). It is impossible to stay detached from those under study, and it is from these issues that criticisms of ethnography chiefly stem. These revolve around notions of accounts being subjective and idiosyncratic, and the danger that prolonged exposure in the field might lead to losing perspective and becoming blind to the peculiarities under investigation, so called 'going native'.

Reflections from the field

It is important to recognize that research conducted using ethnography is contaminated by social presence (Patton 1990) in that the data collected does not somehow naturally occur without being mediated by the researcher's theoretical concerns and biography (May 1999). However, directly experiencing and understanding reality (Bryman 1988) is enhanced by considering how I am affected by the social scene, what goes on within it, and how the coaches and players act within and interpret their social situations (Patton 1990). Furthermore, being part of the social world which we study 'is not a matter of methodological commitment it is an existential fact' (Hammersley and Atkinson 1983: 15). My own cultural equipment is therefore used reflexively to understand social action in context. In effect, as Angrosino and Mays de Perez (2000) contend, because I am a member/observer I am, therefore, an artifact of the very situation of cultural displacement that I'm studying. Often it is not, in fact, possible to resolve the tension between what I am and what I have to become in the field. Rather than fret about the tension, it is better to 'find some practical use' (Wolf 1996: 217) for it. Is observational objectivity either desirable or feasible as a goal? The 'practical use' of my presence in research is best explained because my coaching background influences and shapes the research process. In sport this background is in fact something of a research imperative. Failure to meet a degree of experiential criteria would undoubtedly limit access to the inner sanctums of clubs and the coaches' worlds, thus limiting access not only to subsequent participants, but valuable data. Furthermore, my coaching background often offsets my 'academic' status, important in an environment where anyone with a university background can be termed a 'boffin' or 'Prof' or worse! Moreover, I feel it enhances my relationships with coaches and prevents any feelings of aloofness and distance.

In an example from one of my participants, 'Greg' (Cushion and Jones 2006), my presence certainly affected the way he approached his work, although his manner and behavior, acquired over many years, were not affected by me, as these remarks may suggest:

> 'I think that having you here has kept me on me toes, I knew you would be watching so I tried a bit harder, I thought oh oh, that cunt's gonna be watching me again!'

Probing this remark further:

> 'I'd come in see you there and get me session down on paper, you know, look like I was organized'.

Finally, ethnography has much to offer the development and understanding of coaching through providing insight into interaction and complexity *in situ*. It provides a set of methods to highlight the problematic, interrelated, and interdependent nature of relationships that construct and influence coaching. While it is not a panacea for all coaching methodology ills, or capable of providing a 'silver bullet' of data, ethnography offers a set of methods and underlying assumptions that counter simplistic, reductionist, and unproblematic approaches.

Notes

1 Not interviewing, my emphasis added.
2 That said, interviewing remains a valuable part of a multi-method approach, and is discussed in detail in Chapter 15.

References

Adler, P. A. and Adler, P. (1994) 'Observational techniques', in N. K. Denzin and Y. S. Lincoln (eds) *Handbook of Qualitative Research*, Thousand Oaks, CA: Sage, 377–92.

Angrosino, M.V. and Mays de Perez, K. A. (2000) 'Rethinking observation: From method to context', in N.K. Denzin and Y.S. Lincoln (eds) *Handbook of Qualitative Research* (2nd ed.), London: Sage, 673–702.

Bolin, A. (1997) 'Flex appeal, food and fat', in P. Moore (ed.) *Building Bodies*, New Brunswick, NJ: Rutgers University Press, 184–208.

Bourdieu, P. (2000) *Pascalian Meditations*, Cambridge: Polity Press.

——(2004) *Science of Science and Reflexivity*, Chicago: University of Chicago Press.

Bricknell, L. (1999) 'The trouble with feelings: Gender, sexualities and power in gender regime of competitive sailing', *Journal of Sport and Social Issues* 23(4): 421–38.

Bryman, A. (1988) *Doing Research in Organisations*, London: Routledge.

Christensen, M. K., Laursen, D. N. and Sorensen, J. K. (2011) 'Situated learning in youth elite football: A case study among talented male under-18 football players', *Physical Education and Sport Pedagogy*, 16(2): 163–78.

Culver, D. M., Gilbert, W. D. and Trudel, P. (2003) 'A decade of qualitative research in sport psychology journals: 1990–99', *The Sport Psychologist*, 17: 1–15.

Cushion, C. J. and Jones, R. L. (2006) 'Power, discourse and symbolic violence in professional youth soccer: The case of Albion FC', *Sociology of Sport Journal*, 23(2): 142–61.

——(2012) 'A Bourdieusian analysis of cultural reproduction: Socialisation and the "hidden curriculum" in professional football', *Sport Education & Society*: DOI:10.1080/13573322.2012.666966.

Denzin, N. K. (1978) *The Research Act* (2nd ed.), Chicago: Aldine.

Everhart, R. B. (1977) 'Between stranger and friend: Some consequences of long-term field work in schools', *American Educational Research Journal*, 14: 1–15.

Fetterman, D. (1989) *Ethnography: Step by Step*, London: Sage.

Gans, H. (1982) 'The participant observer as a human being: Observations on the personal aspects of fieldwork', In R. G. Burgess (ed.) *Field Research: A Sourcebook and Field Manual*, London: Allen & Unwin, 56–61.

Hammersley, M. and Atkinson, P. (1983) *Ethnography: Principles and Practice*, London: Routledge.

——(1995) *Ethnography: Principles and Practice* (2nd ed.), London: Routledge.

Hobbs, D. (1988) *Doing the Business*, Oxford: Clarendon.

Hodgson, I. (2000) 'Ethnography and healthcare: Focus on nursing [25 paragraphs]', *Forum Qualitative Sozialforschung/Forum: Qualitative Social Research* 1(1): http://www.qualitative-research.net/fqs-texte/1-00/1-00hodgson-e.htm

Klein, A. (1997) *Baseball on the Border*, Princeton: Princeton University Press.

Krane, V. and Baird, S. M. (2005) 'Using ethnography in applied sport psychology', *Journal of Applied Sport Psychology*, 17: 87–107.

LeCompte, M. D. and Schensul, J. J. (1999) *Designing and Conducting Ethnographic Research*, Walnut Creek, CA: Alta Mira Press.

Lincoln, Y. S. and Guba, E. (1985) *Naturalistic Enquiry*, Beverly Hills, CA: Sage.

Lofland, J. (1996) 'Analytic ethnography: Features, failings and futures', *Journal of Contemporary Ethnography*, 21: 30–67.

Lofland, J. and Lofland, L. H. (1984) *Analyzing Social Settings*, Belmont, CA: Wadsworth.

MacPhail, A. (2004) 'Athlete and researcher: Undertaking and pursuing ethnographic study in a sports club', *Qualitative Research*, 4(2): 227–45.

MacPhail, A., Gorely, T. and Kirk, D. (2003) 'Young people's socialisation into sport: A case study of an athletics club', *Sport, Education and Society* 8(2): 251–67.

May, T. (1999) *Social Research: Issues, Methods and Process*, Buckingham: Open University Press.

Parker, A. (1996) 'Chasing the big-time: Football apprenticeship in the 1990's', unpublished thesis, Warwick University.

Patton, M. (1990) *Qualitative Researching*, London: Sage Publications.

Poczwardowski, A., Barott, J.E. and Henschen, K.P. (2002) 'The athlete and coach: Their relationship and its meaning. Results of an interpretive study', *International Journal of Sport Psychology*, 33: 116–40.

Sands, R. R. (1999) *Gutcheck! A Wild Ride into the Heart of College Football*, Captinera, CA: Rincon Hill Books.

Tedlock, B. (2000) 'Ethnography and ethnographic representation', in N.K. Denzin and Y.S. Lincoln (eds) *Handbook of Qualitative Research* (2nd ed.), London: Sage, 455–86.

Turnbull, N. and Antalffy, N. (2009) 'Bourdieu's distinction between philosophical and sociological approaches to science studies', *The Sociological Review*, 57(4), 547–66.

Wacquant, L. (1992) 'The social logic of boxing in black Chicago: Towards a sociology of pugilism', *Sociology of Sport Journal*, 9: 221–54.

——(1995) 'Pugs at work: Bodily capital and bodily labour among professional boxers', *Body and Society*, 1(1): 65–89.

Wolcott, H. (1990) 'Ethnographic research in education', in R. Jaeger (ed.) *Complementary Methods for Research in Education*, Washington DC: American Educational Research Association, 187–206.

——(1995) *The Art of Fieldwork*, Walnut Creek, CA: AltaMira.

Wolf, M. A. (1996) 'Afterword: Musings from an old grey wolf', in D. L. Wolf (ed.) *Feminist Dilemmas in Field work*, Boulder, CO: Westview, 215–22.

Woods, P. (1986) *Inside Schools: Ethnography in Educational Research*, London: Routledge & Kegan Paul.

17 Analysis of qualitative data

William Taylor

Introduction and overview

For any qualitative researcher, experienced or neophyte, key questions will be 'what do I do with the data I have gathered, and how do I make sense of it all?' Certainly, qualitative research can produce a considerable amount of data which at first glance seems unstructured, messy, intimidating, confusing, and, at times, contradictory. Patton (1980) captures this point by suggesting:

> The data generated by qualitative methods are voluminous. I have found no way of preparing students for the sheer massive volume of information with which they will find themselves confronted when data collection has ended. Sitting down to make sense out of pages of interviews and whole files of field notes can be overwhelming.
>
> (Patton 1980: 297)

This chapter aims to introduce the reader to some of the approaches, techniques, and methodologies that they might employ in efforts to analyze and make sense of this material. It should be noted that qualitative inspired approaches in coaching research are presently 'playing catch up' (Markula and Silk 2011) with other social-based research. Indeed, it has been suggested that in the past research in coaching has been lacking in both sophistication and criticality. Denzin argues that 'Many of the old sports studies narratives, both methodological and interpretive, are exhausted' (Denzin 2012: 295), and that previous frames of analysis and their underlying assumptions do little more than just describe the visible, and, thus fail to shed light on to the complex and contested nature of the phenomenon. In doing so, he adds to the call from such as Bush *et al.* (2013) and Jones (2012) for coaching scholars to be brave and look beyond the obvious when conducting coaching-based research and engaging in the analysis of data. Novel approaches to research and data analysis can often lead to an illumination of the once mundane and allow us to expose hidden complexities and nuances which had, by the method of study, been hidden from us.

One of the shortcomings of any chapter which deals with the analysis of data in a separate format, is that one might be led to think that the most effective way to undertake analysis is best served by seeing it as a single and isolated event. Treating data analysis as a distinct and separate event itself causes a false division between the rest of the research process and analysis. It could be argued that the analysis only makes sense if it is seen as a con- tinuation of the research and there is acknowledgment that we need to engage in thinking about what the data means on an ongoing basis. Indeed, Wolcott (1994, 2001), Sparkes (2002) and Markula and Silk (2011) claim that it is neither desirable nor practical to view the analysis of data as something that you do 'after collection and before your write up'; their position being that as researchers we are making judgments, reaching conclusions and ordering our thoughts all the time. In addition, these authors see the qualitative researcher as a research tool in their own right and a central part of any engagement. Researchers are thus encouraged to view the analysis of material as a recursive and iterative exercise. That is, a working back and forth between data and theory, the understanding and questioning of the data. Wolcott (1994, 2001) suggests that it is only the necessities of presenting or publishing our work that calls a halt to this ongoing relationship. It does not matter if we are reading policy documents, observing a coach delivering a session, or listening to an interview recording: we cannot distance ourselves from the process of thinking about what we read, see, or hear.

More traditional approaches, still working within the qualitative paradigm, have treated the research process and the analysis of data in a somewhat linear fashion (Creswell 2007). In doing so, some authors have positioned analysis as a distinct element characterized as being procedural and unproblematic. This description of data as routine has its attractions and there are a number of text books that outline a step-by-step account of 'what to do and how to do it'. Certainly, this approach to qualitative data analysis promises to help researchers attempt to deal with the unstructured and untidy nature of much qualitative data. Creswell (2007) and others have portrayed data analysis in a pictorial form; the 'Data Analysis Spiral' (Creswell 2007: 151), as Creswell describes it, guides the reader through a number of stages from early data management, to coding, onto description, and, finally, to representation. While comforting to many, this formulaic representation does not mirror my own experience of the realities of research. Analysis of any data can be a frustrating and time-consuming process and rarely conforms to patterns or a pre-existing ideal. It is this unpredictable nature of data analysis which makes the process both exciting and at times adventurous.

This seeming division in approach and philosophy should not be a surprise to those who have utilized qualitative methods in sports coaching research; indeed, one of the benefits of working within such a paradigm is the eclectic nature of the subdisciplines upon which it draws. This in turn allows qualitative researchers to employ a wide range of techniques, practices, and methods of analysis.

These paradigmatic differences often relate to the ontological and episte- mological assumptions that guide particular schools of research, as well as the various disciplines within coaching. These views will steer differing forms of qualitative research into coaching. This will, in turn, influence the manner in which we formulate research questions, decide what we think is of value in terms of observations, reading, and whom we listen to, how we conduct ourselves during the investigation, and, ultimately, how we treat the data (Denzin and Lincoln 2005; Markula and Silk 2011). Because coaches and the act of coaching, as objects of research, belong to no one academic discipline, qualitative inquiry and the treatment of data have been approached from many positions and from a number of paradigmatic camps. Markula and Silk (2011) have divided these camps into three broad groups: post-positivism, and the anti-positivist approaches, interpretive and postmodern/poststructuralist.

All three groups reject the positivist assumptions that have steered much of the earlier work on coaching (e.g. Chelladurai and Saleh's 1980 work on leadership in sport settings; Cumming *et al.*'s 2005 research on athletes' perceptions of coaching behaviors; Price and Weiss's 2000 examination of coach burnout). The suggestion is that by adopting positivist positions we can only capture part of the picture and gloss over the complexity that characterizes much coaching activity. In doing so, Markula and Silk argue that the desire to generalize findings, a key tenet of positivism, from coaching research is problematic and fails to take account the nuanced nature of the act of coaching. If we are to do justice to the messy nature of coaching practice, we need to investigate it mindful of its individuality, context, and nuanced subtleties.

Post-positivist approaches to qualitative analysis

Post-positivists, although questioning some of the assumptions inherent in positivism, are still primarily guided by notions of single theory generation (Guba and Lincoln 1994), attempt to minimize the influence of the researcher, and try to meet traditional definitions of validity and reliability. A number of coaching scholars have utilized post-positivism by employing a mixed-methods approach to their research. For example, Vergeer and Lyle (2009), in their study of the influence of coaching experience in coaches' decision-making, employed telephone interviews to collect numerical data, while more interpretive verbal data provided depth and meaning relating to the responses. Jowett (2003), in her paper on 'the coach–athlete relationship in crisis', coded the interview responses by using an existing model (a form of deductive analysis) and then displayed the findings as a hierarchical tree displaying the relationship between first-order and second-order themes.

Interpretive approaches to qualitative analysis

Those using an interpretive framework share many of the considerations of other qualitative approaches (see Chapter 4). Their point of departure is the belief that not only will our pre-existing beliefs color what we choose to study, but the web of assumptions we all hold as researchers must affect the manner in which we present research findings and the elements of data we privilege (Brown 1977). Because of these commitments, researchers see both the collection and analysis of data as a 'knowledge-making experience', where meaning(s) are constructed about the social world as collective encounter between all parties engaged in the research and through the subjective nature of the individual. Authors who claimed interpretivism as their guiding framework have included scholars such as Jones *et al.* (2004). In their study of coaches and their practice, they acknowledge that the life stories they present have been interpreted by themselves as researchers and the coaches they interviewed. Thus the stories they offer are a collaboration of individual views of the world and in themselves are open to further interpretation by the reader.

Postmodern or poststructuralist approaches to qualitative analysis

Those who take a postmodern or poststructuralist stance tend to treat the manipulation of data with some caution (see Chapter 5). Because of their commitment to maintaining data in their original ecological form, they have tended to shy away from organizing data and presenting them in tables, models, and graphical forms. While postmodernists tend to focus on cultural representation and draw from a wider range of critical disciplines, poststructuralists have emerged from a rejection of the structuralism of the 1970s. Both these terms actively resist definition and are often confused and conflated (see Benton and Craib 2001 for an excellent *tour de force* of the philosophy of social science). Normally, those working in these genres have favored the application of theoretical writings to provide a 'lens' by which data are analyzed and made sense of. Using theory, or a positional approach, data are read from a particular standpoint or via the use and application of an individual theorist or critical stances. Denison (2007) used the writings of Michel Foucault and his notion of disciplinary power to examine his own coaching of an athlete. What is of interest here is the way that Denison revisited Brian's (the athlete) training diaries and suggested that the documented work regimes constituted a form of disciplinary power. Here Denison is not trying to make a collective point, but rather alerting us to the hidden power dynamic vested in the coach. Fletcher (2013) in his examination of PE teachers working within the risk society uses the consideration of Beck (1992), arguing that professional insecurity influences both their thinking and practices while working with young people. Using fictional narratives, Fletcher blurs the boundaries between using data as evidence and presenting data as evocative prose. While it is not imperative that researchers are embedded in the field work itself, in postmodernist- and poststructuralist-inspired research the centrality of the author in the analysis of the data is a key component.

Applied issues and considerations

For a number of authors (e.g. Silverman 2001; Ritchie and Lewis 2005; Boeije 2010) the process of analysis is about the management of data, more particularly, about the segmenting and reassembling of it. This view of data analysis was perfectly encapsulated by Bogdan and Biklen (2002: 153):

> Data analysis is the process of systematically searching and arranging the interview transcripts, field notes and other material that you accumulate to increase your own understanding of them and enable you to present what you have discovered to others. Analysis involves working with data, organizing them, breaking them into manageable units, synthesizing them, searching for patterns, discovering what is important and what is to be learned, and deciding what you will tell others.

The key element is that the process described involves the organizing of data. In doing so, we attempt to transfer the mass of intimidating material into something that we can work with. As before, the way that your paradigmatic leanings guide you in the progress of analysis either suggest that you are attempting to discover 'a more truthful account' (post-positivists) or that you are using the activity to make the data easier to work with and illustrative of more structural criticisms (postmodernist and poststructuralists). Those researchers who tend to utilize more theory-based approaches to their work have argued that any manipulation of data may corrupt the ecological purity of the material and thus should be avoided. Of course, the two positions, managing data to expose a more accurate account of a phenomena, or leaving data as it is in a purer state, represent two ends of a spectrum; in reality most coaching researchers work somewhere in the middle and, as always, are guided by their research aims and questions. One thing that all qualitative researchers must contend with is that at some point, we, as the authors, are selecting which bits we think are important, which elements we believe to be convincing and thus we are choosing to disregard other sections of the data.

Dealing with data

The process of segmentation is where the data itself, in all its forms, is broken up into units. This process often takes the form of close and attentive reading of the material line by line. There are a number of techniques involved in this close inspection. One method is to read the material and use different high-lighter pens to identify patterns or commonalities which can later be gathered together into larger groupings. One of the advantages of the multiple high-lighter pen method is that it allows a visual check of how this segmentation of material is progressing and which areas are becoming most populated. With which themes or concepts individual sections of the text become associated is guided by the questions you are asking of the data in relation to your original research question(s). An example may help here: if one of your research questions is to identify avenues of coach learning, you might identify or seek out terms, phrases, and words which could be associated with each other and, in turn, belong to a more inclusive general term. So, in a process often referred to as 'open coding' (Boeije 2010), words and sections of text which may include, for example, 'working with mentors', 'watching other coaches work', 'talking about coaching in the bar after sessions', and 'engaging in online debates about technique', could all be coded under 'types of coach learning or learning opportunities'.

Another method is to write memos in the margins of text using a system of signs and abbreviations, or to take a pair of scissors to individual sections, cut up the text and divide into piles. It is worth remembering that whichever technique you choose, it should work for you and may only make sense once the full process of analysis is complete. While some researchers are happy to get down and dirty with masses of paper, others prefer to cut and paste and color using a PC. There are now a number of software packages (e.g. NVIVO, NUDIST, N6, CISAID) which some may find work well for them for this process (Lewin and Silver 2007). In terms of 'open coding', this comes to a natural halt once all the data has been analyzed and/or you feel that (re)reading produces no new insight (i.e. a point of saturation). This point may be in concert with data collection and, thus, once you feel that the open coding has provided sufficient data for the coded categories, you may wish to come to an end in terms of data gathering.

It should be clear that analysis of any data forces the researcher to engage with two intertwined activities: thinking and doing; doing stimulating thinking and vice versa. The processes of segmenting and reassembling may be mentally exhausting, but at the same time it should be stimulating. What we must do is to ensure that we remain open-minded to unexpected or contradictory data.

Making sense of data

Once you have completed your initial open coding, and this could take two hours or two months depending on whether you are working on an undergraduate essay, research paper, or postgraduate thesis, the process of reassembling can then take place. Often referred to as 'axial or focus coding', this is defined by Strauss and Corbin as 'a set of procedures whereby data are put back together in new ways after coding, by making connections between categories' (Strauss and Corbin 2007: 96). This process brings the earlier codes together and looks to see if they can be reassembled under particular named categories. The primary purpose of axial coding is to determine which elements of the research appear to be dominant and which are less important. The second purpose is to reduce the amount of data so that it becomes more manageable when you decide which elements you choose to represent in a write-up or presentation. At this stage the categories can be represented in a hierarchical tree privileging primary categorizations over secondary ones (Silverman 2001). The dividing of this data into major and less significant considerations may relate to the original research question(s) and so will lead to the query 'do these data answer the questions I have asked of them?'

Returning to our earlier example, it could be that as well as a code which is concerned with 'coach learning or learning opportunities', we may also have a code entitled 'personal development'. We may wish to then incorporate these into a wider category, which we name 'professional development'. Of course, at this point you are continuously looking for elements that you may wish to reconsider, but which do not seem to fit into existing categories and thus require recoding. In addition, you may find that the same segment of data ends up appearing in more than one coded grouping. It is important to remind ourselves at this point that although the thinking and doing central to any analysis is an iterative process (Boeije 2010), often time constraints will necessitate bringing this process to a conclusion.

Those researchers who adopt a more postmodern or poststructuralist approach to their research focus less on the management of data and more on its collective meanings. This approach can appear somewhat vague as there is little written on the relationship between these paradigmatic approaches and the way data is used within them. Markula and Silk (2011) acknowledge these vagaries and they suggest that there is an attempt to marry the themes of the theorist with collective themes evident in the data. For example, theorists such as Beck (1992) have suggested that we live in a risk-averse society and writers such as Fletcher (2013) have used this theme when analyzing interview material gathered from PE teachers. Other examples have seen Bourdieu's notions of habitus and capital (Bourdieu and Wacquant 1992) used to examine transprofessionalism in coaching (Taylor and McEwan 2012) and Foucauldian notions of surveillance (Foucault 1982) in the work of Johns and Johns (2000). These writers and theories provide a 'lens' through which we can read and interpret data and the wider phenomena under study. Not only are postmodernists and poststructuralists interested in what can be explained, but also in what appears to sit outside conventional culture. For those researchers wishing to study non-conformist or marginalized coaching practices, these theorists may provide a fruitful approach.

Reflections from the field

In this section I will draw upon two examples of research that myself and colleagues have been involved with; first from a recent Economic and Social Research Council funded project exploring the 'politics of touch' in the context of sports coaching (Piper *et al*. 2012). Within this research, although utilizing a broad qualitative and ethnographic approach, and guided by poststructuralist sensitivities, we employed the theories of Foucault and used them as a 'lens' by which we might analyze elements of the empirical data. Such was our commitment to expose the nature of the prevailing child protection discourse and its impact on the practical realities of coaching, that we felt our leanings toward critical poststructuralism and personal histories in coaching needed to be clearly acknowledged, as these positions ultimately framed and guided our analysis. We were not silent authors; indeed, as 'insiders' we argued that the analysis was 'richer and more significant' because of our histories and pre-existing knowledge of this area of study (Charmaz and Mitchell 1996). Because of the duration of the investigation, a full year, and the variety of data collection methods employed, such as observation of coaching practice, single and group interviews, review of policy documents, and research notes taken from attendance at child protection training courses, the processes of analysis were continuous and recursive. The research team met on a regular basis and discussed the most recent experiences of being out in the field. We 'talked aloud' about the data and what we thought it meant. The sharing of these thoughts and feelings was not a single isolated event, but a collective one, often involving us reconsidering and challenging our own and each others' ideas. An extract from my own research log illustrates the ebb and flow of these opinions and reflections:

> Talking to the others I can see that I might have missed something in my first reading of the data. Maybe I was too keen to look for easy fit answers – it would appear now there are contradictions in the interview text – I didn't see them. Viewing the data as a whole, and not focussing on the particular or obvious, I can see that the interviews are examples of emerging knowledge and that the coaches are expressing their inherent contradictions and insecurities. It comes down to what questions am I asking of the data and what is the interview suggesting – not what answers are given.

The additional insight that both collective reviewing of data provides and the adoption of new ways of looking affords should not be understated. Data remains a continuous point of reference for reflexivity and can be subject to multiple readings. In this particular case, it supported the notion that the act of coaching is multifaceted and open to a variety of expressions.

The second example is related to ongoing research on the professionalization of sports coaching. In this particular context, the interview data gathered from practicing coaches was analyzed and framed against the explicit research questions that formulated the research project. What I wished to do with this data was to draw out the differences in the manner in which the notion of professionalization was being internalized by coaches across differing domains and spaces. Also, I was keen to identify the contradictions and outliers that the analysis exposed. I did not have the advantage of working in a team, so took it upon myself to return to the data a number of times, attempting to forget my last set of conclusions. This intra-review process, where I returned to the data after leaving it to attend to other aspects of the research, gave comfort as after three or four [re]readings I was not coming up with any new insights (saturation), nor was I drifting away from applying the original research question. The resulting paper (Taylor and Garratt 2010: 23) suggested:

> questions were posed of the data in order to stimulate useful comparisons, analytical reflection, and opportunities to challenge potentially important

problems. Throughout, a method of 'working back and forth' (Silverman 2004: 357), between data and theory, was employed to facilitate analysis and consider how theory might be usefully appropriated to expose the complexities, conflicts, and contradictions in the evolving discourse of professionalism. The process of analysis, therefore, was not a single or unitary event, but rather comprised a hermeneutical strategy, in which the researcher engaged in continuous conversation with the data, producing a sort of 'second-level hermeneutics'.

(Alvesson and Skoldberg 2004: 261)

Because of the nature of the data collection, i.e. interviewing a range of coaches working across differing domains and at different levels, and at times returning to a coach four or five times to gain additional information, the tactics adopted allowed me to present the same data in the consideration of a number of different contexts. Examples of these contexts are a single-coach case study, focusing on coaches as volunteers, and drawing on the experiences of coaches working in a particular sport (Taylor and Garratt 2010).

The analysis of qualitative data is not easy and, as I have suggested, it is often messy, at times confusing, and rarely presents a complete picture. It does, however, allow us to shed light and make sense of some of the complexities of the social phenomenon that is sports coaching. The methods and approaches you will use to tackle these issues must be guided by the answers to a number of key questions: (1) what epistemological assumptions am I making within this research undertaking? (2) what are the explicit research aims, objectives, and questions which have guided the work and what questions can I legitimately ask of this data? (3) which approach or method of analysis is going to provide most illumination and insight when applied?

References

Alvesson, M. and Skoldberg, K. (2004) *Reflective Methodology: New Vistas for Qualitative Research*, London: Sage.

Beck, U. (1992) *Risk Society: Towards a New Modernity*, London: Sage.

Benton, T. and Craib, I. (2001) *Philosophy of Social Science: The Philosophical Foundations of Social Thought*, Basingstoke: Palgrave.

Boeije, H. (2010) *Analysis in Qualitative Research*, London: Sage.

Bogdan, R. C. and Biklen, S. K. (2002) *Qualitative Research for Education: An Introduction to Theory and Method*, Boston, MA: Allyn and Bacon.

Bourdieu, P. and Wacquant, L. J. D. (1992) *An Invitation to Reflexive Sociology*, Cambridge: Polity.

Brown, R. H. (1977) *A Poetic for Sociology*, New York: Cambridge University Press.

Bush, A. J., Silk, M. L., Andrews, D. L. and Lauder, H. (2013) *Sports Coaching Research: Context, Consequences and Consciousness*, Abingdon: Routledge.

Charmaz, K. and Mitchell, R. (1996) 'The myth of silent authorship: Self, substance, and style in ethnographic writing', *Symbolic Interaction*, 19: 285–302.

Chelladurai, P. and Saleh, S. D. (1980) 'Dimensions of leadership behaviour in sports: Development of a leadership scale', *Journal of Sports Psychology*, 2: 34–45.

Creswell, J. W. (2007) *Qualitative Inquiry and Research Design: Choosing Among Five Approaches*, London: Sage.

Cumming, S. P., Eisenmann, J. C., Smoll, F. L., Smith, R. E. and Malina, R. M. (2005) 'Body size and perceptions of coaching behaviors by adolescent female athletes', *Journal of Psychology of Sport and Exercise*, 6: 693–705.

Denison, J. (2007) 'Social theory for coaches: A Foucauldian reading of one athlete's poor performance', *International Journal of Sports Science and Coaching*, 2: 369–83.

Denzin, N. (2012) 'Afterwards: Sport and neoliberalism', in D. L. Andrews and M. Silk (eds) *Sport and Neoliberalism, Politics, Consumption and Culture*, Philadelphia: Temple University Press.

Denzin, N. K. and Lincoln, Y. S. (2005) 'Introduction: the discipline and practice of qualitative research', in N.K. Denzin and Y.S. Lincoln (eds) *The Sage Handbook of Qualitative Research* (3rd ed.), Thousand Oaks: Sage, 1–32.

Fletcher, S. (2013) 'Touching practice and physical education: Deconstruction of contemporary moral panic', *Sport, Education and Society*, 18(5): 694–709.

Foucault, M. (1982) 'How is power exercised?', in H. L. Dreyfus and P. Rabinow (eds) *Michel Foucault: Beyond Structuralism and Hermeneutics*, Brighton: Harvester.

Guba, E. G. and Lincoln, Y. S. (1994) 'Competing paradigms in qualitative research', in N. K. Denzin and Y. S. Lincoln (eds) *Handbook of Qualitative Research*, London: Sage.

Johns, D. P. and Johns, J. S. (2000) 'Surveillance, subjectivism and technologies of power: An analysis of the discursive of high performance', *International Review for the Sociology of Sport*, 35: 219–34.

Jones, R. L. (2012) 'Editorial', *Sports Coaching Review*, 1: 1–3.

Jones, R., Armour, K. and Potrac, P. (2004) *Sport Coaching Cultures: From Theory to Practice*, London: Routledge.

Jowett, S. (2003) 'When the "honeymoon" is over: A case study of a coach–athlete dyad in crisis', *The Sport Psychologist*, 17: 444–60.

Lewin, A. and Silver, C. (2007) *Using Software in Qualitative Research: A Step by Step Guide*, London: Sage.

Markula, P. and Silk, M. (2011) *Qualitative Research for Physical Culture*, Basingstoke: Palgrave.

Patton, M. Q. (1980) *Qualitative Evaluation Methods*, Beverly Hills, CA: Sage.

Piper, H., Garratt, D. and Taylor, B. (2012) *Hands off Sports' Coaching: the Politics of Touch*, RES-000-22-4156, Swindon: Economic and Social Research Council.

Price, M. S. and Weiss, M. R. (2000) 'Relationships among coach burnout, coach behaviors, and athletes' psychological responses', *The Sport Psychologist*, 4: 391 – 409.

Ritchie, J. and Lewis, J. (eds) (2005) *Qualitative Research Practice: A Guide for Social Science Students and Researchers*, London: Sage.

Silverman, D. (2001) *Interpreting Qualitative Data* (2nd ed.), London: Sage.

——(2004) *Qualitative Research: Theory, Method and Practice*, London: Sage.

Sparkes, A. C. (2002) *Telling Tales in Sport and Physical Education: A Qualitative Journey*, Champaign, IL: Human Kinetics.

Strauss, A. L. and Corbin, J. (2007) *Basics of Qualitative Research: Techniques and Procedures for Developing Grounded Theory*, (3rd ed.), London: Sage.

Taylor, B. and Garratt, D. (2010) 'The professionalisation of sports coaching: Relations of power, resistance and compliance', *Sport, Education and Society*, 15: 121–39.

Taylor, W. G. and McEwan, I. M. (2012) 'From interprofessional working to transprofessional possibilities: The new age of sports coaching in the United Kingdom', *Sport Coaching Review*, 1: 38–51.

Vergeer, I. and Lyle, J. (2009) 'Coaching experience: examining its role in coaches decision making', *International Journal of Sport and Exercise Psychology*, 7: 431–49.

Wolcott, H. (1994) *Transforming Qualitative Data: Description, Analysis and Interpretation*, Thousand Oaks, CA: Sage.

——(2001) *Writing up Qualitative Research* (2nd ed.), Thousand Oaks, CA: Sage.

18 Judging qualitative research

Brett Smith, Andrew C. Sparkes, and Nick Caddick

Introduction and overview

Qualitative and quantitative research in sports coaching needs to be held to high and difficult standards. Qualitative research, however, is different from quantitative research in terms of its ontological (the nature of reality) and epistemological (the relationship between the inquirer and the known) assumptions, its goals, and its methods (McGannon and Schweinbenz 2011; Sparkes and Smith 2013). This being the case, the standard criteria used for judging quantitative research (e.g. internal validity and external validity) are inappropriate for judging qualitative research and, as such, different criteria are required. But what criteria might be appropriate for passing judgment on a qualitative research study in sports coaching? How might we differentiate the 'good' from the 'bad'?

There are various positions available to a qualitative researcher in relation to judging qualitative research and how validity is conceptualized. A popular one in sport coaching is the *parallel position* (Sparkes 1998, 2002; Sparkes and Smith 2009, 2013). This position recognizes that qualitative and quantitative research differs, and thus different criteria are needed to judge each. The parallel position converts ideas from quantitative research about how research can be judged into comparable criteria for judging qualitative research. In so doing, the criteria proposed parallels or mimics quantitative criteria. A good example of a parallel position can be found in the work of Lincoln and Guba (1985).

Within sport research, the work of Lincoln and Guba (1985) remains the 'gold standard' for judging the quality of qualitative research. They proposed several parallel criteria, such as *credibility*, *transferability*, and *dependability*, which taken together make up the *trustworthiness* of a qualitative research study. For example, paralleling the quantitative criteria of internal validity, there is *credibility*. This criterion involves establishing that the results of qualitative research are believable from the perspective of the participant in the research. To achieve the goal of credibility, Lincoln and Guba suggest a number of techniques. These include *prolonged engagement* in the field, *persistent observation*, *negative case analysis*, and *peer debriefing*. It also comprises *triangulation*. This is a technique whereby researchers obtain multiple forms of data to cross-check information and/or more than one researcher analyzes the data to achieve a consensus on the findings. Another crucial technique for establishing credibility, propose Lincoln and Guba, is *member checking*. Sometimes called *respondent validation*, member checking involves 'verifying' with the participants that the researcher's interpretations of the data are accurate.

The criteria that Lincoln and Guba (1985) propose for judging the quality of qualitative research have been well used within the field of sport sciences, including in sports coaching. For example, Vallée and Bloom (2005), Gucciardi *et al.* (2009), and Walsh *et al.* (2010) sought to ensure the trustworthiness of their sports coaching research by appealing to the criterion of credibility and applying several techniques for achieving it (e.g. peer debriefing, triangulation, and participant member checks). More recently, in their study of ice hockey coaches' perceptions of the factors influencing athlete leadership, Bucci *et al.* (2012) drew on member checks as 'an essential technique for establishing credibility (Lincoln and Guba 1985)' (Bucci *et al.* (2012): 248).

Whilst the concept of trustworthiness and associated techniques are widely used within sports coaching, Lincoln and Guba's (1985) parallel stance on criteria has been subjected to critique by Sparkes (1998, 2002) and Sparkes and Smith (2009). The following are just three of the problems they identify. First, some of the actual techniques proposed to achieve aspects of trustworthiness are not appropriate to the logic of qualitative research. For example, the use of member checking as a method of verification is problematic as it suggests that in the midst of multiple realities (i.e. the researcher's and the participants') those being studied are the real knowers and, therefore, the possessors of truth. However, there is no reason to assume that participants have privileged status as commentators on their actions or motivations. There is also the possibility that researchers and participants disagree on interpretations. Participant feedback, then, cannot be taken as a direct validation or refutation of the researcher's inferences.

Second, Lincoln and Guba's (1985) work is philosophically contradictory. On the one hand, their work promotes sports coaching research grounded in ontological relativism. This means the researcher believes in a world of multiple, constructed, and mind-dependent realities. On the other hand, Lincoln and Guba's ideas behind trustworthiness promote epistemological foundationalism. This refers to a way of knowing in which it is believed that techniques can sort out trustworthy from untrustworthy interpretations of reality. These two beliefs are, however, *incompatible*. To believe in a world of multiple mind-dependent realities *and* a world in which reality can be found objectively leads to an untenable situation from which there are only two ways to escape. Either there has to be an acceptance that in a relativistic world of multiple realities that are dependent on the researcher there is no way to sort out trustworthy interpretations from untrustworthy ones. Techniques alone will not sort out the trustworthy from the untrustworthy. Or, the existence of a reality outside of ourselves that can be known objectively through the appropriate use of procedures or techniques and this assumption (the reality), as Smith and Deemer (2000) emphasize, has to be confirmed. This second option is often the preferred one within the sport sciences. Yet, as Smith and Hodkinson (2009) point out, the problem with it

> is that there is no way to 'get at' that reality as it really is (see also Randall and Phoenix 2009). And, if one cannot capture that social reality as it really is, then that reality cannot be called upon to do the adjudicate-the-different-claims-to-knowledge work asked of it. This is the whole problematic posed by the idea that no matter how hard we try, we cannot achieve theory-free observation or knowledge.
>
> (Smith and Hodkinson 2009: 34)

Indeed, the second option has yet to be cashed in and confirmed in sports coaching research. However, it still persists as the option to take.

Third, in light of such problems, Lincoln and Guba changed their position toward the end of the 1980s (Guba and Lincoln 1989) and now no longer believe in their 1985 proposals (see also Lincoln 1995; Guba and Lincoln 2005). That is, they listened to critiques, agreed with them, and rejected the idea of achieving trustworthiness as simply involving the use of specific data-gathering *techniques*. This raises questions about the non-reflective adherence of sport coaching researchers to this earlier position. Why, given the numerous critiques and the fact that Lincoln and Guba have changed their mind, do sport researchers still adopt the position they held in 1985?

Although many sports coaching researchers still adopt a parallel approach when judging qualitative research, there are some who have reacted to the critiques and adopted different positions and strategies for judging qualitative research that call on different criteria in the process. One of these is the *letting go* position as described by Sparkes (1998, 2002), and Sparkes and Smith (2013). Here, the sports coaching researcher lets go of traditional views of validity that privilege techniques as the only way to guarantee trustworthiness, and calls upon other more relevant and appropriate criteria to judge the 'goodness' of a qualitative study. This shift is informed by a *relativist* perspective in which the use of time- and place-contingent lists of characteristics to make judgments is called upon.

It is important to stress that relativism does not mean that 'anything goes' when it comes to making assessments about the quality of qualitative research. Nor does it mean that all knowledge claims are equal to other knowledge claims. As Smith and Deemer (2000) point out, relativists can and do make judgments, and will continue to do so for the foreseeable future. But, when passing judgment on a piece of research, the criteria used are not taken to mean a preordained or universal standard against which to make judgment. Given this, relativists view criteria as *characterizing traits* that have, at best, mild implications as a prescription for inquirer behavior. They are willing to describe what one *might* do, but are not prepared to mandate what one *must* do across all contexts and on all occasions prior to any piece of research being conducted.

Once criteria come to be seen as characterizing traits, then, as Smith and Deemer (2000) note, any particular traits will always be subject to constant reinterpretation as times and conditions change. There is a list-like quality to how criteria are used. The list of characterizing traits is ongoing. It can be added to, subtracted from, and modified in light of what specific research one is judging. Therefore, the criteria used to judge a piece of research can change depending upon the context and the purposes. It is not fixed nor should it be applied on all occasions. In the next section we consider some possible criteria that might inform the list drawn up for judging any given qualitative research study in sports coaching.

Applied issues and considerations

What characterizing traits might be used to judge qualitative sports coaching research, and how are these criteria arrived at? Before offering a response to the first question, criteria are based on what is being done in the field – exemplars in action. Likewise, criteria are arrived at through *phronesis* (Flyvbjerg 2001). This refers to the practical wisdom gained through experience. For example, experience can be gained, and criteria arrived at, by reading exemplars, doing research, and engaging in dialogue with others about qualitative work. Indeed, as Rolfe notes, 'In the absence of any objective criteria, all we have are prudence, our subjective experience and our practical wisdom' (Rolfe 2006: 14). With this in mind, and in keeping with the 'letting go' perspective on validity, the following are some examples of criteria that sports coaching researchers might decide to use when judging a qualitative study. These criteria are selected from lists provided by Lieblich *et al.* (1998), Richardson (2000), Sparkes (2002), Holman Jones (2005), Sparkes and Smith (2009, 2013), Tracy (2010), Barone and Eisner (2012) and Smith and Caddick (2012) to whom the reader is referred for more detail.

- *Substantive contribution*: Does this piece contribute to our understanding of social life? Does the writer demonstrate a deeply grounded (if embedded) social scientific perspective? How has this perspective informed the construction of the text?
- *Impact*: Does this affect me? Emotionally? Intellectually? Does it generate new questions? Move me to write? Move me to try new research practices? Move me to action?
- *Width*: This criterion refers to the comprehensiveness and quality of evidence the researcher(s) provide in their final report as well as to the proposed interpretation or analysis. Numerous quotations in reporting studies, as well as suggestions of alternative explanations, should be provided for the reader's judgment of the evidence and its interpretation.

- *Aesthetic merit*: Does this piece succeed esthetically? Does the use of creative analytical practices open up the text, invite interpretive response? Is the text artistically shaped, satisfying, complex, and not boring?
- *Coherence*: Coherence can be evaluated both internally, in terms of how the parts fit together, and externally, namely, against existing theories and previous research.
- *Dialogue as a space of debate and negotiation*: This criterion refers to the ability of the research to open up meaningful dialogue among different people.
- *Personal narrative and storytelling as an obligation to critique*: Does the story enact an ethical obligation to critique subject positions, acts, and received notions of expertise and justice within and outside of the work? If so, how?
- *Engaged embodiment as a condition for change*: This criterion refers to the ability of the research to make political action and social or personal change possible in and outside the work. If this criterion is appropriate for the research being judged, and if the research does have strong potential to make change, then it meets this criterion and can be deemed 'good'.
- *Worthy topic*: The topic of the research is relevant, timely, significant, interesting, or evocative.
- *Rich rigor*: The study uses sufficient, abundant, appropriate, and complex theoretical constructs, data and time in the field, sample(s), context(s), and data collection and analysis.
- *Sincerity*: The study is characterized by self reflexivity about subjective values, biases, and inclinations of the researcher(s); and transparency about methods and challenges.
- *Resonance*: The research influences, affects, or moves particular readers or a variety of readers through esthetic merit, evocative representations, naturalistic generalizations, and transferable findings.
- *Credibility*: Has the researcher spent a significant amount of time with participants? Were participant reflections on the researcher's interpretations of the data sought? Participant reflections, or what is sometimes known as member checks, can open up dialogue about the fairness, appropriateness, and believability of interpretations offered. As participants reflect, fresh light on the study may too be thrown up, providing a spur for richer and deeper analyses. Participant reflections or member checking is, therefore, less a *test* of research findings or a technique to achieve *trustworthiness*. Instead, they are an opportunity for dialogue with participants, reflexive elaboration, critique, feedback, affirmation, disagreement, and even collaboration.
- *Transparency*: Was the research made transparent through, for example, an audit trail? Did another person, such as a critical friend, scrutinize matters like theoretical preferences, breadth of the interview sample, and the process of sorting, choosing, organizing, and analyzing the data? Did a researcher present his or her interpretations of the data to critical friends who provided a theoretical sounding board to encourage reflection upon,

and exploration of, alternative explanations and interpretations as they emerged in relation to the data? Here, in contrast to peer debriefing within a parallel position, the notion of presenting an interpretation acknowledges that while there can be agreement, not all those involved in the process need to define the meanings of a particular data set in the same way as they can be positioned differently in relation to their theoretical interests, research experience, and power resources. This is not a problem. On the contrary, the different perspectives offered by critical friends are used as a resource for challenging and developing the interpretations made by any one researcher as they construct a coherent and theoretically sound argument to defend the case they are making in relation to the data generated in a particular study. Thus, no claims are made about validity or reliability. Every opinion offered is rather a resource to deepen and extend interpretation. They are also a reminder that for every additional viewer there is an additional view.

- *Incisiveness*: Research that gets to the heart of a social issue. It goes to its core. It does not get swamped with details that have no inherent significance and do little to increase the cogency of the research itself. Incisiveness means that the work of research is penetrating; it is sharp in the manner in which it cuts to the core of an issue.
- *Generativity*: The ways in which the work enables one to see or act upon phenomena even though it represents a kind of case study with an n of only 1.

The application of a list like that above is contingent. Its use depends, for example, on the type of study (e.g. ethnographic, discursive, or narrative) one is judging, its purpose, and what the person judging the work brings to the table. It depends on what has and is being done in the field along with the practical wisdom gained through experience in the field (i.e. *phronesis*). Thus, the list is not set in stone to be applied to all qualitative studies be they ethnographic, grounded theory, narrative, visual, or otherwise. Nor do we wish to suggest that the 'more' criteria that are met from any given list that the better the study is. That is, meeting ten criteria does not make a study twice as good as one that meets five criteria. As Smith and Deemer (2000) warn, to think of a list in these terms is to miss the point that lists and how they are used is a practical matter. Criteria are worked and reworked within the context of actual practices/applications by researchers in the field and cannot be set down in abstract formulae. That is, our lists to judge sports coaching research are challenged, changed, and modified not though abstracted discussions of the lists and items in and of themselves, but in application to actual research. Thus, in proposing lists like that above we do not wish to infer that these are the only criteria that can be used for passing judgment. Rather, these criteria are just a few that students, journal reviewers, and so on might apply on different occasions to sort out 'good' qualitative sports coaching work from the 'bad'.

Reflections from the field

There are many ways in which a qualitative researcher might represent their findings (Sparkes 2002; Sparkes and Smith 2013). Over the years we have used a variety of different genres to represent our research. These include realist tales (e.g. Smith and Sparkes 2008, 2011; Caddick and Ryall 2012; Smith 2013a), creative ethnographic non-fictions (e.g. Sparkes 2007, 2009, 2012; Smith 2013b), and poetic representations (e.g. Smith 1999; Sparkes and Douglas 2007; Sparkes 2012). Another genre we have used to represent our research is autoethnography (Sparkes 1996, 2012; Smith 1999, 2013c). Sometimes called narratives of the self, autoethnographies are highly personalized, revealing texts in which researchers tell stories about their own lived experiences, relating the personal to the cultural. How, then, might a researcher judge a 'good' autoethnography from a 'bad' one?

One approach for passing judgment on qualitative research in general is advocated by Hammersley (1992). He suggests the following criteria be used: plausibility (is the claim plausible?), credibility (is the claim based on credible evidence?), and relevance (what is the claim's relevance for knowledge about the world?). Garratt and Hodkinson (1998) reflect on how these criteria might operate when applied to an autoethnographic piece by one of us (Sparkes 1996) called 'The Fatal Flaw: A Narrative of the Fragile Body-Self'. With regard to plausibility, this would entail asking whether the claims made within the autoethnographic research seemed plausible given our existing knowledge. However, as Garratt and Hodkinson (1998) point out in relation to judging the paper by Sparkes:

> How could we begin to make judgments about an autobiographical narrative of the self, immanently characterised in terms of its subjectivity, uniqueness, fragmentation, and novelty of expression, on the basis of either the empirical claims it makes or in terms of the match with existing research ... In this sense, it may be neither possible nor desirable to judge the quality of this piece on the basis of its accuracy relative to research that already exists within the field. Rather, it might be more helpful, in this particular case, to ask ourselves different questions, such as: Does this account work for us? Do we find it to be believable and evocative on the basis of our own experiences?
>
> (Garratt and Hodkinson 1998: 252–3)

Given that the *Fatal Flaw* is bound to fail the test of plausibility in Hammersley's (1992) terms, the next step for a student or reviewer in sports coaching is to assess its credibility. Garratt and Hodkinson (1998) point out the problems with such a move. As they argue, any judgment about the credibility of a claim necessarily involves a judgment about its accuracy, which entails a closer examination of the evidence collected and a judgment about whether the research was conducted using the relevant methodology.

For them, such procedures appear incongruous in understanding the research process associated with the production of the *Fatal Flaw*, and we would add any other sports-related autoethnographies where the author actually states that accuracy is not the issue, since autoethnographies seek to meet different criteria (e.g. coherence, sincerity, verisimilitude, and impact). Given this, any judgment about the value of research would rest primarily on feelings of trust and the experience of the reader in participating with the text. To attempt to judge this work against Hammersley's (1992) criteria of plausibility and credibility, or even Lincoln and Guba's (1985) criteria, will inevitably result in the work being described as seriously flawed or as not constituting 'proper' research at all.

Drawing from the list of characterizing traits offered for consideration in the previous section, more appropriate criteria to judge the 'Fatal Flaw', and other autoethnographies, *might* include the following:

- Substantive contribution
- Impact
- Esthetic merit
- Dialogue as a space of debate and negotiation
- Engaged embodiment as a condition for change
- Personal narrative and storytelling as an obligation to critique
- Worthy topic
- Sincerity
- Resonance
- Incisiveness
- Generativity

The above criteria are a few among many that *might* be used on certain occasions to judge a sporting autoethnography. If, however, we had preselected criteria, such as outlined by Lincoln and Guba (1985) and Hammersley (1992), sporting autoethnographies like the 'Fatal Flaw' would be deemed 'not research'. Each would 'fail' the criteria pre-imposed on it. For us, then, when criteria are used in a predetermined manner to judge all research, there is the danger of excluding work before it has even been read and producing a closed system of judgment that can only operate with a very narrow range of what constitutes legitimate research. Others agree. For example, along with Smith and Deemer (2000), Garratt and Hodkinson (1998) state that, choosing any list of universal criteria in advance of reading a research report is antithetical to the process of understanding as experience:

> Any prespecification of universal criteria is in danger of foisting on research artificial categories of judgment, preconceptions of what research should be, and a framework of a priori conditions that may be impossible or inappropriate to meet at least in some cases. One inevitable result of such lists is that they police what can be done. Indeed, this is part of the intention.
>
> (Garratt and Hodkinson 1998: 533)

When prespecified criteria are applied in advance to *all* research, then new kinds of qualitative inquiry along with novel forms of representation are, by definition, excluded. In some cases, as we have found, they are not deemed worthy of the term 'research' at all. Yet, as we have argued, there are problems associated with not just a parallel approach, but also with using pre-determined and universal criteria when it comes to passing judgment on qualitative research. For us, it is more productive and fair to consider criteria as characterizing traits, list-like, and starting points for judging what is 'good' and 'bad' qualitative research.

References

Barone, T. and Eisner, E. W. (2012) *Arts Based Research*, Thousand Oaks, CA: Sage.

Bucci, J., Bloom, G. A., Loughead, T. M. and Caron, J. G. (2012) 'Ice hockey coaches' perceptions of athlete leadership', *Journal of Applied Sport Psychology*, 24: 243–59.

Caddick, N. and Ryall, E. (2012) 'The social construction of "mental toughness" – a fascistoid ideology?', *Journal of the Philosophy of Sport*, 39: 137–54.

Flyvbjerg, B. (2001) *Making Social Science Matter: Why Social Inquiry Fails and How It Can Succeed Again*, Cambridge: Cambridge University Press.

Garratt, D. and Hodkinson, P. (1998) 'Can there be criteria for selecting research criteria?: A hermeneutical analysis of an inescapable dilemma', *Qualitative Inquiry*, 4: 515–39.

Guba, E. and Lincoln, Y. (1989) *Fourth Generation Evaluation*, London: Sage.

Guba, E. G. and Lincoln, Y. (2005) 'Paradigmatic controversies, contradictions, and emerging confluences', in N. K. Denzin and Y. Lincoln (eds) *Handbook of Qualitative Research* (3rd ed.), London: Sage, 191–216.

Gucciardi, D. F., Gordon, S. and Dimmock, J. A. (2009) 'Evaluation of a mental toughness training program for youth-aged Australian footballers: II. A qualitative analysis', *Journal of Applied Sport Psychology*, 21: 324–39.

Hammersley, M. (1992) *What's Wrong With Ethnography?*, London: Routledge.

Holman Jones, S. (2005) 'Autoethnography: Making the personal political', in N. K. Denzin and Y. Lincoln (eds) *Handbook of Qualitative Research* (3rd ed.), London: Sage, 763–92.

Lieblich, A., Tuval-Mashlach, R. and Zilber, T. (1998) *Narrative research*, London: Sage.

Lincoln, Y. (1995) 'Emerging criteria for quality in qualitative and interpretive research', *Qualitative Inquiry*, 1: 275–89.

Lincoln, Y. and Guba, E. (1985) *Naturalistic inquiry*, Thousand Oaks, CA: Sage.

McGannon, K. R. and Schweinbenz, A. N. (2011) 'Traversing the qualitative–quantitative divide using mixed methods: Some reflections and reconciliations for sport and exercise psychology', *Qualitative Research in Sport, Exercise and Health*, 3: 370–84.

Randall, W. L. and Phoenix, C. (2009) 'The problem with truth in qualitative interviews: Reflections from a narrative perspective', *Qualitative Research in Sport and Exercise*, 1(2): 125–40.

Richardson, L. (2000) 'Writing: a method of inquiry', in N. Denzin and Y. Lincoln (eds) *Handbook of Qualitative Research* (2nd ed.), London: Sage, 923–48.

Rolfe, G. (2006) 'Judgements without rules: Towards a postmodern ironist concept of research Validity', *Nursing Inquiry*, 13: 7–15.

Smith, B. (1999) 'The Abyss: Exploring depression through a narrative of the self', *Qualitative Inquiry*, 5: 264–79.

——(2013a) 'Disability, sport, and men's narratives of health: A qualitative study'. *Health Psychology*, 32: 110–19.

——(2013b) 'Sporting spinal cord injuries, social relations, and rehabilitation narratives: An ethnographic creative non-fiction of becoming disabled through sport?', *Sociology of Sport Journal*, 30(2): 132–52.

——(2013c) 'Artificial persons and the academy: A story', in N. Short, L. Turner and A. Grant (eds) *Contemporary British Autoethnography*, Rotterdam: Sense Publishers, 187–202.

Smith, B. and Caddick, N. (2012) 'Qualitative methods in sport: A concise overview for guiding social scientific research', *Asia Pacific Journal of Sport and Social Science*, 1: 60–73.

Smith, B. and Sparkes, A. (2008) 'Changing bodies, changing narratives and the consequences of tellability: A case study of becoming disabled through sport', *Sociology of Health and Illness*, 30: 217–36.

——(2011) 'Multiple responses to a chaos narrative', *Health: An Interdisciplinary Journal for the Social Study of Health, Illness & Medicine*, 15: 38–53.

Smith, J. and Deemer, D. (2000) 'The problem of criteria in the age of relativism', in N. Denzin and Y. Lincoln (eds) *Handbook of Qualitative Research* (2nd ed.), London: Sage.

Smith, J. and Hodkinson, P. (2009) 'Challenging neorealism: A response to Hammersley', *Qualitative Inquiry*, 15: 30–39.

Sparkes, A. (1996) 'The fatal flaw: A narrative of the fragile body-self', *Qualitative Inquiry*, 2: 463–95.

——(1998) 'Validity in qualitative inquiry and the problem of criteria: Implications for sport psychology', *The Sport Psychologist*, 12: 363–86.

——(2002) *Telling Tales in Sport and Physical Activity: A Qualitative Journey*, Champaign, IL: Human Kinetics Press.

——(2007) 'Embodiment, academics, and the audit culture: A story seeking consideration', *Qualitative Research*, 7: 521–50.

——(2009) 'Ethnography and the senses: Challenges and possibilities', *Qualitative Research in Sport, Exercise and Health*, 1: 21–35.

——(2012) 'Fathers and sons: In bits and pieces', *Qualitative Inquiry*, 18: 174–85.

Sparkes, A. and Douglas, K. (2007) 'Making the case for poetic representations: An example in action', *The Sport Psychologist*, 21: 170–90.

Sparkes, A. and Smith, B. (2009) 'Judging the quality of qualitative inquiry: Criteriology and relativism in action', *Psychology of Sport and Exercise*, 10: 491–7.

——(2013) *Qualitative Research in Sport, Exercise and Health Sciences: From Process to Product*, London: Routledge.

Tracy, S. J. (2010) 'Qualitative quality: Eight "big tent" criteria for excellent qualitative Research', *Qualitative Inquiry*, 16: 837–51.

Vallée, C. N. and Bloom, G. A. (2005) 'Building a successful university program: Key and common elements of expert coaches', *Journal of Applied Sport Psychology*, 17: 179–96.

Walsh, D., Ozaeta, J. and Wright, P. M. (2010) 'Transference of responsibility model goals to the school environment: Exploring the impact of a coaching club program', *Physical Education and Sport Pedagogy*, 15: 15–28.

Part V

Contemporary approaches to coaching research

19 Autoethnography

Brian T. Gearity

Introduction and overview

The purpose of this chapter is to help students understand the key concepts of autoethnography, an increasingly popular approach to generating knowledge in the social sciences. The word 'autoethnography' can be broken down into its three components. 'Auto' refers to the self or author – that could be you. 'Ethno' refers to culture and human interaction. Finally, 'graphy' is the process and product of conducting research (Ellis 2004). In the social science literature, you will find autoethnography referred to in a variety of different ways (e.g. introspective ethnography, memoir, personal narrative, narrative of the self).

Dissatisfied with dominant research designs (e.g. experimental), statistics and limited ways of thinking about our social world (i.e. abstract theories, value-neutral, void of emotion), along with the lack of authorial voice in ethnographic research (i.e. researcher), and powerful critiques of social science research in general (i.e. crisis of representation; see Chapter 9), auto-ethnography blossomed in the late 1990s. At that time, and still today, researchers used experimental designs and statistics in an attempt to predict, and often control, human behavior. Many scholars felt this way of thinking was ethically problematic and reduced the complexities of human behavior and our social world to a few, measurable variables. Scholars also argued for research that was explicit in values or ethics, daily practices and interactions, and emotion, which were considered taboo or outside the scope of social science research (Flyvbjerg 2001; Ellis 2004). Social scientists, in an attempt to be like natural scientists, believed that 'real science' meant removing themselves from their research, seeking widespread generalizations, and that there was only one acceptable way to write up or disseminate research (i.e. third-person voice, clear interpretations).

Diverging from the natural sciences, new forms of social science were developed. Scholars wrote stories and other 'impressionist tales' of their own cultural experiences (Van Maanen 1988). Drawing upon mostly ethnographic methods, they focused on specific cases, rich descriptions, and practical knowledge (Denzin 2001; Flyvbjerg 2001). Indeed, narrative scholars increasingly revived an understanding of ourselves and our social worlds as stories, filled with characters, plot lines, and (un)expected complications and resolutions (Polkinghorne 1988; Clandinin and Connelly 2000). With a corpus of scholars, and their graduate students, along with an infrastructure that hosted academic conferences and journals, a new 'moment' emerged for social science research (Denzin and Lincoln 2000; Ellis 2004).

Autoethnography thus developed as a qualitative methodology tied to storied writing (Sparkes 2000, 2002; Goodall Jr. 2008). Some of the personal benefits of writing stories can be therapeutic or coming to terms with the lack of catharsis, to develop one's imagination and interpretive openness, to think deeply and complexly, identify a host of ethical issues, and to work upon one's self (Sparkes 2002; Ellis 2004; Frank 2010; Pearce 2010). There also exist wider social benefits for the public good such as encouraging others to think and act critically and reflexively, facilitating dialogue and empathy, and influencing political and pedagogical practices (Ellis 2004; Holman-Jones 2005; Markula and Denison 2005).

Autoethnographers sought to do research that was self-reflexive and infused with aspects from the growing field of narrative research (Reed-Danahay 1997; Ellis and Bochner 2000; Ellis 2004). These autoethnographers favored engaging research that led with 'the heart' (Ellis and Bochner 2000). Abstract theorizing or leading with 'the head' took a backseat to thickly described, evocative, or performative texts. If life is understood as a story with complex interactions between history, culture, and human thought, feeling, and behavior, then it was argued that research could be conducted and represented in such a manner. In this regard, Ellis (2004) summarized how artistic autoethnography contains,

> (a) people depicted as characters; (b) an epiphany or crisis to provide dramatic tension, around which events in the story revolve, and towards which a resolution and/or explanation is pointed; (c) a temporal ordering of events; and (d) a point or moral to the story that provides an explanation and gives meaning and value to the crisis.
>
> (Ellis 2004: 32)

Anderson (2006) has promoted a different form of autoethnography, one that is said to be analytic or realist (i.e., more scientific) that encompasses: '(1) complete member research status, (2) analytic reflexivity, (3) narrative visibility of the researcher's self, (4) dialogue with informants beyond the self, and (5) commitment to theoretical analysis' (Anderson 2006: 378). This approach favors research that is clearer, minimally incorporates story, and offers a straightforward interpretation. The author's experiences are deemed important so long as it leads to theoretical insight. Analytic autoethnography tends to use the self as a means to a theoretical end, whereas artistic autoethnography answers the call of stories by producing a gripping my-story.

Looking at autoethnography in yet another way, Burnier (2006: 414) stated that: 'it's autoethnography's "both ... and" features that make it so appealing to me as a scholar. Autoethnographic writing is both personal and scholarly, both evocative and analytical, and it is both descriptive and theoretical when it's done well.' Ellis (2004) refers to this both/and (i.e. artistic and analytic) style of research as a layered consciousness. It is layered, like lasagna, with part analytic theory and part emotive story. Expanding upon this approach, Richardson (2000) is credited with coining the term creative analytic practices (CAP) to refer to research that is both creative and analytic.

While this is a useful heuristic, the lines drawn between approaches are porous and perhaps undesirable as they may impede us from thinking in new, and possibly better, ways. Indeed, scholar-dancer Pirkko Markula (2012) advocated for an autoethnography of the 'feet' as a way to avoid dichotomous and limited thinking associated with any dominant approach. The label of 'not-yet' could appropriately describe experimental or fresh ways of doing auto-ethnography. The beginning autoethnographer needs to see that their purpose, process, and product 'fit.' We may call this harmony 'autoethnographic fit'.

In summary, our present understanding of autoethnography has three major themes: artistic, analytic, and and/both or not-yet. As can be seen in Table 19.1, each approach goes by multiple names, has been developed by several proponents, contains the essential research components of purpose, process and product, and has possible strengths and weaknesses associated. See Appendix II in Ellis (2004) for a different and lengthier typology. As autoethnography is a blurred genre (Holman-Jones 2005), defining it is like trying to use your finger to spear a fleck of egg shell darting incessantly around the bottom of a bowl. Just when you think you've got it, it shoots off in another direction.

Table 19.1 Dominant ways of understanding autoethnography

	Artistic	Analytic	And/Both, Not-Yet
Similar Names	Literary, evocative, storied, fiction, artful	Essay, realistic, objective	Creative analytic practices
Proponents	Ellis, Bochner, Denzin	Anderson, Atkinson, Charmaz	Burnier, Richardson
Purpose	Empathy, usually greater focus on self	Theoretical explanations, usually greater focus on culture	Use or reject existing approaches, create new ways, inline with author's purpose
Process	Data collected and analyzed to produce story	Data collected and analyzed with, or to produce, theory	Varied, multiple
Product	Short story, fiction, impressionist tales, life-like	Essay, scientific, realist tale, accurate	Layered, mixed, novel
Possible strengths/ weaknesses	Multiple interpretations, quality of story	Clearer interpretation, use of theory	Does not fit neatly into one camp, needs good story and use of theory

Critiques of autoethnography within social science research

The most frequent critique against autoethnography is the charge of self-indulgence or narcissism (Delamont 2009; Sparkes 2002). Critics argue that social science should be *social* and analytical, which cannot be done if autoethnography is reduced to, or chiefly about, a single author. Moreover, social scientists already hold positions of authority and legitimacy which are said to need no additional voice, power, or justice, thereby contradicting the claim that social science should be done for the public good. Furthermore, critics argue that social scientists' experiences and writing are largely dull, and that autoethnography cannot maintain a strict code of ethics since it often cannot provide confidentiality to participants.

Autoethnographers rebuke these critiques by noting that individuals and society are always mutually created, and historically and culturally situated. Autoethnographies are not merely about the author, but some experience (i.e. illness, relationship breakdown, working relationships) in connection with others and culture. Therefore, autoethnographies go beyond the self and connect with social issues such as racism, sexuality, identity, and education. Still, autoethnographies could be self-absorbed. For example, I think of typical stories students share about when he or she was an athlete and worked hard to improve, rehabilitated an injury, or helped to win or lose the big game. Stories like this often do strike me as narcissistic, especially if they do not show a significant struggle, and connect with a public issue or existing research and literature. Borrowing from C. Wright Mills (1959), I believe the autoethnographer must situate the story and the character's personal troubles within (a) public issue(s). What does the particular (individual) mean for the whole (general)? How can we change existing social structures, ways of knowing or power relations to reduce negative consequences or to live more ethically?

Why do autoethnography in sport coaching research?

Existing sports coaching autoethnographies have demonstrated how social norms influence coach's presentation of self (Jones 2006), dominant or taken for granted coaching practices lead to negative effects (Denison 2007, 2010; Gearity and Mills 2013; Potrac *et al.* 2013), and the coach–athlete relationship can be filled with care and/or conflict (Purdy *et al.* 2008; Jones 2009; Gearity and Mills 2013). Hardly narcissistic or self-indulgent, these scholar-coach-athletes engaged in an exegesis of a personal problem within a social issue and then offer possibly more effective and ethical practices to be taken up by practitioners and scholars for the public good, and for multiple uses in coach education. Behind the scenes of these published autoethnographies, the autoethnographer labored over the literature across multiple disciplines, wrestled with selecting an autoethnographic approach, and the multitude of decisions that go into storytelling. These coach-scholars have years of coaching experience, extensive knowledge of the literature in sports coaching, and an expansive education in research methods. It seems plausible to me that they selected autoethnography precisely because it was the only research approach available to help convey their story.

Given these benefits, which are intentionally not confined to the 'ivory tower' of higher education, scholars are exploring the efficacy of implementing creative analytic practices such as autoethnography (Keyes and Gearity 2011) and ethnodrama (Morgan *et al.* 2013) in the university classroom. When done well, students doing autoethnography would likely show improvement in the aforementioned areas, as well as in reflective practice and complex thought, which are related to enhanced coach effectiveness (Flyvbjerg 2001; Cushion and Nelson 2013; Gilbert and Côté 2013). Given the intensive research and writing required for autoethnography, it would appear to align well with the mission of institutions of higher education to improve student outcomes such as written communication and evaluation of (non)scientific discourses. Like ethnodrama, autoethnographies can be performed (i.e. spoken, dance, sang), thus adding an additional challenge and benefit of (non)verbal communication. Indeed, the pedagogical payoff of autoethnography could be quite handsome and deserves further research.

Applied issues and considerations

Ethics

An appropriate first step in all research is to give serious consideration to research ethics. Depending upon university and federal guidelines, as well as related laws, autoethnographers need to be aware of numerous ethical and legal issues. Two of the most prominent issues are human subjects review and confidentiality. The former tends to require that all research involving use of human subjects be reviewed by an institutional review board prior to investigation (i.e. data collection). Furthermore, the research should be of reasonable (low) risk and (nearly always) voluntary participation. The latter issue involves maintaining, if possible or unless waived, the confidentiality of subjects in the study. In qualitative research this is usually done by using pseudonyms and changing possibly identifiable information, although it may be impossible to do completely.

Although approval may be given by meeting university requirements, autoethnographers have noted ethical considerations abound. How may the subjects in the study be affected? What will they think of their portrayal? What happens to the relation between the researcher and participants after the study is completed? What if the researcher witnesses a crime, abuse, or is asked by a participant not to include something in the study? My point here is not to draw upon any number of ethical frameworks to solve or debate these issues, but to identify their existence for further discussion and consideration.

What's your research purpose?

The purpose of this section is to offer a few practical tips on how to do autoethnography. Having now discussed the multiple ways of understanding autoethnography, the beginning autoethnographer needs to consider his or her own research purpose. I believe it is vital to consider the purpose, process, and product together as they inform each other. In the last section on representation I return to this issue to discuss some tips for writing.

One final caveat. Several scholars have noted that autoethnography and narrative inquiry do not follow a set method or linear series of steps that will lead to unequivocal results or interpretations (Riessman 2008; Frank 2010). I agree with others who do social science by thinking of oneself as a *bricoleur* or artisan and to rely on one's intellectual craftsmanship (Denzin and Lincoln 2000; Frank 2010). The point is that although formal methods are offered and the beginning autoethnographer would be wise to draw upon existing examples, there is no one way to do autoethnography.

Data collection and analysis

Data collection and analysis is the lifeblood of empirical research. Data for autoethnographies come from internal (researcher's) sources (e.g. personal memories, reflections) or external (e.g. others, environment, artifacts, interviews, field notes, and observations) (Chang 2008). Data can come solely from the autoethnographers' memory of past experiences or one can plan a study and then go to the 'field' to collect data (Markula and Denison 2005). Although collecting multiple data sources (often called triangulation) could lead to a more 'complete' representation of a lived experience, the perspective of those involved must be considered. For example, a coach or athlete who's experienced abuse, injustice, or marginalization will offer a different perspective than the abuser, oppressor or dominant group.

Ellis and Bochner (2000) discuss data collection in terms of the participant-observer role. A researcher who participates in the culture he or she is studying is said to be a complete participant, while the non-participant is said to be a complete observer. Ellis refers to a wide array of participant-observer roles such as a 'complete-member researcher' (i.e. complete participant), or that one might be a 'native' autoethnographer who speaks from a traditionally marginalized position. One might also draw upon past experiences as a complete-member researcher, what Ellis labels 'reflexive ethnographies' and what Markula and Denison (2005) called 'personal experience narratives.'

A good starting point for those relying on past experiences is to write down everything you remember. Try to recollect what you were thinking, feeling, and doing. What did you say? With whom did you interact? How had you developed knowledge of yourself and your actions? Write using the five senses (i.e. sight, hear, taste, touch, smell) (Ellis 2004). Consider creating a timeline of events, a storyboard, or a concept map. Pick a specific event and write as much as possible. Add details as you remember more, and consider collecting external data.

Collecting external data can help (dis)confirm or deepen working interpretations and improve details (Chang 2008). Since good resources (see Clandinin and Connelly 2000) exist to inform autoethnographers on how to collect external data, I briefly draw attention to Ellis' (2004) three interviewing techniques particularly suited for autoethnography. *Reflexive, dyadic interviewing* is when the researcher engages the interviewee in order to reflect upon their own beliefs, values, and experiences. An *interactive interview* is a collaborative discussion that blurs the researcher–participant dichotomy. A *co-constructed interview* solicits two individuals' experience separately, and then brings them together for further discussion and elaboration. Depending upon the research purpose and data analysis strategies, interview data is often used verbatim (or with minor editing) as dialogue within the story, or the data is categorized in order to create the story's structure in terms of plot and action.

Data analysis takes place during data collection as the autoethnographer (un)intentionally attends to certain phenomena. Quite literally, we cannot study everything and our research purpose must be focused. What we attend to is based on our experiences, and all perspectives and theories are limited. Again, good resources exist on how to analyze data and the issues of analysis (Polkinghorne 1988; Clandinin and Connelly 2000; Ellis 2004; Riessman 2008; Saldana 2013). For narrative inquiry, Riessman (2008) offers four ways (e.g. thematic, structural, dialogic/performative, and visual) of analyzing data, each with unique strengths and weaknesses. Whereas Clandinin and Connelly (2000) suggest thinking narratively by attending to the stories people tell and then using theory to offer further interpretations. The beginning autoethnographer would likely benefit by early planning of the research approach, as well as writing a justification of the fit between the research purpose, process, and product.

Representation

Representation in autoethnography entails storytelling, which warrants special attention beyond the mundane description offered on research purpose, process, and product (see Chapter 9). Writing correct grammar and using a few literary devices well cannot save a bad story. Autoethnographic thinking requires asking, 'What's my story?' Imagine you've only got 30 seconds to pitch your story to a Hollywood producer. Show that you've peeled away insignificant layers to find a kernel of a story waiting to explode (Furia 2001). Continue providing fuel by crafting and editing until the kernel pops.

A few relevant items are worth discussing, such as organization and form, and writing evocatively and vulnerably. Traditional ways of doing research are organized with five clearly defined sections (i.e. introduction/need, review of literature, methods, results/findings, discussion/conclusion) and some autoethnographies follow this form; some journal editors require this as well.

Some autoethnograhphies embed the content normally found in those sections into a coherent narrative. Alternatively, artistic autoethnographies rely on a vast array of literary genres and devices such as narrative structure and plot (i.e. action, conflict, curiosity, ambiguity, suspense, climax and resolution, moral), voice, time, symbolism, and analogy. You will also need to decide if the form will be non-fiction (i.e. seeks accuracy by using facts, direct quotes), fiction (i.e. imaginary or fabricated), or creative non-fiction (i.e. draws upon but not beholden to non-fiction to produce life-like story). In order to see how sport coaching autoethnographers created a story and use theory see Jones (2006, 2009), Denison (2007), Purdy *et al.* (2008), Keyes and Gearity (2011), Gearity and Mills (2013), and Potrac *et al.* (2013).

Most social science graduate programs do not offer a course on writing, let alone creative writing in which writing evocatively or vulnerably would be discussed. The issue of showing/telling is often identified as a way to write more evocatively.

Here's an example of telling:

It was hot outside and my coach yelled at us.

Here's showing:

Sand kicked up as the gruff coach, hoarse from a long afternoon of berating me and twenty-five of my teammates to sprint again and again, stomped his worn brown cowboy boots across the heat scorn Mississippi field. Beads of sweat poured steadily ...

All writers do a bit of telling and showing. Telling is more concise and useful for minimizing insignificant actions. Autoethnographers rely on telling when they want to use theory or give a straightforward analysis of a lived experience. Some readers and scholars prefer the clearer interpretation offered by telling, while others, more narrative/literary oriented, would rather be intentionally ambiguous. It should make more sense now that analytic autoethnographies rely more on telling than showing. Showing delivers a rich, vivid description that aims to hook the interest and curiosity of the reader. Emotions and emotional reactions can be felt. Unfortunately, showing can take up much of the precious word limit allowed for research articles. A few tips to write more evocatively include alternating sentence length, relying on verbs, and agonizing over word choice. Go study how to write. Practice. Reflect.

Perhaps appropriately, the last word on representation goes to writing vulnerably (i.e. did you recognize the irony?). Vulnerable writing of the self entails having the courage (Goodall Jr. 2008) to share your story, to bear witness (Smith 1999), or what we may call a methodology of the heart (Pelias 2004). Vulnerable writing taps into the author's existential crises, and it is better than writing that deflects or is callous. There's no easy answer on how to do this or even encouragement to do it. It is your choice. You will need to consider that being vulnerable means overcoming personal insecurities and the social risk of stigma, or being labeled abnormal.

For one of my autoethnographies I had a frank discussion with my doctoral advisor and co-author as she was a central character in my story. She agreed to let me tell the story I wanted to, which required me to say some not so nice things about her, and me. Both of us were comfortable with this decision, others may not be. I'm currently working on an autoethnography about the experience of my mother dying from cancer when I was 13, and my high-school football coach's response. I had not thought to write about that experience until I came into autoethnography. While working on this story at my desk in my office at the university I began to weep quietly. In my current draft, I incorporated this into my story and I'm going to play with time and memory as my plot centers on the coach–athlete relationship. I had one student weep while performing her autoethnography on struggling with gender as an African-American lesbian high school athlete. In a move of vulnerability, another student changed topics in the middle of a course to show his struggle with the suicide of a former coach he adored. The beginning autoethnographer will need to choose what he or she is comfortable sharing and the potential effects of telling his or her story.

Reflections from the field

Sounding like a coach, Goodall Jr. (2008) offers writers a seemingly obvious pearl-of-wisdom that deep down we admit whilst hoping for a panacea: 'The secret is that there is no secret' (Goodall Jr. 2008: 60). Autoethnography requires hard work and humility to edit, delete sections, or even to start over. As I painstakingly reflect on my autoethnographic experiences, I've settled on three aspects to share. The first deals with being a scholar-autoethnographer. I think it is the role of an autoethnographer (scholar in general) to be knowledgeable of social science and qualitative research as a whole, and related literature and theories within (and hopefully across) one's discipline. This ideal cannot be reached, promotes connoisseurship, and is likely required to consistently do quality work.

The beginning autoethnographer will undoubtedly be less knowledgeable of social science literature, but may indeed have a story worth sharing. Such was the case with a former undergraduate student of mine, Megan Keyes. Megan crafted a brilliant autoethnogrpahic poem (rap) that she performed for our class and later at the 7th Annual International Congress of Qualitative Inquiry. With my suggestion and offer to edit the introductions of her stories (which were void of theory, and written by her friend which resulted in weak writing compared to hers), I added a creative and theoretical voice to complement the text. Although not every story is published, and you may not want to perform or share it, you can still reap the benefits (identified earlier) from crafting a moving tale.

A second final thought deals with evaluating autoethnography. While crafting your own work, it is useful to try to know how others will evaluate your work (see Chapter 18). Richardson's (2000) widely cited five criteria set the standard for evaluating creative analytic practices. For the sake of space, I paraphrase them here:

- Substantive contribution – is the work insightful or critical of existing ways of knowing?
- Esthetic merit – is the work appealing, evocative, or pleasing?
- Reflexivity – does the author demonstrate a limited, complex, or ethical understanding of his or her place in the research?
- Impact – will the reader remember the piece, be affected by it?
- Expression of a reality – does the work reflect real-life qualities, otherwise known as verisimilitude?

Criteria abound in qualitative research, as do rebuttals and cautions against policing ourselves (Sparkes and Smith 2009). Here, I direct the interested reader to Sparkes' (2002) excellent work in which he reviews many of these issues.

Reviewers of my autoethnographies were concerned with issues of methodological transparency and exactness. They wanted to know more about me personally and my intent (not research purpose), where my data came from, and how exactly I created my story. Transparency is often cited as a canon of good reporting in all research (AERA 2006), but I did not want to take up space with a lengthy, dull, and irrelevant description of some non-existent systematic process on my ability to produce stories. Linking back to a point identified earlier, narrative scholars have argued against the existence of such methodological determinism.

In a review of an extended abstract, a reviewer warned me that it verged on 'self-promotion' and lacked 'constructive analysis'. Since this artistic autoethnography was about self-change and I took great efforts to be vulnerable in sharing intimate details of my own inadequacy, I thought the reviewer might simply be regurgitating popular critique without evidence. Nonetheless, it benefited me as I became more aware that I did not want the story to be perceived as a 'good for me' plot (i.e. self-promotion) and that I had to make a better case for narrative, not an autopsy of my narrative (i.e. what the reviewer called a constructive analysis).

The last point(s) I'd like to make is to offer a few final tips on improving one's writing, which may begin by self-identifying as a writer. I am a writer. Say it. Awareness of issues relevant to writing and conscientiousness to address them are desirable qualities for writers. To help writing Goodall Jr. (2008) suggests creating a storyboard showing key scenes, characters, and action. I often think of how my story might be told if it were a movie or TV show. Stories often have a (non)linear three-part structure containing a setup, conflict or complicating action, and a climax and resolution. I'm easily drawn to television series and movies that predictably use this structure while paradoxically (perhaps) holding my attention. I had a terrifically creative student present an autoethnography that blended fiction and non-fiction through an imaginary dream. I've come to appreciate how challenging and enjoyable it is to tell a good story. I need to better understand how to create characters, scenes, and dialogue. I'm no longer so naïve as to think a couple of drafts will suffice. As such, I continue searching for other, and possibly better, ways of doing autoethnography.

References

Anderson, L. (2006) 'Analytic Autoethnography', *Journal of Contemporary Ethnography*, 35(4): 373–95.

American Educational Research Association [AERA] (2006) 'Standards for reporting on empirical social science research in AERA publications', *Educational Researcher*, 35(6): 33–40.

Burnier, D. (2006) 'Encounters with the self in social science research: A political scientist looks at autoethnography', *Journal of Contemporary Ethnography*, 35(4): 410–18.

Chang, H. (2008) *Autoethnography as Method*, Walnut Creek, CA: Left Coast Press.

Clandinin, D. J. and Connelly, M. (2000) *Narrative Inquiry: Experience and Story in Qualitative Research*, San Francisco, CA: Jossey-Bass.

Cushion, C. and Nelson, L. (2013) 'Coach education and learning', in P. Potrac, W. Gilbert and J. Denison (eds) *Routledge Handbook of Sports Coaching*, London: Routledge, 359–74.

Delamont, S. (2009) 'The only honest thing: Autoethnography, reflexivity and small crises in fieldwork', *Ethnography and Education*, 4(1): 51–63.

Denison, J. (2007) 'Social theory for sport coaches: A Foucauldian reading of one athlete's poor performance', *International Journal of Sports Science & Coaching*, 2(4): 369–83.

——(2010) 'Planning, practice, and performance', *Sport, Education and Society*, 15: 461–78.

Denzin, N. K. (2001) *Interpretive Interactionism*, Thousand Oaks, CA: Sage.

Denzin, N. K. and Lincoln, Y. S. (2000) 'Introduction: The discipline and practice of qualitative research', in N. K. Denzin and Y. S. Lincoln (eds) *Handbook of Qualitative Research* (2nd ed.), Thousand Oaks, CA: Sage, 1–29.

Ellis, C. (2004) *The Ethnographic I: A Methodological Novel about Autoethnography*, Walnut Creek, CA: AltaMira Press.

Ellis, C. and Bochner, A. P. (2000) 'Autoethnography, personal narrative, reflexivity: Researcher as subject', in N. K. Denzin and Y. S. Lincoln (eds) *Handbook of Qualitative Research* (2nd ed.), Thousand Oaks, CA: Sage, 733–68.

Flyvbjerg, B. (2001) *Making Social Science Matter: Why Social Inquiry Fails and How it Can Succeed Again*, Cambridge: Cambridge University Press.

Frank, A. W. (2010) *Letting Stories Breathe: A Socio-narratology*, Chicago: University of Chicago Press.

Furia, P. (2001) 'As time goes by: Creating biography', in C. Forche and P. Gerard (eds) *Writing Creative Nonfiction: Instruction and Insights from the Teachers of the Associated Writing Programs*, Cincinnati, OH: Story Press.

Gearity, B. T. and Mills, J. (2013) 'Discipline and punish in the weight room', *Sport Coaching Review*, 1(2): 124–34.

Gilbert, W. and Côté, J. (2013) 'Defining coaching effectiveness: Focus on coaches' knowledge', in P. Potrac, W. Gilbert and J. Denison (eds) *Routledge Handbook of Sports Coaching*, London: Routledge, 147–59.

Goodall Jr., H. L. (2008) *Writing Qualitative Inquiry: Self, Stories, and Academic Life*, Walnut Creek, CA: Left Coast Press.

Holman-Jones, S. (2005) 'Autoethnography: Making the personal political', in N. K. Denzin and Y. S. Lincoln (eds) *Handbook of Qualitative Research* (3rd ed.), Thousand Oaks, CA: Sage, 763–91.

Jones, R. (2006) 'Dilemmas, maintaining "face," and paranoia: An average coaching life', *Qualitative Inquiry*, 12(5), 1012–21.

Jones, R. L. (2009) 'Coaching as caring (the smiling gallery): accessing hidden knowledge', *Physical Education and Sport Pedagogy*, 14(4), 377–90.

Keyes, M. S. and Gearity, B. T. (2011) 'Narratives of sport pedagogies: The poetic representation of life beyond dreams', *Cultural Studies < = > Critical Methodologies*, 11(5), 511–15: DOI 10.1177/1532708611423214.

Markula, P. (2012, Saturday, May 19, 2012) *Running memories in the time of aeon*. Paper presented at the Eighth International Congress of Qualitative Inquiry, Urbana-Champaign, IL.

Markula, P. and Denison, J. (2005) 'Sport and personal narrative', in D. Andrews, D. Mason and M. Silk (eds) *Qualitative Methods in Sports Studies*, Oxford: Berg, 165–84.

Mills, C. W. (1959) *The Sociological Imagination*, New York: Oxford University Press.

Morgan, K., Jones, R. L., Gilbourne, D. and Llewellyn, D. (2013) 'Innovative approaches in coach education pedagogy', in P. Potrac, W. Gilbert and J. Denison (eds) *Routledge Handbook of Sports Coaching*, London: Routledge, 486–96.

Pearce, C. (2010) 'The crises and freedoms of researching your own life', *Journal of Research Practice*, 6(1): http://jrp.icaap.org/index.php/jrp/article/view/219/184.

Pelias, R. J. (2004) *A Methodology of the Heart: Evoking Academic and Daily Life*, Walnut Creek, CA: AltraMira Press.

Polkinghorne, D. E. (1988) *Narrative Knowing and the Human Sciences*, Albany, NY: State University of New York Press.

Potrac, P., Jones, R., Nelson, L. and Gilbourne, D. (2013) 'Handshakes, BBQs, and bullets: Self-interest, shame and regret in football coaching', *Sports Coaching Review*, 1(2): 79–92.

Purdy, L., Potrac, P. and Jones, R. (2008) 'Power, consent and resistance: An autoethnography of competitive rowing', *Sport, Education and Society*, 13(3): 319–36.

Reed-Danahay, D. E. (ed.) (1997) *Auto/Ethnography: Rewriting the Self and the Social*, New York: Berg.

Richardson, L. (2000) 'Writing: a method of inquiry', in N. Denzin and Y. Lincoln (eds) *Handbook of Qualitative Research* (2nd ed.), London: Sage.

Riessman, C. K. (2008) *Narrative Methods for the Human Sciences*, Thousand Oaks, CA: Sage.

Saldana, J. (2013) *The Coding Manual for Qualitative Researchers* (2nd ed.), Thousand Oaks, CA: Sage.

Smith, B. (1999) The Abyss: Exploring depression through a narrative of the self, *Qualitative Inquiry*, 5(2), 264–79.

Sparkes, A. C. (2000) 'Autoethnography and narratives of self: Reflections on criteria in action', *Sociology of Sport Journal*, 17(1): 21–43.

——(2002) *Telling Tales in Sport and Physical Activity: A Qualitative Journey*, Urbana-Champaign, IL: Human Kinetics.

Sparkes, A. and Smith, B. (2009) 'Judging the quality of qualitative inquiry: Criteriology and relativisim in action', *Psychology of Sport and Exercise*, 10, 491–7.

Van Maanen, J. (1988) *Tales of the Field: On Writing Ethnography*, Chicago: University of Chicago Press.

20 Discourse analysis

Joseph Mills and Jim Denison

Introduction and overview

The philosopher, social theorist, and historian Michel Foucault provided a body of work that showed future researchers how to understand the ways in which particular discourses, or ways of knowing, evolved over time (Markula and Silk 2011). Specifically, by addressing what power *is* and how it *works* through language, Foucault showed how knowledge about any subject could be controlled. In these ways, Foucault's work has enormous potential for students researching coaching because their analysis can work to uncover the formation of coaches' knowledge and how their practices have been influenced by so many subtle operations of power and language. Accordingly, it is important that students gain an understanding of how power operates in coach and athlete settings. Moreover, such analysis can help coaches become aware of previously unconsidered spaces for practising sport that may be more effective.

Students who intend to use Michel Foucault's work as the inspiration for their research have to understand two fundamental tenets of Foucault's work. The first is the paradigmatic framework in which Foucault's theorizing sits. The process of doing research that 'matters' means researchers must understand the philosophical parameters that guide their research (Markula and Silk 2011). Paradigms are conceptual frames of reference that provide the ontological (how the researcher sees the world) and epistemological (how that view guides the gaining of knowledge) frames that shape a researcher's 'way' (Kvale 1996). Such clarity enables researchers to provide a justification for their methods and the subsequent claims that the research enables them to make. In so doing, their research makes sense. A second tenet central to a Foucauldian research project is to employ a method that is driven by his theoretical concepts. Therefore, it is essential that the student coach researcher understand the fundamental concepts of Foucault's toolkit when putting together a Foucauldian-inspired research project.

Foucault's paradigm

Foucault was among a group of French philosophers – Derrida, Lacan, Barthes, Deleuze – who were generally considered to have articulated social theories that, although different, were united in their opposition to the universal nature of structuralism: the search for underlying patterns of thought – structures – in all forms of human activity. This opposition is today referred to as poststructuralism and is often grouped with postmodern thought. Of the many problems with these labels, arguably the most prominent would be each theorist's refusal to be categorized under any specific term. Nonetheless, it is useful to understand, albeit broadly, where poststructuralism comes from and what it hopes to achieve.

One could describe postmodern/structural thinking as stemming from serious questions concerning the 'grand narratives' of modern society. Jean-François Lyotard (1989), when describing the postmodern condition, illustrated how the Enlightenment's belief in progress created a way of talking that promised the emancipation of humanity. At the same time, the political economies of capitalism created a narrative that promised great wealth. Although the spirit of these narratives remained strong, their legitimations did not. Simply put, not everyone prospered. Within coaching, and in particular endurance running, the meta-narratives one hears are equally contradictory. Great rewards are promised for the athletes who train the hardest. But this is not credible, as the athletes who simply 'do more' are also more likely to become injured. It is a narrative that does not make sense as successful coaches require their athletes to do more and less training at the same time. The same may be true in other sports and this is one example of a contradiction in coaching that requires coaches to juggle and tinker with myriad training variables.

Problematic contradictions are an integral feature of the ways in which we come to understand and talk about the things we do such as coaching. Therefore, one characteristic of postmodern/structural thought is the search for better means of understanding these ways of talking and thinking.

> And in this context, I say that our role as thinkers is to deepen our understanding of what goes on in language, to critique the vapid idea of information, to reveal an irremediable opacity at the very core of language.
>
> (Lyotard 1989: 218)

In the absence of modern universal systems of language and knowledge, emphasis has been increasingly given to the perspectives and contexts that researchers bring to their research. Instead of one reality, poststructural/modernists believe in multiple realities. Our lives are filtered through a multitude of lenses, such as language, gender, social class, race, and ethnicity. This brings with it a complete rejection of the idea of one true objective reality. Instead 'it is the structures of language that speak through the person' (Kvale 1996: 52). Individuals are seldom able to give full explanations of their actions or intentions; all they can offer are accounts, or stories, about what they did and why. No single method can grasp the subtle variations in ongoing human experience (Denzin and Lincoln 2008). So how can Foucault's perspective enable a coaching student to analyze these subtle variations?

Power

One of the unique aspects of Foucault's theoretical toolkit is his use and under-standing of power. In contrast to a more traditional understanding of power as something that is used to repress others, Foucault (1987: 11) preferred the term, 'the relationships of power'. For Foucault power does something, it is constantly performed. It is a verb not a noun, a strategy. As a result, power is difficult to explain, locate, or analyze. Rather, power is largely 'anonymous, almost unspoken' (Foucault 1978: 95). Consequently, there is no escaping power, and resisting it is difficult because it is present *everywhere*. Foucault (1978) saw power more like a net or a dense web, a 'capillary-like network', working in myriad meticulous and hidden ways that we simply cannot see and so take for granted.

Discourse

According to Foucault, how power is typically 'played out' is through the ways we talk and think, or what we can refer to as discourse (language). Foucault attempted to articulate his understanding of discourse in his books *The Order of Things* (1966) and *The Archaeology of Knowledge* (1972). Discourses control what can be understood and in so doing can also obscure what potentially could be understood. In framing what is said about a topic such as coaching, a discourse draws boundaries that omits alternatives. Some statements are circulated widely, while others are restricted. It is difficult to think of expressing oneself in ways outside of discourse because to do so one would be, by definition, outside of comprehension or reason (Young 1981). For example, today as we have suggested, it simply does not make sense to perceive coaching in any way other than a process that should be structured, rational, objective, systematic, and planned. Hence we have the oft-noted observations in coaching, 'proper preparation prevents piss-poor performance'; or 'fail to plan, plan to fail'. And it was the effects of the circulation of such statements that Foucault (1972) was interested in. Importantly, discourse is not as simple as translating reality; instead it is the system that structures the way we perceive reality. In these ways, discourse is inextricably linked to power.

As one of his major contributions, Foucault (1978) brought discourse into a relationship with power and asked how they produce each other. In this way, power is a productive force because it 'produces' that which we believe to be true: the knowledges that shape our realities. Together, power and discourse create the ways in which we can understand our *selves* and the things we do. For example, we understand that the more coaches can plan their athletes' preparation, the more likely they are to be successful (Denison 2010).

Practice

Another way in which Foucault described the 'playing out' of power was its effect on the body. Foucault (1977) was concerned with the ways in which bodies were organized in the modern world in order to 'expose a body totally imprinted by history and the process of history's destruction of the body' (Foucault 1977: 148). For example, we do not question that children, from the age of four, have to go to school; or that if we are seriously ill we have to go to hospital to get better; or that to be a successful athlete one needs a coach. Although these actions and the social institutions that support them make sense, there may be many unforeseen consequences associated with them. Therefore, understanding how power and discourse (knowledge) combine and act on the body can lead to everyday practices becoming normalized, and this understanding is central to any Foucauldian research project. For it is in this way that humans can become fixed into specific roles that may unintentionally limit their actions without their realization.

A simple example of how power and discourse work together to produce a taken-for-granted truth is how we have come to understand the athletic body as a machine (Hoberman 1992; Howe 2004; Shilling 2003; Hughson 2009). Like machines, bodies are often talked about in ways that give them components that can be scrutinized, so that malfunctions can be diagnosed. They can then be taken apart, reassembled, and the problems remedied (Kirk 2002). As a result, the muscular system is commonly explained in textbooks as a series of levers and pulleys, implying that muscles work in isolation and that movement is subsequently robotic in nature (Rosser 2001). However, muscles seldom work in isolation and movement is fluid, not robotic. Today the role of strength and conditioning coaches is usually to 'strengthen' specific and isolated areas of the athletic body. For example, using exercises like chest and shoulder presses, or bicep and hamstring curls, implies the strengthening of one muscle that may actually disrupt the harmonious working of the whole body.

Applied issues and considerations

One of Foucault's close friends, Gilles Deleuze (1988), argued that Foucault's books *The Archaeology of Knowledge* and *Discipline and Punish* were significant turning points in Foucault's work. The first book described ways of understanding 'discursive' formations that involve statements, which Deleuze (1988) termed 'articulable'. In more simple terms, it outlined how one could analyze discourse, a Foucualdian discourse analysis. Such methodologies involve a document/textual analysis and provide a determining form to understand practice. The second book described how one could analyze 'non-discursive' formations that involve environments or everyday practices. This analysis Deleuze (1988) termed 'visible' and involved any combination of participant observations/interviews. Through these two distinct methodologies – articulable and visible forms – a researcher can gain an understanding of the way power operates in specific contexts and environments. Coaching statements produce coaching environments, just as coaching environments determine coaching statements. In summary, alongside the rules of the production of discourse, Foucault was interested in the expression of its power – the way discourse and actions work together to reinforce and control what can be said, thought, and practiced about a subject.

The articulable form: A Foucauldian discourse analysis

The term discourse analysis has a number of meanings that cross paradigms and research traditions. The aims of Foucault's discursive method were to uncover the knowledges that dominated particular fields, to understand how they have become dominant and where they have come from (Liao and Markula 2009). By its nature, a Foucauldian discourse analysis is flexible and unprescriptive: 'I take care not to dictate how things should be' (Foucault 1994: 288). As a result, greater demands are placed upon the researcher to ensure his or her procedures are rigorous and clear enough to ensure the findings make sense. In an effort to provide some structure to doing a Foucauldian discourse analysis, Markula and Silk (2011) offered the following analytical steps (see Table 20.1).

The first analytic step involves determining what Foucault (1972) called the 'object' and 'enunciations' for the study. In practical terms, this means having a clear idea of 'what' is being studied and the types of texts that provide information or knowledge about that subject. One 'object' Foucault (1972) continually referred to by way of example was madness, and the profession that had the authority to talk about madness was medicine. Therefore, the 'enunciations' of the subject – the places where madness was legitimately talked about – were the hospital, private practice, the laboratory, and the library.

Table 20.1 Foucauldian discourse analysis

Analytical procedure	How to do it?
Object	What is the object of the study?
Enunciations	Who and what is talking/speaking? Where are they talking?
Concepts	What terms/words are repeated most often? How is the object talked about?
Statements	In what ways do the concepts link together to form meaningful statements? What statements are made?
Conceptual/theoretical formations	In what ways do the statements link together to form meaningful theories? What specific theories are made?
Power relations	How does "who" is speaking connect to the sciences? What nameable sciences define the object?
Overall objective	What effect or practice is produced through the discourses? What are the conditions of possibility for the object?

Once the appropriate data sample has been selected, the next analytic steps in a Foucauldian discourse analysis could be described as a series of discursive abstractions, i.e. the search for the most common series of words, phrases, sentences, and theories are abstracted (listed) from the texts.

To begin this process of identifying abstractions the researcher needs to first search for repetitive concepts found in his or her texts (key words or terms continually repeated). This process allows the coach researcher to determine what concepts (key words) dominate effective coaching. The next level of abstraction involves the analysis of how these concepts (key words) are talked about or how they begin to form meaningful statements – what key statements are actually made. A next step is to examine the rules that make statements meaningful. In other words, what specific (key) theories are made. By identifying how the objects, enunciations, and concepts link to form meaningful statements, theories then start to emerge.

Because Foucault viewed power as being productive, the final stage of a Foucauldian discursive analysis is to connect the discourses to the nameable sciences (i.e. the power relations) that define the texts being examined. In other words, the coaching researcher is able to understand which sciences dominate the coaching of specific sports. Therefore, by observing how the discourses function – who is speaking – we can understand what can be included in the discourse; which then appear in a variety of sites (e.g. texts, documents, locations), triangulating (forming) the object. Consequently, we have an understanding of the ways coaches know about their training practices. For example, in endurance running the 'who' that is speaking, or the science that saturates coaching textbooks, is physiology. As a result, athletes are described as having engines that must be fine-tuned and given the best petrol. The athlete as a complex, emotional, flawed, and intelligent human being is overlooked. In summary, a Foucauldian discourse analysis aims to explore how certain discourses gain dominance in order to understand the specific practices that become acceptable.

The visible form: Analysis of coaching environments

The transition to modern, capitalist society brought with it new ways of organizing every aspect of society, including sport. Markula and Pringle (2006) referred to the powers that were developed to organize 'bodies' in society as a productive force as 'technologies of domination'. This organization became what Deleuze (1988: 32) referred to as practical formations that were visible – 'the system of light' – and so involves coaching environments, contexts, and practices. This was the theme in Foucault's next books, *The History of Sexuality Vol. 1* (1978) and *Discipline and Punish* (1995).

In the first book, Foucault (1978) articulated a subtle power that existed in society called the confessional. So inconspicuous yet penetrating and profound a power is it, that Foucault (1978: 60) described the obligation to confess as something that is 'no longer perceived as the effect of a power that constrains us'. Foucault (1978) detailed how throughout the Middle Ages the confession was only an annual activity. However, with the Counter-Reformation, and the rise of Protestantism, the authority of the Catholic Church was significantly challenged. In order to maintain its influence, the obligation to confess became a more frequent experience until it was employed in a whole series of relationships in society. Foucault's (1978) key point was that confessional powers initiated a process whereby individuals gained a conscience that prevents deviation from whatever is perceived as normal.

In addition, modernizing society produced disciplinary powers that also worked by processes of normalization and so strongly reinforced the ties to normality. Disciplinary powers – mapped out in *Discipline and Punish* (Foucault 1995) – were adopted to organize bodies, such as the soldier, or for our purpose the athlete, in the most prevalent social institutions. For Foucault (1995) this organization of the body came at a cost. The subjection, use, transformation and improvement of the body necessary for increasing performance (utility), renders it docile which may be problematic for peak performance.

As we can see, the first part of our Foucauldian analysis aims to uncover how what is normal is defined through discourse, while the second part of the analysis aims to uncover how what is normal is reinforced in practice. This is acquired, first, by understanding what the various confessional and disciplinary techniques are; and second, by uncovering through interviews or observational methods how these techniques work in practice. Therefore, it is crucial that the coach researcher knows what the numerous small techniques are and how they are put into practice. For a detailed outline of the confession the reader is encouraged to consult Markula and Pringle (2006); and for a detailed outline of disciplinary powers, see Denison *et al.* (2013) and Gearity and Mills (2013).

In brief, discipline works by organizing athletic training via the meticulous control of space and time into a rational, hierarchical, and observable order. This order is normalized and so it ensures a complete fixing or control over the coach and athlete. For example, coaches usually prescribe training efforts that finish at specific markers. The idea of athletes finishing in an area they define and control seems absurd, yet it may be more effective as athletes then learn how to take control of their efforts. In short, 'discipline is a political anatomy of detail' (Foucault 1995: 139). In emphasizing the word 'detail', Foucault (1995) reinforced the importance of things that ordinarily we take for granted. Therefore many of these techniques appear self-evident and to be without them simply would not make sense. However, it is only when considering the totality of these small details that we can start to get a sense of the strength of their hold. Normalization is further reinforced or strengthened by the almost inconspicuous effect of confessional power. The five analytic steps of a confession – personal history, general causality, latency, expert interpretation, therapy – work to produce the truths to which coaches' *selves* have to become because the steps are defined in relation to the norm. In more simple terms, *anything* can be explained by an expert coach, and so it becomes almost impossible for the novice coach to operate outside of the problematic disciplinary framework. Taken together, coaches can be said to be continually striving towards socially constructed norms that are created by discourse and the operation of these powers. Coaches believe these norms to be true and simply cannot perceive any other ways of coaching.

The final aspect of a Foucauldian discourse analysis involves validating or evaluating the research. Validating poststructural research is a subject of great debate (Baudrillard 1983; Denzin 1995; Kvale and Brinkmann 2009). Any attempt to classify poststructural analysis is by its very nature unlikely to be completely satisfactory. 'They are all reflexive and messy. That is as it should be, for the world we encounter is neither neat nor easy to make sense of' (Denzin 1995: 45). Nonetheless, the logic of validation depends on theoretically driven, practically applicable, socially situated knowledge (Markula and Silk 2011). Researchers are encouraged to engage in reflexive practices in order to consider their topic from multiple perspectives and so produce rich, nuanced, coherent, and contextualized research knowledge.

Reflections from the field

To date, although the application of Foucault's work in sport studies is a burgeoning field, there are very few examples of researchers that have used his theoretical framework to gather data. Therefore this is an exciting moment for future researchers willing to use the method(s) we have outlined in this chapter because their work, by its nature, could be considered progressive within the wider field of coach education. It should be clear by now that Foucault's method is inextricably linked to theory. It is simply not possible to proceed without the appropriate theoretical understanding. The methods – document, interview, observations – and analytic foci are mutually dependent and develop as a result of each other. As a result, the focus of our chapter has been to describe how to develop the theoretical/analytical tools that complement the more traditional data-gathering methods. It has not been our intention to discuss traditional qualitative methods such as interviews or observations as it is highly likely the student researcher has already gleaned this information.

When conducting research in the field, given the inherent nature of Foucault's theoretical framework, the researcher should expect to be looking at the unfolding data through 'different eyes' than their participants. It is easy to get the sense, when reading Foucault, that he enjoyed upsetting the normal order – like a troublesome dinner guest who asks the hosts awkward questions. Sociologists refer to this process as 'problematizing', not for the sake of creating problems but in order to find ways of improving practices that most people take for granted. Nonetheless, it could be considered that the default position of the Foucauldian researcher is to challenge dominant ways of thinking or practicing (i.e. outside of reason or normal). As we have suggested, coaches, without the knowledge of the theory, may find it extremely difficult to perceive any other way of being. Inevitably this has led us on many occasions to ask questions that are generally considered by our research participants as coming out of left field.

There are some inevitable consequences for the student coach researcher when carrying out a research project that is considered to be coming from left field. First, one must proceed with great respect, care, caution, and charm. Asking experienced, knowledgeable, and successful coaches to consider different ways of thinking about practices they're generally considered as experts in has the potential to produce uncomfortable moments. Many questions we posed to our participants had to be phrased indirectly such as, 'I wonder'; 'I get a sense that'; 'What would you think if I suggested?' 'You're already very good at that but how do we make more coaches aware?' 'I wonder if you would indulge me?' 'I wonder if we could explore together?'

Second, we have found through our research using Foucault that generally participants enjoy the chance to 'get dirty' with knowledge and practice about which they are extremely passionate. This has meant that often our participants have taken some time to process some of the questions, suggestions, or exchanges that took place in their interviews. Subsequently, the most fruitful part of the interview process for us has been at the very end when the participant wants to return to discuss issues on which he or she has clearly been ruminating. Other participants have simply refused to consider any other ways of thinking about coaching, which has led to some amusing exchanges.

Finally, in the process of conducting our research, we have uncovered a number of coaching practices that our Foucauldian stance considers problematic, contradictory, or an ineffective taken-for-granted assumption. At every turn, as we have returned to review theory in between data collection points, new ways of looking at or considering the unfolding data occur. Moreover, many of them have arisen from what for most researchers would appear small, inconsequential, or insignificant moments. For that reason using follow-up interviews alongside observational data has in our experience been very fruitful, as it provided us with the opportunity to account for as wide a range of complexities – the overlaps, tensions and relations – as possible. In short, to pursue every moment of the data collection and analysis phases that did not make sense.

A constant theme running through Foucault's work was the importance of ongoing critical thought to enable researchers to find more instructive ways of seeing the 'things' that society often assumes to be self-evident. In this sense, Foucault gave researchers the license to dip in and out of his theoretical tool-box. We would advocate this approach and encourage researchers to explore other aspects of Foucault's theorizing that we have omitted here. However, we still would caution researchers that whatever Foucauldian tool they use they should employ it with the intention of being as true as possible to Foucault's paradigmatic logic and his major theoretical concepts, which we have outlined here. In this way, the project will have greater integrity as a Foucauldian study and a far greater likelihood to truly matter.

References

Baudrillard, J. (1983) *Simulations*, New York: Semiotext(s).

Deleuze, G. (1988) *Foucault*, London: Athlone Press.

Denison, J. (2010) 'Planning, practice and performance: The discursive construction of coaches' knowledge', *Sport, Education and Society*, 15: 461–78.

Denison, J., Mills, J. P. and Jones, L. (2013) 'Effective coaching as a modernist formation: A Foucauldian critique', in P. Potrac, W. Gilbert and J. Denison (eds) *Routledge Handbook of Sports Coaching*, London: Routledge, 388–99.

Denzin, N. K. (1995) 'Poststructural crisis in the social sciences', in R. H. Brown (ed.) *Postmodern Representations: Truth, Power, and Mimesis in the Human Sciences and Public Culture*, Champaign, IL: University of Illinois Press, 38–60.

Denzin, N. K. and Lincoln, Y. S. (2008) 'Introduction: The discipline and practice of qualitative research', in N. K. Denzin and Y. S. Lincoln (eds) *Collecting and Interpreting Qualitative Materials* (3rd ed.), Thousand Oaks, CA: Sage, 1–45.

Foucault, M. (1966) *The Order of Things*, Paris: Editions Gaillimard.

——(1972) *The Archaeology of Knowledge*, New York: Vintage.

——(1977) 'Nietzsche, genealogy, history', in D. F. Bouchard (ed.) *Language, Counter Memory, Practice Selected Essays and Interviews by Michel Foucault*, New York: Cornell University Press, 139–64.

——(1978) *The History of Sexuality, volume 1: An Introduction*, New York: Vintage.

——(1987) 'The ethic of care for the self as a practice of freedom', in J. Bernauer and D. Rasmussen (eds) *The final Foucault*, Cambridge: MIT Press.

——(1994) 'An Interview with Michel Foucault', in J. D. Faubion (ed.) *Power, Volume 3*, New York: The New Press, 239–97.

——(1995) *Discipline and Punish* (2nd ed.), New York: Vintage.

Gearity, B. and Mills, J. P. (2013) 'Discipline and punish in the weights room', *Sports Coaching Review*, 1(2): 124–34.

Hoberman, J. (1992) *Mortal Engines: The Science of Performance and the Dehumanization of Sport*, Caldwell: The Blackburn Press.

Howe, D. (2004) *Sport, Professionalism and Pain: Ethnographies of Injury and Risk*, London: Routledge.

Hughson, J. (2009) *The Making of Modern Sporting Cultures*, London: Routledge.

Kirk, D. (2002) 'The social construction of the body in physical education and sport', in A. Laker (ed.) *The Sociology of Sport and Physical Education: An Introductory Reader*, London: Routledge.

Kvale, S. (1996) *Interviews: An Introduction to Qualitative Research Interviewing*, London: Sage.

Kvale, S. and Brinkmann, S. (2009) *Interviews*, London: Sage.

Liao, J. and Markula, P. (2009) 'Reading media texts in Women's sport: Critical discourse analysis and Foucauldian discourse analysis', in P. Markula (ed.) *Olympic Women and the Media*, Basingstoke: Palgrave Macmillan, 30–49.

Lyotard, J. F. (1989) 'Rules and paradoxes and svelte appendix', *Cultural Critique*, 5: 209–19.

Markula, P. and Pringle, R. (2006) *Foucault, Sport, and Exercise: Power, Knowledge and Transforming the Self*, New York: Routledge.

Markula, P. and Silk, M. (2011) *Qualitative Research for Physical Culture*, Basingstoke: Palgrave Macmillan.

Rosser, M. (2001) *Body Fitness and Exercise: Basic Theory and Practice for Therapists* (2nd ed.), London: Hodder and Stoughton.

Shilling, C. (2003) *The Body and Social Theory* (2nd ed.), London: Sage.

Young, R. (1981) *Untying the Text: A Post-structural Anthology*, Boston: Routledge and Kegan Paul.

21 Conversation analysis

Ryan Groom, Lee Nelson, Paul Potrac, and Christopher Cushion

Introduction and overview

The interactions that occur between coaches and athletes within the coaching context are widely acknowledged to be a central feature of sports coaching (e.g. d'Arripe-Longueville *et al.* 2001; Cushion and Jones 2006; Purdy *et al.* 2008). However, few methods for studying the use of language have been employed in the sports coaching literature in comparison to the techniques and procedures employed within the social sciences. Phillips and Hardy (2002) have highlighted that such approaches are often collectively termed 'discourse analysis' and are aimed at exploring the relationship between the practices of talking, writing, and reality through the analysis of data from interviews, documents, political speeches, and naturally occurring conversations (see Chapter 20). Whilst there are similarities across the range of methods for analyzing interactions, these approaches are often underpinned by differing ontological (the nature of reality) and epistemological (the nature of knowledge) positions with regard to the importance placed upon the social and historical context, the role of the analyst in interpreting the data, and the empirical material under investigation. This chapter principally focuses upon conversation analysis (CA) as a methodological approach to better understand the nuanced, temporal, initiation, reaction, and exchange processes that occur within coaching contexts (Jones *et al.* 2010). Informed by a 'social research' approach, the aim of such investigation is to produce knowledge through the inspection of empirical evidence to understand the structures and processes evident in 'the social world' (Ten Have 2004). Through such an investigation, we argue that some of the everyday realities, structures, and processes of sports coaching may become more visible and thus better understood.

Why do CA?

Within sports coaching, CA is an underused methodological approach which holds a great deal of potential to further understand the interactions that occur between coach and athlete within the coaching context for the following reasons:

1. CA is empirically grounded and therefore well placed to generate the sort of discoveries that can inform practice.
2. Its focus on practical accomplishments through interaction establishes a natural link with professional practice.
3. Because its raw materials are publically observable phenomena, these are available as resources in any subsequent training interventions.

(Richards 2005: 4)

Therefore, CA offers a potentially fruitful avenue to 'understand broader interactional practices of coaches' and 'move beyond the current tendency to treat coaching as a series of unconnected episodes, which can be dissected and its parts aggregated' (Groom *et al.* 2012: 454).

Language as a cultural resource

Language is of central importance to understanding human interaction as 'whatever their characteristics, it appears that all societies and sub-units have a central resource for their integration and organization of interaction – an organization informed by the use of language' (Schegloff 2007: xiii). This is the first key concept that highlights the importance of CA (the *why* of CA), which drives researchers to further explore how people go about making sense of each other in their day-to-day interactions and in context-specific situations (e.g. student–teacher, a doctor–patient or coach–athlete, etc.). When studying interactions, a number of methodological choices are available. However, all approaches to the study of 'talk-in-interaction' necessitate that words or utterances in interaction are the central phenomena under investigation. Therefore, this approach to studying sports coaching differs methodologically from other approaches as the study of language more directly captures the ongoing empirical events of interest (i.e. talk in interaction).

Interaction as social order

The second key concept to understand when undertaking CA is that interactions are patterned and ordered, and the purpose of CA is to make this social order clearer through analytical inspection. In laying the foundations for the study of interaction, Goffman (1955, 1983) established that social interaction is a form of social order, which comprises of interactional rights and obligations, termed the *interactional order*. Here, Goffman (1967) noted that interaction has an underlying structural organization or *syntax*, stating that 'I assume that the proper study of interaction is not the individual and his psychology, but rather the syntactical relations among acts of different persons mutually present to one another' (Goffman 1967: 2). It is this *syntax* that provides participants in interaction with the sequential ordering of actions (Goffman 1971). An example of the patterning of interactions that we might see in conversations would be that one party talks while the other party listens, and during this time the party that listens pays attention to what is said and responds accordingly (Schegloff 2007). Importantly, Heritage and Clayman (2010) explain that through Goffman's view, interaction is the site where face, self, and identity are expressed. Therefore, through an analysis of such structures people's motivations and identities can be established. While Goffman viewed the organization of interaction to be a domain to be studied in its own right, he did not propose a systematic methodological approach to understand the structures and rules within talk-in-interaction (Heritage and Clayman 2010).

CA's ontological, epistemological, and theoretical position

Although influential, Goffman was interested in how face and identity are associated with action and the motivation of moral conduct, rather than examining how participants understand one another within interaction (Heritage and Clayman 2010). Therefore, questions regarding the structure of the interaction itself and shared understanding within interaction remained unexplored. Here, the work of Harold Garfinkel highlighted that all human action, including Goffman's work on interactional order, is built upon the foundation that people are able to make shared sense of situations throughout interactions, which enables people to understand situations (Heritage and Clayman 2010). Garfinkel's theoretical contribution towards the development of conversation analysis is based upon his work outlining ethnomethodology (Garfinkel 1967), which has been described as a kind of social inquiry that focuses upon 'the ways in which collectively members create and maintain a sense of order and intelligibility in social life' (Ten Have 2004: 14). In further explaining ethnomethodology's theoretical position Garfinkel (1967) states that 'I use the term "ethnomethodology" to refer to the investigation of the rational properties of indexical expression and other practical actions as contingent ongoing accomplishments of organized artful practices of everyday life' (Garfinkel 1967: 11). Here, indexical expressions relate to local, time-bound, and situational aspects of action, whose sense depends upon the local circumstances in which they are uttered, such as 'you' and 'yesterday' (Ten Have 2004). Ethnomethodology's ontological position (nature of reality) is rooted within social constructionism, where 'social phenomena and their meanings are constantly being accomplished by social actors' (Bryman 2001: 18). Therefore, conversation analysis aims to reveal the organization and construction of social reality by participants within interactions (Seedhouse 2005). From an epistemological (nature of knowledge) perspective, conversation analysis is located within a phenomenological paradigm with the aim of examining common-sense thinking through the analysis of the procedural infrastructure of situated action (Seedhouse 2005; Ten Have 2007). Following the work of Garfinkel (1967), Harvey Sacks 'was on the look-out for new possibilities for doing sociology, which might provide alternatives to the established forms of sociological discourse' at the time, with particular emphasis on the treatment of empirical materials (Ten Have 2007: 7). Here, Sacks developed the notion of sequential analysis, which forms the basis of CA (Ten Have 2004).

Applied issues and considerations

A number of analytical tools are available for the conversation analyst. However, all CA work requires utterances to be recorded and transcribed in a great deal of detail to capture the interactions 'as they are'. This section will focus on selecting and recording interactions, transcribing and annotating text, and the CA concepts of turn taking, adjacency pairs, and error repair (the *how* of CA). Within this section, we will draw on interactional examples from our work undertaking CA in sports coaching (Groom *et al.* 2012).

Selecting and recording interactions

The first consideration when undertaking conversational analysis work is the specific research question that you are trying to address. This raises a number of initial questions:

1. What kind of interactions between the coach and athlete are you trying to understand?
2. What are the ethical issues and potential consequences of such an analysis?
3. How can these interactions be best captured and recorded (video/audio)?

In considering Question 1, it is worthwhile examining the existing body of literature in sports coaching and identifying a specific research question that may add to our theoretical and/or empirical understanding of sports coaching (see Chapter 7). For example, you may decide that you would like to explore the patterning of interactions between a coach and a group of athletes over the course of a competitive season to explore how the team's results impact the coach–athlete interactions. Following the selection of a research question, the next stage is to consider access and ethical issues regarding the data collection and analysis (Question 2). For example, you may need to consider the impact of your observations and analysis on the coach–athlete relationship or how the data collection may impact on your relationship with the coach during ethnographic work. Other potential ethical issues may include consideration of anonymity of the participants, the age and consent of the participants and what you will do with the data once collected and analyzed (i.e. publication in a journal article or presentation at a conference). These issues need to be considered early in the process and fully explained to the participants as part of your voluntary informed consent (see Chapter 10). Once these issues have been considered the next stage is to start to plan the collection of data (Question 3). During this phase it is important to ensure that you can gain access to the population under investigation and that you can record the interactions that take place in a naturalistic manner, whilst retaining a high level of audio quality for later analysis. In our work (Groom *et al.* 2012), the classroom environment provided an excellent physical space to both audio and video record the coach–athlete interactions away from potentially difficult weather conditions and large distances between the coach and the athlete on the training field.

Transcribing and annotating text

The analysis process involves a detailed understanding of both the symbols and procedures of CA and the development of the skills to listen and analyze in detail the subtleties of interactions upon which CA is based. Some textbooks in this area provide excellent examples of annotated text and the accompanying audio files (e.g. Schegloff 2007). For coaching scholars working within a university setting, you may be lucky enough to have a sociology department with experts in CA who may be able to guide you in the early stages of your work. Alternatively, a number of professional companies exist, who specialize in the transcription of CA that may be able to help you work with your data. A good tip here is to speak directly to the analyst involved in your work and explain the purpose of your research and the particular form of transcription and annotation that you would like to use on your work. The following example (Example 1) is taken from the work of Groom *et al.* (2012: 447–8) and highlights a series of recorded interactions between a Head Coach (HC) and his group of players (P1–P24) in a video-based feedback session. At this point we have removed the conversation analysis annotations for reader clarity.

Example 1:

1 HC: Alright inswinging free kick we have two on 'im initially one
2 comes off it, so we don't need two out there cos it's not a sh-
3 it's not a shot so he's done the right thing coming off it but then,
4 whoever it is I'm not exactly sure who it is runs back in and does
5 does nothing look at this one player here unmarked marked
6 by him one player here unmarked so one for one
7 man one for one man one for one man another one
8 one for one man there
9 P1: ((coughs))
10 ((pause))
11 HC: Is that one of ours?
12 P1: No, no that's me I come across
13 HC: That's you, no that's you there isn't it?
14 P1: Yeah
15 HC: So who's that?
16 P3: Player 4 plays there Player 4 was there
17 P?:

18 HC: Right so he's, we have to say that he's unmarked then?
19 not marked the right side okay, is he marked?
20 P7: I was at the back
21 HC: You just said you were marking 'im?
22 P7: Yeah
23 HC: Okay
24 HC: Right both those players unmarked
25 P?: (?)
26 HC: Right
27 P6: One of the refs blocking off the deep one
28 ((pause))
29 P6: One of our players near the ref
30 HC: There
31 P6: Yeah screening off
32 HC: Yeah this player we'll take that that's the ball that's okay so
33 basically we've gone one, two, three, four players unmarked
34 four players unmarked in a set piece from the start

Whilst this example is a verbatim transcript of the interactions, there remains a lack of detail about *how* the utterances were articulated by the participants. From a CA perspective, this level of transcription fails to consider important information regarding *meaning* in this context. Conversation analysts contend that 'one wants to write down not only what has been said, but how it has been said' when analyzing talk in interaction (Ten Have 2007: 94); thus capturing the phonetic properties of utterances. The following example (Example 2) is the same passage of interaction taken from Groom *et al.* (2012: 447–8) but includes the CA notations outlined in Table 21.1.

Table 21.1 Conversation analysis transcription symbols (Heritage and Clayman 2010; Schegloff 2007)

Symbol	Meaning
[	Beginning of overlapping talk.
]	End of overlapping talk.
=	Lines connected by two equals signs by different speaker indicates that the second followed the first with no discernible silence between them, or was 'latched' to it.
(0.5)	Number in parentheses indicates silence, represented in tenths of seconds.
(.)	A dot in parentheses indicates a 'micropause', audible but not readily measurable; ordinarily less than 0.2 seconds.
.	Punctuation marks are not used grammatically, but to indicate intonation, the period indicates a failing, or final, intonation contour, not necessarily the end of a sentence.

Table 21.1 (continued)

Symbol	Meaning
?	A question mark indicates rising intonation, not necessarily a question.
,	A comma indicates continuing intonation not necessarily a clause boundary.
::	Colons are used to indicate the prolongation or stretching of the sound just preceding them. The more colons the longer the stretching.
<u>word</u>	Underlining is used to indicate some form of stress or emphasis, either by increased loudness or pitch. The more underlining the greater the emphasis. Underlining sometimes is placed under the first letter or two of a word.
WORD	Especially loud talk is indicated by upper case. The louder, the more letters in upper case.
-	A hyphen after a word or part of a word indicates a cut-off or self-interruption.
↑↓	The up and down arrows mark sharper intonation rises or falls.
> <	The combination of 'more than' and 'less than' symbols indicates that the talk between them is compressed or rushed.
°	The degree sign indicates that the talk following it was markedly quiet or soft.
°°	When there are two degree signs, the talk between them is markedly softer than the talk around it.
( )	When all or part of an utterance is in parentheses, or the speaker identification is, this indicates uncertainty on the transcriber's part, but represents a likely possibility. Empty parentheses indicate that something is being said inaudibly or in some cases, speaker identification cannot be achieved.
(( ))	Double parentheses are used to mark transcriber's description of events, rather than representations of them. Thus ((coughs)), ((sniff)) etc.

Example 2:

1 HC: Alright inswinging free kick (.) we have ↑two on 'im initially (0.4) one
2 COMES OFF I: t, (1.2) > so we don't< need two out there (.) cos it's > not a sh- <
3 (.) IT'S NOT A SHOT SO HE'S DONE THE RIGHT THING COMING OFF I: t (.) but then, (.)
4 whoever it is (.) I'm > not exactly < sure who it is runs back in and (0.4) doe: s)
5 (.) does nothing (.) look at this (3.6) one player here unmarked (1.0) marked
6 BY HIM (0.8) °(?)° (0.6) ONE PLAYER HERE (2.4) UNMA: rked (.) so o:ne for one
7 man (0.4) one for one man (.) > one for one man < (2.8) > (another) one < (0.8)
8 one for one (man)/(there)
9 P1: ((coughs))
10 (0.4)

11 HC: °Is that (one of ours)°
12 P1: No: °no° (.) that's me I come across
13 HC: That's you, (.) no that's you there isn't it
14 P1: °Yeah°
15 HC: So who's that
16 P3: [(Player 4 plays there (.) Player 4 was there)]
17 P?: [(?)]
18 HC: Right (.) so he:'s, (.) we have to say that he's unmarked (then)/(man) (.) he's
19 not marked the right side (0.8) okay, (0.6) ↑is he marked?
20 P7: °I was (?) (at the back)
21 HC: You just said you were marking 'im,
22 P7: °Yeah°
23 HC: Okay
24 HC: Right both those players unma:rked
25 P?: (?)
26 HC: Right
27 P6: One of the refs (.) blocking o:ff (.) the deep one
28 (0.8)
29 P6: One of our players (near the) refs
30 HC: There =
31 P6: = Yeah screening off
32 HC: °Yeah° (.) this playe:r (we'll) take that that's a (?) the ball that's okay (.) SO
33 BASically we've gone ONE (.) two (.) three (.) FOUR players unmarked
34 (0.6) four players unmarked (.) in a set piece (2.8) from the sta: rt
35 (13.8)

Many readers might be put off by CA annotations. This is understandable, as the text often appears unintelligible at first sight. Indeed, to start with it is often advisable to have copies of not only the transcribed and annotated utterances of text but also of audio files to listen to as you read the annotated data.

Once the data has been transcribed using the symbols of CA the pauses, emphasis, and sequencing of the interactions (including speakers talking over each other) become more visible. This is one of the strengths of the conversation analysis approach, highlighting the detail in the analysis and transcription, all of which have *meaning* for participants in interaction. This is the key to CA work. Once the data has been annotated you are now in a position to explore the utterances to highlight key patterns in interaction such as turn taking sequences, adjacency pairing, and error repair.

Turn taking

One of the major features of conversation analysis is 'turn taking'. Turn taking is a process by which interactants allocate the right or obligation to participate in an interaction, which is interactionally managed (locally within the interaction) and structurally constrained (Sacks *et al.* 1974). Therefore, within conversations and dialogue one person tends to speak (takes their turn) while the other person listens. The following example taken from the previously presented Groom *et al.* (2012: 448) excerpt, highlights how the interactions between a coach and athlete consist of turns (Turn 1 line 29, Turn 2 line 30, Turn 3 line 31).

Example 3:

29 P6: One of our players (near the) refs
30 HC: There =
31 P6: = Yeah screening off

Adjacency pairs

Schegloff (2007) highlights that adjacency pairs are characterized by a minimum of: (a) two turns, (b) by different speakers, (c) adjacently placed (one after the other), and (d) that they are relatively ordered by a first part (i.e. the initiation of an exchange such as a question, request, offer, invitation announcement) and second part (i.e. answer, grant, reject, accept, decline, agree/disagree, acknowledge). In the following example, the participants (i.e. athletes) recognize that they should follow these interactional rules as a moral obligation (i.e. I ought to respond to the request), therefore the turn-taking system can be seen to be an act of normative organization in its own right (Heritage 2005). This can be seen in the following example taken from Groom *et al.* (2012: 448).

Example 4:

13 HC: That's you, (.) no that's you there isn't it
14 P1: °Yeah°

As you can see, the two utterances in Example 4 consist of two turns, by different speakers, adjacently and relatively ordered; in that, the Head Coach asks the athletes a question (line 13) and one of the players (P1) responds affirmatively to this question (line 14). Therefore, this small sequence of interaction is adjacently paired.

Error repair

However, sometimes during interaction the natural order of turn taking can be disrupted when a speaker speaks out of turn. To correct this 'interactional error' error repair devices are used in conversations. The work of Jefferson (1974) highlights how error correction is a form of interactional resource. The following example (Example 5), again taken from the previously identified Groom *et al.* (2012: 450) data extract, highlights a basic example of an error repair in a conversation. Following the description of the team conceding a goal (lines 16–20), one of the players (P1) starts to speak (line 21). However, as the coach continues his analysis P1 stops talking. This is an example of an error repair. Following this the Head Coach later asks P1 what he was saying (line 24), to which P1 responds (an interaction that is an adjacency pair).

Example 5:

16 keep going (3.8) (°is he here°) (P8 that's your man) just let 'im go (0.4) just
17 COME RI: ght off (you)/(him) (2.8) three mistakes < number one we don't get
18 marked up early enough in the box, (.) man for man we don't win that
19 HEADER, (0.4) AND PEOPLE SWI: tching off < again look stop there > just a <
20 minute (.) just ↑(peo-), (.) you're not near anybody,
21 P1: (I ju-)
22 HC: You're not (.) you're not (.) and ↑you're not (.) there's too many players that
23 A: ren't (bu:y) people locking in on people > getting < goalsi:de of people (0.4)
24 what were you saying P1?
25 P1: Cos I was ma:rking (?)(the man) (?) (my 'ead) (.) (and as I was marking the)
26 STA: rt 'ee runs out (.) and another person runs in now look (.) (here) (look)
27 LOOK WHAT'S GOING ON THERE

Reflections from the field

Whilst conversation analysis work is typically based upon analyzing the interactions between people in everyday conversations, the analytical tools offer us a great deal of potential to further understand the essence of those interactions that occur in sports coaching contexts. Our journey to undertake a CA project in sports coaching (Groom *et al.* 2012) started with an interest in trying to understand: how coaches coach, and what the mechanisms coaches use in interactions are. Through engaging in the CA literature a number of features and techniques were evident which appeared useful to offer a means of exploring the temporal nuances of coach–athlete interactions (Jones *et al.* 2010). We felt that CA offered the most advanced theoretical and procedural analytical approach to dealing with these features of talk in interaction. That is, other approaches were unable to capture the same degree of detail as CA once the utterances had been converted to text.

However, one of the main challenges in undertaking our work was to address one of the major criticisms of CA, that despite having its 'origins in the discipline of sociology, CA is frequently criticized for being unresponsive to what might be called the 'sociological agenda' – concerned with the analysis of class, power, ideology and related social structures' (Hutchby and Wooffitt

2008: 208). Therefore, in an attempt to overcome this issue we provided a traditional institutional CA analysis of talk in interactions using line numbers for reference and CA annotations within the analysis (cf. Sacks *et al.* 1974) but also a secondary theoretically based analysis drawing upon Heritage's (2005) concept of 'work-task-related identity' and B. H. Raven's work on social power. This multilayered analysis enabled us to better explain the sequential organization of the interactions and the ongoing construction of the social identities of the interactants within the coaching context. However, one of the concerns that we have with our work is that the CA annotations will prevent other researchers reading and engaging in our work, even though we feel that the work has made a novel contribution to understanding the patterning of coach–athlete interaction within our field.

References

Arripe-Longueville, F. (d')., Saury, J., Fournier, J. F. and Durand, M. (2001) 'Coach–athlete interaction during elite archery competitions: An application of methodological frameworks used in ergonomics research to sport psychology', *Journal of Applied Sport Psychology*, 13: 275–99.

Bryman, A. (2001) *Social Research Methods*, Oxford: Oxford University Press.

Cushion, C. J. and Jones, R. L. (2006) 'Power, discourse and symbolic violence in professional youth soccer: The case of Albion FC', *Sociology of Sport Journal*, 23(2): 142–61.

Garfinkel, E. (1967) *Studies in Ethnomethodology*, Englewood Cliffs, NJ: Prentice Hall.

Goffman, E. (1955) 'On face work: An analysis of ritual elements in social interaction', *Psychiatry*, 18(3): 213–31.

——(1967) *Interaction Ritual: Essays in Face-to-Face Behaviour*, Garden City: Doubleday.

——(1971) *Relations in Public: Microstudies of the Public Order*, New York: Harper and Row.

——(1983) 'The interaction order', *American Sociology Review*, 48: 1–17.

Groom, R., Cushion, C. J. and Nelson, L. (2012) 'Analysing coach–athlete "talk in interaction" within the delivery of video-based performance analysis feedback in elite youth soccer', *Qualitative Research in Sport, Exercise and Health*, 4(3): 439–58.

Heritage, J. (2005) 'Conversation analysis and institutional talk', in K. L. Fitch and R. E. Sanders (eds) *Handbook of Language and Social Interaction*, Mahwah, NJ: Lawrence Erlbaum, 103–47.

Heritage, J. and Clayman, S. (2010) *Talk in Action: Interaction, Identities, and Institutions*, Chichester: Wiley Blackwell.

Hutchby, I. and Wooffitt, R. (2008) *Conversation Analysis* (2nd ed.), Cambridge: Polity Press.

Jefferson, G. (1974) 'Error correction as an interactional resource', *Language and Society*, 2(2), 181–99.

Jones, R. L., Bowes, I. and Kingston, K. (2010) 'Complex practice in coaching: Studying the chaotic nature of the coach–athlete interactions', in J. Lyle and C. Cushion (eds) *Sports Coaching: Professionalisation and Practice*, London: Elsevier, 15–25.

Phillips, N. and Hardy, C. (2002) *Discourse Analysis: Investigating Processes of Social Construction, Qualitative Research Methods Series 50*, Thousand Oaks, CA: Sage.

Purdy, L., Potrac, P. and Jones, R. (2008) 'Power, consent and resistance: An autoethnography of competitive rowing', *Sport, Education and Society*, 13(3): 319–36.

Richards, K. (2005) 'Introduction', in K. Richards and P. Seedhouse (eds) *Applying Conversation Analysis*, New York: Palgrave Macmillan, 1–15.

Sacks, H., Schegloff, E. A. and Jefferson, G. (1974) 'A simplest systematic for the organization of turn-taking for conversation', *Language*, 50: 696–35.

Schegloff, E. A. (2007) *Sequential Organization in Interaction: A Primer in Conversation Analysis (Volume 1)*, Cambridge: Cambridge University Press.

Seedhouse, P. (2005) 'Conversation analysis as a research methodology', in K. Richards and P. Seedhouse (eds) *Applying Conversation Analysis*, New York: Palgrave Macmillan, 251–66.

Ten Have, P. (2004) *Understanding Qualitative Research and Ethnomethodology*, Thousand Oaks, CA: Sage.

——(2007) *Doing Conversation Analysis: A Practical Guide* (2nd ed.), Thousand Oaks, CA: Sage.

Part VI

Disseminating coaching research

22 Presenting coaching research

Phil Marshall

Introduction and overview

The purpose of this chapter is to provide guidance to those who are likely to be involved in the presentation of coaching research. While aimed primarily at those undertaking undergraduate and postgraduate study, it is hoped that the messages conveyed within this chapter will be of value to anyone involved in presenting the findings of coaching-related research. I will begin by taking readers through the wide range of contexts in which they may be required to present, and the range of factors that will impact on interaction with their audience. This will be followed by some practical recommendations regarding the planning and organization of the presentation, which will hopefully make this process easier to tackle. I will then consider an example from my own experience, which I feel highlights the importance of the factors discussed in the first two sections of this chapter. Finally I will conclude by reflecting on this personal experience and considering the important interplay between effective planning and its impact on effective interaction with an audience.

Presenting is a normal part of many undergraduate and postgraduate programs of study. Few university students will be able to make their way through a program without being called on to present at some point. For many this is a daunting and uncomfortable experience. It is, however, also a valuable learning experience that introduces students to skills that will be invaluable to them as they leave university and move into employment or further study. Similarly researchers may be required to present their work at conferences and work-shops. While many researchers do not enjoy giving conference presentations, there is increasing academic pressure to do so. Many jobs require employees to present to audiences of varying sizes and backgrounds, and indeed many interviews now have a presentation element built into them. Developing the confidence and skills required to do a good job of this task is something that is surely of benefit, in both the short and long term.

Key to this process is the consideration of both verbal and visual commu-nication styles. Your information must be presented clearly and effectively. It must capture the attention of your audience, making them want to engage with the subject matter you are presenting and holding their attention over what can, in some cases, be a considerable amount of time. Considering how you do this is one of the arts of presenting effectively and of engaging with your audience. Regardless of your own feelings while standing out in front of what could be a large audience, your main aim cannot be forgotten. Presenting effectively is not about simply getting through the act as quickly as possible and getting away from the gaze of the audience. Rather, it is about connecting with an audience, about engaging them in your subject matter, and about holding their attention so that you can effectively convey your message.

David and Sutton (2011) suggest that the key here is building a rapport with your audience. They propose that this will aid in both building your own confidence and in ensuring your audience can see you have something important to say. To assist in this process they suggest that maintaining eye contact with your audience is essential. Here it is suggested that looking around your audience will provide you with valuable feedback on how your presentation is going. The same authors also note that a clear and confident tone of voice will help to engage your audience further. Controlling the speed of your speech is an important consideration; do not rush and try to avoid obvious signs of nerves such as fumbling with a pen or repeating certain phrases (David and Sutton 2011).

While the guidance above holds true for any presentation, the contexts in which you may be required to present can require very varied approaches. You may have to present as part of an academic program. This could be a part of the assessment process, or a kind of formative assessment to allow tutors to consider your knowledge base or program-related skills. As a postgraduate student you may be required to present the findings of your research to academic staff within your institution. You may also find yourself presenting at conferences, seminars, or workshops attended not only by academics but also by members of the public. In the case of coaching research you may find yourself presenting to an even more diverse range of audiences. These may include coaching practitioners, sports development staff, and members of national governing bodies, among others.

This broad range of potential contexts means that your start point should be to find out about and understand the expectations of your audience. For example, as an undergraduate student presenting as part of the assessment process, what do your tutors require of you? Why have you been asked to present? What learning outcomes do your tutors want you to demonstrate an understanding of or competency in? What percentage of your overall module mark is attributed to this method of assessment? Is the assessment focussed on content, on process, or a combination of both? In most cases tutors will look to see a combination of these factors, with students required to demonstrate competency in the methods of communication and at the same time a sound understanding of the information they present.

A further contextual factor worthy of consideration is the kind of data you may find yourself presenting. Here studies may be qualitatively or quantitatively focused or indeed may take a mixed methods approach. The type of data you are dealing with will impact on the approaches you choose to use to present this information. Quantitative data lends itself more readily to presentation through summary tables, graphs, and charts. While qualitative data may be summarized through tables, the richness of the data often requires direct presentation of interview and questionnaire responses. For example, presenting direct quotes can be an effective way of conveying the quality and depth of your data. The nature of your audience may again be a consideration here. The way the data is presented needs to make sense to your audience; the data needs to be accessible for them. Presenting complicated research data couched in academic language, for example, may be a quick way to lose a group of coaching practitioners who simply want to know how your findings relate to their practice. Whatever the nature of the data, ensure you give full consideration to the ways in which you can maximize impact and most effectively convey your message.

Making a success of your presentation must inevitably include a consideration of these contextual factors. Failure to give these factors due consideration may mean that what you finally present is wide of the mark, failing to meet the expectations of your audience. In such circumstances the success of your presentation may be seriously compromised. However, the factors discussed above only form half of the overall equation. The other half is made up of a range of careful planning considerations. To some extent these considerations are of equal importance and if not taken into account can be just as damaging. These wide-ranging factors are considered in the next section.

Applied issues and considerations

This section attempts to cover the wide range of practical issues, which I believe that anyone presenting research findings should consider. Readers interested in this topic are also directed to the work of the following authors for further information: Silverman (2005: ch. 19), Thomas *et al.* (2011: ch. 22) and David and Sutton (2011: ch. 28).

Venue

Although seemingly obvious, this is a significant consideration which, if overlooked or not given due attention, can make or break a presentation. Not including this in your planning and preparation is a major oversight. We have discussed above the importance of a confident and well-considered delivery. Arriving late for your presentation because you have not taken this step in the planning process will not help in this regard. Consider the following questions when planning to help ensure that you are not caught out:

- Where is the venue, how easy is it to get to, how long will this take?
- What time are you due to present? How will this affect your ability to get to the venue on time? For example, will you have to negotiate rush hour traffic?

- What space is available for your presentation and what equipment is available for you to use?
- If the presentation is interactive, does the space facilitate this? Are you limited in this regard by being allocated a tiered lecture theatre or is the room in which you are due to present a level space? How will you overcome these challenges?
- How many people are scheduled to attend the presentation? Are additional audio needs required to allow voice projection? Are these provided?
- Are you required to provide handouts, and if so how many are required?

While many of the above may appear to be common-sense considerations, all of these factors have the potential to have a major impact on the success of your presentation. In many cases going to the venue in advance and familiarizing yourself with the environment is to be advised. In some cases you may even be able to practice using the available equipment and give a mock presentation. In cases where this is not an option though, at least finding out as much as you can about the venue is time well spent. If nothing else this may help to set your mind at rest and help to calm your nerves.

Equipment requirements and methods of presentation

Having the right equipment available to you may help to significantly enhance the impact of your presentation. This might be something as simple as having a microphone available which allows you to project your voice effectively to your audience. After all, if they cannot hear you, how can you get your message across? It may be something essential like access to a laptop or computer that allows you to deliver the presentation in the first place. You will need to know if this is provided or if you will need to provide your own. For many of us, delivering a presentation relies on access to these facilities, with most presentations being delivered using the Microsoft PowerPoint format or similar software. You may also wish to consider if the venue has a projector available or if you need to provide your own. If you are providing your own laptop and are using someone else's projector, then it is also strongly advised that you practice setting up this connection in advance. If this is not possible, then at least arrive in sufficient time to allow for any difficulties in setting up. There is nothing worse than standing in front of an audience desperately grappling with a connection problem between projector and laptop, not knowing if you are even going to be able to give your presentation at all! This is not the best way to begin to establish a rapport with your audience either.

If your presentation relies on interaction with your audience, then your equipment requirements may be more important to success or failure. For example, if input is required from your audience, do you need to make a note of the comments you receive from them? In such cases then, access to a flipchart or whiteboard and pens might be an important consideration. In some cases you may also be able to achieve this through use of a Smartboard or similar. Here, it is strongly recommended that you familiarize yourself with the equipment before attempting to use it on the day of your presentation.

If you want to be able to move around among your audience, then a laser pointer is a useful aid. A laser pointer that allows you to change slides without having to return to the front of the lecture theatre or venue also allows you much greater freedom; you can remain among the audience without having any obvious breaks in your presentation. In such circumstances it is often easier to interact with audience when you are among them. It has been my experience that people are often less inclined to offer opinions and ideas in situations where they have to shout these out across a busy room or lecture theatre. Your close proximity to them may help to encourage them to interact with you more. It also aids in building a good rapport with your audience. Being among them breaks down barriers and removes some of the perceived distance between audience and presenter. Although not appropriate in all contexts, this approach can significantly enhance the impact and effectiveness of your presentation.

Group or individual presentation

Much of the guidance provided in this chapter applies equally to group and individual presentations. Many of the issues remain the same. The advantages of a group presentation lie in the fact that many of the considerations listed above and below can be addressed by the group as a whole rather than all falling on the shoulders of one individual. However, this advantage can also become a disadvantage for the group presentation. Deciding who will address each of these tasks is vital, as is some form of reporting procedure that will allow this process to be monitored. With more people involved there exists a real possibility that key aspects of the preparation process will fail to be addressed, because group members think that someone else is going to take care of them. In such circumstances the reality of this oversight may only become apparent on the day of the presentation, when it is often too late for anything to be done about it. Communication is vital among group members to ensure everyone involved is fully informed throughout the process.

Slide construction

Here, the key is simplicity to allow your overall message to speak for itself. Too much text, complicated slide transitions, confusing slide layouts, and too many slides are all common mistakes when constructing a presentation, distracting your audience's attention. Something as simple as ensuring your text is clearly visible against your slide background can make a huge difference to the effectiveness of your presentation. In constructing your slides your approach should not be to include as much information as possible, but rather to keep the information you present on your slides simple and clearly laid out.

Reducing the number of slides you use and ensuring you elaborate on your content is a good approach to take. You risk losing your audience if you use over-complicated slides with large tracts of text. They will be too busy trying to read your slide content instead of focusing on what you are saying.

A common error for underprepared presenters or those who lack confidence is to include all of their information on their slides. This allows them to read from the slides directly rather than trying to elaborate on their content. Remember that slides are there as a visual aid, and as such should not dominate your presentation. You should be the focus of your audience's attention and not your slides. In addition, inclusion of things like video links in your presentation may help to enhance the overall impact. However, such enhancements can bring with them technical problems. For example, do you need access to the internet to be able to run the video? Does your venue make this possible? If you plan to include such features in your slides, ensure they that they work in advance and that your venue allows you to make use of them.

Practice and time constraints

Again this may appear to be a common-sense consideration when preparing to give a presentation. You will usually be made aware well in advance of how long you have for the presentation and in many cases will be allocated a set time, followed by time for additional questions from the floor. While few of us would risk giving a presentation without first practicing what we will say and how long it may last, it is not uncommon for this to be misjudged. Public speaking for many of us is a daunting prospect, particularly when delivering to peers or those we perceive to possess more knowledge and experience than ourselves. The impact of nerves cannot be underestimated. This may lead to a rushed delivery of our presentation, and consequently may mean that our content will be delivered in considerably less time than we had originally planned for. Never fail to account for this in your planning and preparation. Even with good control of your speech on the day you will still probably find that you move through your content more rapidly than in practice. Being ready for, and even expecting this, will allow things to progress more smoothly. Have additional content ready in your notes. Keep an eye on your pacing and if you are getting through things quicker than expected include some of this content to fill the time.

Ensure you are aware of how much time is available for questions at the end of your presentation. This is another excellent opportunity for further interaction with your audience, one not to be overlooked. You can enhance this aspect of your presentation through adding numbers to your slides. Such a minor addition will easily allow the audience to identify the aspect of your presentation on which they wish to ask questions. Equally, taking this step will make it much easier for you to jump back to the relevant slide, having this up on screen while you answer questions. Further preparation should include consideration of what questions you may be asked by your audience. Ask yourself 'what would I ask myself if I was in the audience?' and 'what would I not want to be asked'? Expect and prepare for such questions in advance to avoid any embarrassment on the day. Avoid including anything in your presentation that you do not fully understand to ensure you head off any potentially difficult questions. By giving consideration to the questions above, you should be able to identify any such areas well in advance.

Delivery of your presentation

It is worth reiterating the message emphasized earlier in this chapter, that a key aspect of successful presentations is building a rapport with your audience. Ensuring you have practiced your presentation and prepared properly, as noted above, will enhance your chances here. Knowing your content and being confident in what you are presenting will allow you to do the key things, like maintaining eye contact with the audience and feeling comfortable in interacting with them. This will allow you to build that rapport far more effectively than someone who simply reads from their slides, avoids the gaze of the audience, and takes an almost defensive approach to presenting.

We have all seen such presenters in action. They stand behind the lectern at the front of the room, unwilling to emerge from behind its perceived protection. They read directly from their slides or notes, avoiding the eyes of the audience, fearful of any questions that may arise should they look up and acknowledge their presence. Try to ensure that this is not you. Plan and prepare properly and consequently feel more at home in front of your audience. Using notes or crib cards is fine, to help you to avoid missing any important points, but avoid reading directly from these. Use these only to aid your memory and help in your overall presentation. A worthwhile process to follow to allow you to be as effective as possible in this aspect of presenting is to script your presentation. Once scripted reduce this to a list of bullet points on a handout. Use this for practice and time your delivery. By going through this process and practicing time and again, you will help to ensure a professional and trouble free delivery of your presentation.

Reflections from the field

The advice I have given above has been compiled over a period of years of presenting coaching research and presenting to coaching-related audiences in all their diversity. What I would like to do in this final section is to share with you a personal experience of my own. The incident described below stuck in my mind. It was born of complacency, from overconfidence. I was an experienced presenter, delivering in a familiar setting to a familiar audience. I felt at ease and I had accounted for many of the planning and preparation issues I have described above. I had carefully considered my audience and the way in which I wanted to present my message to them. I was aware of their expectations and indeed of some of the skepticism and resistance I was likely to meet from them. However, I was too focused on congratulating myself on a job well done, before I had even delivered my presentation. The consequences of my overconfidence are described below.

A lesson learned

We have all seen it before, attending a presentation where the presenter has turned up late. They stand at the front of the lecture theatre, struggling to get their laptop to connect to the projector. They optimistically ask for assistance from the audience, 'does anyone know anything about IT'? A small crowd gathers at the front of the room, trying to sort the problem out, the start time for the presentation comes and goes, and people's patience begins to ebb away. Frustrated glances are cast towards the presenter, wristwatches are stared at in the most obvious ways, and audible sighs are heard around the room. I have sat there, shaking my head, wondering whether I should make a public display of my disappointment by getting up and leaving. After all, we are all busy people; we do not have time to waste on amateurish mistakes and poor preparation like this!

This time I was standing at the front of the room, looking and feeling like a complete amateur. I was presenting some coaching research at a local coaches conference. I knew the venue well; it was not too far from home for me. I had used it many times before. I knew my audience; after all I was one of these local coaches. I had sat at similar presentations myself in the past. I had prepared my slides well in advance and had given considerable thought to how I would present the information. We are a difficult crowd, us coaches, and I knew that standing at the other side of the projector, so to speak, meant I needed to translate this research into something that had real-world meaning for them. I could not just present the facts and figures and not explain to them how this might impact on their own practice. I could hear the questions in my mind while I was putting the slides together: 'What's this got to do with coaching' and 'how can I use this when I'm out on the park'? If I could not answer these questions I might as well not start the presentation in the first place.

So the slides and my notes were geared up to deliver what I thought these coaches wanted from the presentation. I was using my own laptop, the projector was provided for me, and I knew the space I would be using well. It was a good level classroom space, which would allow for plenty of interaction with the audience. I would be able to move among them freely. I had my remote control to allow me to move between my slides from anywhere in the room. Everything seemed to be in place for a successful presentation. The one thing I had failed to account for though was rush-hour traffic during that short trip from my home!

I sat frustrated in traffic, wishing I had set off earlier. Why had I not considered this in my planning? How could I have been so stupid? I wracked my brain for alternative routes, ones that would get me through the traffic more quickly. I sped down quiet back streets to make myself feel better, knowing full well that at the end of each street all I would do was rejoin the traffic queues. I hoped that proceedings were running behind, so that my late arrival would go unnoticed. I arrived in a state of panic, in completely the wrong frame of mind to stand in front of a room full of people and give a confident and involving presentation. As I rushed from the car park to the venue I tried desperately to compose myself. Somehow I had managed to gather myself as I walked into the reception area. I found a member of the organizing staff and was quickly ushered to my room. Feeling somewhat calmer now, I was confident I could turn things around. All I needed was for my laptop to connect to the projector they had provided without any complications, then I would be fine ...

And so I stood in front of a room full of coaching practitioners, rapidly seeing any chances of winning them over and getting them interested in my subject matter disappearing, as my laptop steadfastly refused to connect to the projector. By the time I had got this presentation up and running I would have lost my audience completely. I played out in person the scenario I have described above, appealing to the audience for assistance in getting the laptop and projector to speak to each other. I paused occasionally to look up; seeing a few familiar faces in the room did not help to calm my nerves. What kind of opinion would they have of me after this? When the slides finally flickered hesitantly into view on the projector screen my nerves were shot. The calm, collected, approach I had planned to take to the presentation had evaporated in the preceding minutes and I now stood there on edge. I was in anything but the right frame of mind in which to give an engaging and enlightening presentation. I looked around the room, noting the annoyance on some faces and the blank looks on others. My plan to engage my audience by making eye contact stumbled a bit here. I was not that sure making eye contact with the audience was a good idea now. It was more likely to damage my confidence even further, than to help me win them over. This was going to be a tough evening!

For me this was a lesson learned at a key point in my career. Although experienced and having a good understanding of both my audience and my subject area, I had become complacent. I had failed to address each aspect of the planning and preparation process I have described throughout this chapter. Although most of the boxes had been ticked I had made two apparently minor oversights, which in the end had a major impact on the success of my presentation. For me the take-away message from this chapter is that if you are going to be presenting coaching research, then account for all of the variables I have covered above. Perhaps most importantly, know your audience and know what they expect of you. Try to meet their expectations and you will be well on the way to success. However, the apparently common-sense planning and preparation considerations cannot be overlooked. Address all of these issues and you will hopefully enjoy a rewarding and fulfilling experience.

References

David, M. and Sutton, C. D. (2011) *Social Research: An Introduction* (2nd ed.), London: Sage.

Silverman, D. (2005) *Doing Qualitative Research* (2nd ed.), London: Sage.

Thomas, J. R., Nelson, J. K. and Silverman, S. J. (2011) *Research Methods in Physical Activity* (6th ed.), Champaign, IL: Human Kinetics.

23 Publishing coaching research

Pierre Trudel, Diane Culver, and Wade Gilbert

Introduction and overview

> [S]cientific research as the human activity of 'making science' is strongly competitive at the personal, institutional and national level. It is no exaggeration to say that scientific research is the most competitive of all human activities, even if we compare it, for example, with sports.
>
> (Braun and Diospatonyi 2005: 1548)

The above quotation reflects very well the working climate in universities around the world and, equally well, the expression "Publish or Perish" (van Dalen and Henkens 2012). Researchers in coaching science seem to have understood the message. As shown in different analyses of the coaching science literature, the number of published articles is constantly increasing (Gilbert and Trudel 2004; Williams and Kendall 2007; McCullick *et al.* 2009; Cushion *et al.* 2010; Nash *et al.* 2012; Rangeon *et al.* 2012). But what does this literature have to say specifically about coaching research? First, for many years the majority of studies focused on what coaches do (behavior), but in the last decade studies on coaches' learning/development and decision-making have steadily increased. Second, there has been a shift in methodology; the number of qualitative studies is now equal to or higher than the number of quantitative studies. The interview is by far the method of choice used by qualitative sports coaching researchers. Third, for years articles were spread across a wide range of academic journals, but numerous coaching science journals now exist, including the *International Journal of Sport Science and Coaching*, *Sports Coaching Review*, and the *International Sport Coaching Journal*. These journals are peer-reviewed, which means that manuscripts are subject to review by other scholars. This review process takes months, and sometimes even years. Not all manuscripts are eventually published and rates of acceptance vary widely among scientific journals.

Because publication records are used to make critical decisions regarding student scholarships, funding allocations, the performance and promotion of academic staff (Kulinna *et al.* 2009), learning how to write a publishable manuscript is critical to survival in the academic world. Fortunately, many resources are available including books like 'Writing articles in 12 weeks' (Belcher 2009), and insights from graduate students discussing their publishing experiences (Bowen 2010).

Considering that research never takes place in a vacuum (Armour and Macdonald 2012), students and researchers in coaching research need to understand the big picture; that is the rules of the 'game of publishing' (Magnusson 1999; Tedesco 2011). Although coaching researchers can be affiliated with a School of Human Kinetics, Kinesiology, Physical Education, Exercise Science, or other schools within a Faculty of Health Sciences, Medicine, Education, Arts, and so on, a progressive trend is to link research with the general health and wellness field. Historically higher status tends to be given to the "more scientific" researchers, typically those who use a quantitative approach (Brustad 2009; Bush *et al.* 2013). Furthermore, our experiences tell us that government funding agencies – around the world – do not place sports coaching research as a priority, hence coaching researchers often try to frame their coaching research in physical activity, obesity, or other medical issues (Haff 2010; Armour and Macdonald 2012). This trend is part of a problematic cycle relating to the publishing/funding race. To secure a research grant you need to have a strong publication record (preferably in top-tier refereed journals). The research grant then provides you with additional opportunities to conduct research leading to more publications, which in turn makes the research more competitive for additional research grants, and so on.

In this environment, quantitative research is predominant, a fact that limits the training of students in an alternative research approach. We contend that, as is commonly the case in psychology programs (Mitchell *et al.* 2007), undergraduate programs rarely, if ever, offer qualitative research courses. For example, one of the most popular books used in research methods courses is *Research Methods in Physical Activity* (6th edition) by Thomas *et al.* (2011) (a 450-page book translated into seven languages). Out of the twenty-two chapters, only one eighteen-page chapter is reserved for "Qualitative Research". Another example of the domination of quantitative research is seen in the common provision of statistical analysis software for students and academic staff in most universities. In our experience rarely is any type of comparable qualitative data analysis software made available. This is yet another example of 'how structurally and institutionally qualitative methods are not supported to the extent that quantitative methods are supported' (Mitchell *et al.* 2007: 233).

In brief, coaching researchers have progressively adopted qualitative research, an approach that will make their work more 'accessible to coaching practitioners and those with an interest in the practice of coaching, and which is not necessarily written primarily for a scientific audience' (Bush *et al.* 2013: 118). On one hand coaching researchers should be commended for this attempt to bridge the theory–practice gap (e.g. Cassidy *et al.* 2006; Jones and Turner 2006). However, they must also be aware that this type of research is not often given the credit it merits.

Applied issues and considerations

In an attempt to demonstrate how the rules presented in the previous section can be operationalized, we crafted a fictitious story based on our combined fifty years of academic experience and a review of the literature.

As they are walking to their bimonthly meeting with their graduate students, Patricia informs Paul of the latest development regarding her application for promotion

PATRICIA: I met the Promotion Committee yesterday.

PAUL: So we can celebrate your success ...

PATRICIA: No. The decision is that my request is premature. They concluded that I do not yet have the same number of journal articles as my colleagues and should wait a couple of years. They strongly recommend publishing in journals with high impact factors.

PAUL: What?

PATRICIA: I am so frustrated! I think I am just another example of a female academic who has a baby within the first five years after getting their doctorate, thereby decreasing their chances of advancement (Halpern 2008).

PAUL: It seems to me that you have published almost the same number of publications as Luke, Peter, and Tom, who were hired at the same time as you.

PATRICIA: The issue is that the committee does not take into consideration many of my publications. For example, my articles published in French or in Spanish have no value despite being in peer-reviewed journals. Even the book chapter we published two years ago doesn't count (Cheek *et al.* 2006).

PAUL: But we constantly receive positive comments from colleagues for that chapter and on Google Scholar we are at seventy-five 'hit counts' after only two years.

PATRICIA: What really matters to them are the numbers from 'Web of Science'. As we discussed the other day, qualitative researchers often experience frustration in trying to get peer-reviewed papers published in top-tier journals (Cheek *et al.* 2006; Bowen 2010).

PAUL: I really do not understand why the impact-factor criterion is sometimes overemphasized for issues related to promotion and job tenure. We are at the university level; we should know the importance of using valid methods to evaluate the performance of professors. The literature is full of articles showing that this system is inadequate for such evaluation (Cheek *et al.* 2006; Archambault and Larivière 2009). Even those who created the instrument warned against using it for the evaluation of individual articles and scientists (Garfield 2006; Pendlebury 2009).

PATRICIA: You are right, but what can we do? On top of that, their comments contradict the message about the importance of knowledge transfer through publishing some of our work in professional journals where we can contribute to debates about coaching policy issues (Trudel 2008; van Dalen and Henkens 2012). As far as I am concerned, quantitative metrics should not dominate our research activities, and by extension, our careers. There are now a variety of media channels that we can use to reach our target audiences (Uncles 2004).

PAUL: I hope you will put in a grievance?

PATRICIA: Yes, probably. But while I do this my colleagues will be writing more articles ...

In the meeting room four students, waiting for Patricia and Paul, are sending emails/texts or looking at documents the group will discuss today. The group is composed of Ulric, a student doing his undergraduate project and interested in applying to a master's program; and Mary, a master's student, who has submitted the first of her two thesis articles. The two doctoral students, Dina and Donald, will graduate within five months, each via a different journey. Donald focused solely on his research project and plans to finish within three years. Dina will have taken five years, during which she will have taught two courses and been involved in different projects.

PAUL: On the agenda today is an update of where you are with your own publications. Ulric, last time you mentioned that you were collecting the data for your undergraduate project on 'What type of support junior gymnasts need?' How is it going?

ULRIC: Data collection is going well. I interviewed five coaches and five athletes with one of their parents. However, it seems that my project is not sound enough to be published.

PAUL: What do you mean?

ULRIC: The research project course professor met the six of us who plan on publishing our respective project. As my colleagues' projects were part of a big study on obesity funded by the government, each has analyzed a section of the questionnaire answered by nearly 2,000 parents. They told me they might even become co-authors (Burks and Chumchal 2009). As far as I am concerned, the professor doesn't think I can publish an article with my research. The main reasons: my participants were not randomly selected, the analyses of my interviews are probably biased because I did not do a reliability test, and I cannot generalize the results. He thinks my project should be considered a preliminary step that can be used in the development of a questionnaire or something like that.

PAUL: Humm. ... Could it be that your professor is not very familiar with qualitative research?

ULRIC: He's a new faculty member and defines himself as a 'typical' exercise scientist with a good background in the physiological and biomechanical aspects of exercise (Haff 2010).

PAUL: That explains his comments. In most Schools of Human Kinetics like ours, quantitative research methods are predominant because of the influence of the health sciences; these methods become the default research approach (Sandelowski 2008).

ULRIC: In reality, I do not know much about qualitative research. In my research methods course last year, we spent only three hours on qualitative research.

PAUL: If our School continues to stress the importance of providing under-graduate students with a research background, it should 'walk the talk' and provide the resources to prepare the students in more than one research perspective. Come to my office tomorrow; I'll lend you some research method books that provide a good mix of quantitative and qualitative approaches (Gratton and Jones 2010; Armour and Macdonald 2012). What about you Mary?

MARY: I finally received an email from the editor. Frustrating! Waiting eight months to receive what? One reviewer suggests minor revisions while the other rejects the article stating that I should have used another theory to frame it. The editor suggests I take the reviewers' comments into consideration to improve my article, and send it to another journal because the topic isn't a good fit with the journal. So I am planning to work on my article and send it elsewhere.

DONALD: Where?

MARY: I really believe it is a good article, and I was told to publish in journals with a high impact factor. Any suggestions?

PATRICIA: Donald? We have discussed this.

DONALD: First, because the impact factor is based on the number of people who cite the articles in a journal, new journals and journals with a small target audience like the coaching research field will have difficulty achieving high impact factors (McBride 2006). Given this, who will want to publish in a new journal? (Cheek *et al.* 2006).

MARY: What about other journals?

DONALD: If you go to sportsci.org you will find the latest issue of Sportscience with an article by Hopkins (2012) listing 126 journals.

MARY: On coaching?

DONALD: Of course not, but the journals where most articles on coaching science are published are in the list. The six journals with an impact factor of 1 or higher are: *Journal of Sport and Exercise Psychology* (2.7), *Journal of Applied Sport Psychology* (1.6), *Research Quarterly for Exercise and Sport* (1.5), *The Sport Psychologist* (1), *International Journal of Sport Psychology* (1), and *Journal of Teaching in Physical Education* (1).

MARY: Interesting. Maybe I will send it to *Journal of Sport and Exercise Psychology*.

DONALD: You can try, but be aware that their record of publishing qualitative research is extremely low compared with the other journals (Culver *et al.* 2012).

PATRICIA: Mary, using the impact factor as the first criterion for selecting a journal is not what you should do. I suggest the following (Nihalani and Mayrath 2008; Routledge 2012). First, look for the best fit between the journal's mission and your topic and methodology. Second, familiarize yourself with the articles published in this journal over the last four to five years. Third, structure your article similarly to those that have been published in the journal. Dina what about you?

DINA: Good news! I have been accepted to join the research group in the psychology department that got that huge grant entitled 'Youth motivation to participate in sport and physical activity'.

DONALD: You got the post-doc position?

DINA: Don't be silly, that position went to someone with a very quantitative background. I got an eight-month contract and will be involved in the qualitative part, doing interviews, transcribing and analyzing the transcripts. They said that I could be co-author on some articles. My concern, however, is that I will probably have to put on the back burner the two articles I was writing from the 'Coaches' learning pathway' project.

PATRICIA: Three things, Dina. First, congratulations for this new job opportunity; I think you are well prepared. Second, I recommend that you openly discuss the publication process with the research team to make sure it is fair for all. I have a few articles on that topic (Osborne and Holland 2009; Smith and Williams-Jones 2012). Third, if your two manuscripts are quite advanced, make a special effort to finish them. Based on my experience, if you wait more than six months to publish your results, the chances of achieving a published article diminish progressively. Your review of literature will have to be updated; you will have new research ideas and probably other priorities in your life. Now we have to end the meeting. For our next meeting I suggest reading the first three chapters of Wolcott's book *Writing up Qualitative Research* (2009).

Reflections from the field

In this section, each of us has elected to share stories or lessons learned from our experiences with the coaching research publishing process. I (Wade Gilbert) would like to share some lessons I learned over the years sitting on both sides of the publishing equation (as an aspiring author and as a journal editor). Aspiring authors need to understand that the primary criteria for evaluating a manuscript are: (a) fit with the journal's mission, (b) research design, and (c) contribution to new knowledge. Given the limited space here, I will focus on the first criterion – fit. I have had many manuscripts returned (as an author), and I have returned many manuscripts (as an editor) simply because the "wrong" journal was selected. Even before starting the process of writing a manuscript, you should carefully identify two or three potential journals for the work. For each journal pay careful attention to the journal's mission/vision, who sits on the editorial board, and the types of papers previously published in that journal. If you cannot clearly make a connection from the topic of your research to the mission/vision of the journal and show how your research will contribute to other research, or concept papers, published in that particular journal, you will likely be wasting your time – regardless of how sound your research design may be. As an author, I always like to include something in my letter to the editor about how my manuscript will complement other papers published in that journal. Be specific, list the title and publication date of the papers to which your manuscript will directly connect. Also, clearly describe how and what your manuscript will add to this line of research. This shows the editor first and foremost that your paper – regardless of his or her personal opinions about the topic or the research design – clearly fits the mission/vision of the journal. It will be very difficult for an editor not to send your manuscript out for review after you've clearly made the case for "fit". Think like a lawyer trying to make your case to the judge (in this instance, the editor) for at least hearing your case. Once you've made your case to the editor, next you need to build your case for the jury (in this case the reviewers). Look over the list of editorial board members and ask yourself if you have (a) integrated important pieces of literature authored by members of the editorial board and (b) if your manuscript includes a critique of any of the work authored by members of the editorial board. You can be sure that editorial board members who review your manuscript will be looking to see if you have cited their work related to the topic and if your description – or critique – of their work is accurate. Part of the publishing game is explicitly acknowledging the contributions of those who serve as gatekeepers. You do not have to agree with all of their conclusions, or 'pad' your manuscript with unrelated citations, but you most certainly need to be aware of your audience and potential connections between your work and that of the editorial board members for the journal to which you are submitting your manuscript. I encourage readers to listen to David Kirk's (editor of Physical Education and Sport Pedagogy) interview on the importance of manuscript fit as the primary review criterion (Routledge 2012). His comments directly support the lessons I've shared here.

In the early 2000s, my colleagues and I (Diane Culver) completed a review of the qualitative research published in the 1990s in the *Journal of Sport and Exercise Psychology*, the *Journal of Applied Sport Psychology*, and *The Sport Psychologist* (Culver *et al.* 2003). In 2012 we published the follow-up review for the decade 2000–2009. Given that the 2003 article had been 'cited in at least 65 academic publications in the seven years since it was published' (Culver *et al.* 2012: 261), we were able to publish the follow-up article in the same journal as the first one. As qualitative researchers in the broader field of sport psychology we can take heart in the fact that there has been an increase in the number of published articles that used qualitative data collection methods from 17.3 percent for the 1990s to 29.0 percent for this last decade. However, as discussed in the latter review, budding qualitative researchers in sport coaching should be aware that criteria for judging qualitative research are the subject of much discussion. For example, we should warn you 'according to our review, and as Krane and Baird (2005: 274) note, the parallel perspective on validity/trustworthiness may be the current orthodoxy in qualitative sport psychology research'. This perspective parallels the validity concepts used in quantitative research. Thus, if you decide to use other perspectives, which we hope you will consider if they seem appropriate for your research questions, you should be prepared to thoroughly justify your decision. Otherwise, you are likely to end up in the same situation as our student Mary (see Chapter 18).

I (Pierre Trudel) have two stories to share. First, for the last three years I served as the vice-dean of professorial affairs in the Faculty of Health Sciences (School of Human Kinetics, School of Rehabilitation Sciences, School of Nursing, Interdisciplinary School of Health Sciences, and bachelor's program in Nutrition Sciences). One of my responsibilities was to help professors going through the tenure application. It became evident to me that even if members of the different committees (school, faculty, university levels) were trying to be fair, they often compared the files of researchers coming from different research fields. Second, when I applied for a promotion to be full professor, I realized that my credibility as a researcher in the coaching field was 'largely seen as dependent on the one-way move to quantitative research. Progress is never defined as the move to qualitative inquiry' (Sandelowski 2008: 194). Here are the comments from one of the external evaluators to the question 'Has the applicant contributed through his academic works to the advancement of knowledge?':

> For me, having conducted descriptive and experimental research, the answer is no. From my perspective, the applicant is too attached to an ideological research method (qualitative) instead of using other methodological approaches to study his research problems. ... Other methods, like the experimental method which is more precise and expeditious would uncover more nuances and critical information.

No one would ever imagine refusing a promotion to a 'quantitative researcher' because he/she has never published an article using a qualitative approach!

To conclude, conducting research without publishing arguably is a waste of public money and of the time of many people, not least the participants. Therefore, the publication record must be part of the way in which academic staff are evaluated, but this should be in conjunction with the evaluation of other roles (teaching and service). Moreover, if metrics such as impact factor are used, they must be tailored to the specific research field (Abbott *et al.* 2010), in our case the coaching research field. As indicated by Hofmeyer *et al.* (2007): 'Recognizing and weighting applied scholarly activities for tenure and promotion involves conversations between researchers and administrators in faculties and departments in the academy' ('Creating a sense of urgency for participation in the health sciences section', para. 2). For this to happen, we as researchers in the coaching science field must be present at the table to 'educate' our colleagues about coaching research. In order to facilitate our ability to educate others about our field, we believe it is important to conduct extensive literature analyses every 7–10 years to provide insights on publishing trends (who, where, and what).

References

Abbott, A., Cyranoski, D., Jones, N., Maher, B., Schiermeier, Q. and Van Noorden, R. (2010) 'Do metrics matter?', *Nature*, 465 (17 June): 860–62.

Archambault, E. and Larivière, V. (2009) 'History of the journal impact factor: Contingencies and consequences', *Scientometrics*, 79(3): 635–49.

Armour, K. and Macdonald, D. (2012) *Research Methods in Physical Education and Youth Sport*, London: Routledge.

Belcher, W. L. (2009) *Writing your Journal Article in 12 Weeks: A Guide to Academic Publishing Success*, Thousand Oaks, CA: Sage Publications, Inc.

Bowen, G. A. (2010) 'From qualitative dissertation to quality articles: Seven lessons learned', *The Qualitative Report*, 15(4): 864–79.

Braun, T. and Diospatonyi, I. (2005) 'Counting the gatekeepers of international science journals a worthwhile science indicator', *Current Science*, 89(9): 1548–51.

Brustad, R. J. (2009) 'Validity in context – qualitative research issues in sport and exercise studies: A response to John Smith', *Qualitative Research in Sport and Exercise*, 1(2): 112–15.

Burks, R. L. and Chumchal, M. M. (2009) 'To co-author or not co-author: How to write, publish, and negotiate issues of authorship with undergraduate research students', *Science Signaling*, 2(94).

Bush, A., Silk, M., Andrews, D. and Lauder, H. (2013) *Sports Coaching Research: Context, Consequences, and Consciousness*, London: Routledge.

Cassidy, T., Potrac, P. and McKenzie, A. (2006) 'Evaluating and reflecting upon a coach education initiative: The CoDe of rugby', *The Sport Psychologist*, 20: 145–61.

Cheek, J., Garnham, B. and Quan, J. (2006) 'What's in a number? Issues in providing evidence of impact and quality of research(ers)', *Qualitative Health Research*, 16(3): 423–35.

Culver, D., Gilbert, W. and Sparkes, A. (2012) 'Qualitative research in sport psychology journals: The next decade 2000–2009 and beyond', *The Sport Psychologist*, 26: 261–81.

Culver, D., Gilbert, W. and Trudel, P. (2003) 'A decade of qualitative research in sport psychology journals: 1990–99', *The Sport Psychologist*, 17: 1–15.

Cushion, C., Nelson, L., Armour, K., Lyle, J., Jones, R., Sandford, R. and O'Callaghan (2010) *Coaching Learning and Development: A Review of Literature*, Leeds: Sports Coach UK.

Garfield, E. (2006) 'The history and meaning of the journal impact factor', *Journal of the American Medical Association (JAMA)*, 295 (1): 90–93.

Gilbert, W. and Trudel, P. (2004) 'Analysis of coaching science research published from 1974–2001', *Research Quarterly for Exercise & Sport*, 75(4): 388–99.

Gratton, C. and Jones, I. (2010) *Research Methods for Sports Studies* (2nd ed.), London: Routledge.

Haff, G. G. (2010) 'Sport Science', *Strength and Conditioning Journal*, 32(2): 33–45.

Halpern, D. F. (2008) 'Nurturing careers in psychology: Combining work and family', *Educational Psychology Review*, 20: 57–64.

Hofmeyer, A., Newton, M. and Scott, C. (2007) 'Valuing the scholarship of integration and the scholarship of application in the academy for health sciences scholars: Recommended methods', *Health Research Policy and Systems*. Available at: www.health-policy-systems.com/content/5/1/5. Accessed December 13, 2012.

Hopkins, W. G. (2012) 'The impact-factor Olympics for journals in sport and exercise science and medicine', *Sportscience*, 16: 17–19.

Jones, R. L. and Turner, P. (2006) 'Teaching coaches to coach holistically: Can problem-based learning (PBL) help?', *Physical Education and Sport Pedagogy*, 11(2): 181–202.

Krane, V. and Baird, S. M. (2005) 'Using ethnography in applied sport psychology', *Journal of Applied Sport Psychology*, 17(2): 87–107.

Kulinna, P. H., Scrabis-Fletcher, K., Kodish, S. Phillips, S. and Silverman, S. (2009) 'A decade of research literature in physical education pedagogy', *Journal of Teaching in Physical Education*, 28: 119–40.

Magnusson, J.-L. (1999) 'Reference five: Five easy games of referencing', *International Journal of Applied Semiotics*, 1: 43–52.

McBride, R. (2006) 'Impact factors for the *Journal of Teaching in Physical Education*: What are they and are they important?', *Journal of Teaching in Physical Education*, 25: 3–8.

McCullick, B., Schempp, P., Mason, I., Foo, C., Vickers, B. and Connolly, G. (2009) 'A scrutiny of the coaching education program scholarship since 1995', *Quest*, 61: 322–35.

Mitchell, T., Friesen, M., Friesen, D. and Rose, R. (2007) 'Learning against the grain: Reflections on the challenges and revelations of studying qualitative research methods in an undergraduate psychology course', *Qualitative Research in Psychology*, 4: 227–40.

Nash, C., Martindale, R., Collins, D. and Martindale, A. (2012) 'Parameterising expertise in coaching: Past, present and future', *Journal of Sports Sciences*, 30(10): 985–94.

Nihalani, P. K. and Mayrath, M. C. (2008) 'Publishing in educational psychology journals: Comments from Editors', *Educational Psychology Review*, 20: 29–39.

Osborne, J. W. and Holland, A. (2009) 'What is authorship, and what should it be? A survey of prominent guidelines for determining authorship in scientific publications', *Practical Assessment, Research & Evaluation*, 14(15): 1–19.

Pendlebury, D. A. (2009) 'The use and misuse of journal metrics and other citation indicators', *Arch. Immunol. Ther. Exp*, 57: 1–11.

Rangeon, S., Gilbert, W. and Bruner, M. (2012) 'Mapping the world of coaching science: A citation network analysis', *Journal of Coaching Education*, 5(1): 83–113.

Routledge, Education Arena. (2012) 'Expert interview with David Kirk, editor of *Physical Education & Sport Pedagogy*', Available at: www.educationarena.com/expertinterviews/interviewcategory9/cpes.asp. Accessed December 13, 2012.

Sandelowski, M. J. (2008) 'Editorial: Justifying qualitative research', *Research in Nursing & Health*, 31: 193–5.

Smith, E. and Williams-Jones, B. (2012) 'Authorship and responsibility in health sciences research: A review of procedures for fairly allocating authorship in multi-author studies', *Science and Engineering Ethics*, 18: 199–212.

Tedesco, P. A. (2011) 'The race to publish in the age of ever-increasing productivity', *Natures Sciences Sociétés*, 19: 432–5.

Thomas, J., Nelson, J. and Silverman, S. (2011) *Research Methods in Physical Activity* (6th ed.), Champaign, IL: Human Kinetics.

Trudel, P. (2008) 'L'appropriation des connaissances scientifiques et des connaissances d'expérience par les entraîneurs (Appropriation of scientific knowledge and experimental knowledge by coaches)', in N. Wallian, M-P. Poggi and M. Musard (eds) *Co-construire des Savoirs: Les Métiers de L'intervention dans les APSA*, France: Les Presses universitaires de Franche-Comté.

Uncles, M. D. (2004) 'Journal rankings: How much credence should we give them?', *Australasian Marketing Journal*, 12(1): 67–72.

van Dalen, H. P. and Henkens, K. (2012) 'Intended and unintended consequences of a publish-or-perish culture: A worldwide survey', *Journal of the American Society for Information Science and Technology*, 63(7): 1281–93.

Williams, S. J. and Kendall, L. R (2007) 'A profile of sports science research (1983–2003)', *Journal of Science and Medicine in Sport*, 10: 193–200.

Wolcott, H. F. (2009) *Writing up Qualitative Research*, Thousand Oaks, CA: Sage.

Index

Lightning Source UK Ltd.
Milton Keynes UK
UKOW06f1656200815

257234UK00005B/147/P

9 780415 626828